PASSING THROUGH MISSING PAGES

Passing Through Missing Pages

THE INTRIGUING STORY OF ANNIE GARLAND FOSTER

FRANCES WELWOOD

Daphne, a true BC Historian,

Frances Welwood.

CAITLIN PRESS

Caitlin Press Inc.
8100 Alderwood Road,
Halfmoon Bay, BC von 1y1
www.caitlin-press.com

Text and cover design by Kathleen Fraser.
Edited by Catherine Edwards.
Thank you to Angela Lockerbie for her assistance with the family tree.
Printed in Canada

Caitlin Press Inc. acknowledges financial support from the Government of Canada through the Canada Book Fund and the Canada Council for the Arts, and from the Province of British Columbia through the British Columbia Arts Council and the Book Publisher's Tax Credit.

Canada Council for the Arts   Conseil des Arts du Canada

BRITISH COLUMBIA
ARTS COUNCIL
An agency of the Province of British Columbia

Library and Archives Canada Cataloguing in Publication

Welwood, Frances, 1942–
    Passing through missing pages : the intriguing story of
Annie Garland Foster / Frances Welwood.

Includes bibliographical references and index.
ISBN 978-1-894759-61-8

    1. Foster, Annie H., 1875–1974. 2. Authors, Canadian (English)—
British Columbia—Biography. 3. Women social reformers—British
Columbia—Biography. 4. Women politicians—British Columbia—
Biography. 5. Teachers—Canada—Biography. 6. Nurses—Canada—
Biography. I. Title.

FC3826.1.F67W45 2011   971.1'03092   C2011-904914-7

Dedicated to the memory

of

my two Marys

CONTENTS

FOREWORD

REFLECTIONS ON MEETING ANNIE GARLAND FOSTER

A biography of the West Kootenay's most formidable and intriguing woman is long overdue. Annie Garland Foster Hanley (1875–1974) has been on my agenda and a companion of sorts for nineteen years. Although undertaken somewhat sporadically, the research to discover and describe her has been deep and all-consuming. The bibliographic and archival trail to find the story of this woman existed. Only persistence, ingenuity and the willingness to deal with my admirable but at times reticent and sometimes contradictory subject, Annie, were required!

The story of researching and writing Annie's biography began in the early 1970s when my husband, Ron Welwood, established the Kootenaiana Archival Collection of documents and photographs at the library of Notre Dame University of Nelson in Nelson, British Columbia. As Chief Librarian, Ron had a brief correspondence with a Mrs. Hanley, a very elderly journalist living in White Rock, British Columbia. This forthright woman, who was, for her own enjoyment, compiling an index of British Columbia authors, clearly demonstrated a profound interest and knowledge of Nelson and the West Kootenay.

Nelson's—and my—interest in Mrs. Hanley (or Mrs. Garland Foster, as she was known during her days in Nelson) was marginal until 1991, when the Nelson Museum curated an exhibition called *The Women of Nelson: 1880–1950*. Mrs. Garland Foster was selected as one of the notable Nelson women to be featured in the exhibition. She would appear under the banner "Politics and Civic Figures." I offered to research Mrs. Garland Foster.

The few materials on hand at the Nelson Museum and Archives—various Minute Books, City Hall records, directories, and the superb reporting of the *Nelson Daily News*—revealed Mrs. Garland Foster to be a civic figure of considerable importance. She had been a school principal, a Great War veteran, in 1920 the first woman "Alderman" in Nelson, an accomplished author and journalist and a member of the prestigious University Club of Nelson. How fitting to recognize Mrs. Garland Foster as a notable woman in a community which, in her time, had been in existence barely thirty years.

Research revealed Mrs. Garland Foster to be a fine figure of a woman who stood out among the women of Nelson. Although she rarely attended teas or whist drives, she belonged to and took responsibilities in every area of public life that seriously affected women, children, widows, the community's health and, in particular, "The Boys" who had returned from World War I. Before the days of publicly funded social service boards, Mrs. Foster was there to speak and act for those forgotten by society. Primarily she was a doer and risk-taker and a community leader of the first order. For a relatively brief time in the early decades of the twentieth century, Annie Garland Foster was a "Local Legend" among those citizens of Nelson who cared to take her honestly and seriously.

The *Women of Nelson: 1880–1950* exhibition opened in March 1991. In February, I was already writing letters and making phone calls to White Rock, British Columbia; Woodstock, New Brunswick; and Correctional Services Canada in response to information that had come my way when it became known in Nelson that I was asking questions about Annie Garland Foster. I sensed there was more to this austere but vocal schoolmarm and politician than my contribution to the *Women of Nelson* exhibition had revealed.

A British Columbia County Court judge (locally born and raised) offered the fascinating information that Mrs. Garland Foster had been involved with a gentleman who was found guilty in 1926—in the Nelson Court House—of murder. This was corroborated by sympathetic long-time residents who had known and respected Mrs. Garland Foster. In the dust and crumbling plaster of the attic tower of Nelson's historic courthouse, I located the hefty Registrar's Notebook for the Supreme Court at Nelson 1916–1948. Here, confirmed in ink-stained certitude, was a true copy of the court proceedings referred to by His Honour.

The archives of Annie's alma mater, the University of New Brunswick, revealed an inventory of her published and unpublished articles, unpublished manuscripts, family photos and, most exciting of all, a manuscript entitled "Passing Through"—a memoir of her life begun in 1938. Sixty dollars for a photocopy of the 248-page manuscript "Passing Through" seemed like a good investment. It was certain to answer all my questions about my new friend, Annie.

So far, first-hand contact had been limited to chats with old-timers, research into past issues of the *Nelson Daily News* and a review of the occasional article by Annie Foster found in sundry clippings files. Grimy original documents such as the Nelson court record and unread manuscripts hold great fascination for the determined historical researcher, but diaries, letters and memoirs are first-rate finds.

On the evening in May 1991 when the box from the University of New Brunswick containing Annie's "Passing Through" manuscript arrived in our Nelson home, Ron and I settled down to read. As we passed the typewritten pages back and forth, we heard Annie tell delightful stories about her Scottish and Maritimes ancestors, her university days, her early careers as a nurse and a teacher, the ghastly 1914–1918 Great War, her role as a community figure in Nelson and her move to Vancouver. The memoir concluded with a description of her then-current (1939) career as writer and journalist in White Rock. *The End*.

Wait a minute! What about the events of 1925 and the 1926 murder trial in Nelson? Were these not significant? Apparently not … or perhaps they were too important or too private to include for possible public consumption? Annie *did* write about those years in her memoir. However, some time after 1939, but prior to committing her papers and the memoir to the University of New Brunswick Archives, she removed the six pertinent pages from a chapter titled "Reconstruction." She noted in pencil on page 226 "cut 7 [sic] pages." We were not to know her role in or her interpretation of the murder verdict at the Nelson Court House in 1926. This purge served to encourage her would-be biographer to uncover the full story. The biographer's quest had become "The Case of the Missing Pages."

As Ron and I read the pages of "Passing Through," another characteristic of Annie's memoir became evident. Except in cases of immediate family or verifiable historical characters, Annie rarely referred to towns, regions, institutions, or, most discouraging of all, the *people* in her text, by name. Yet another point of frustration for the biographer!

It was through dozens of visits, e-mails, calls to archives and libraries, and the creative use of directories, census records and maps, and hundreds of website searches, that many places, names and even dates in the memoir were eventually identified. Several interesting blanks remain. What was the last name of Frank, Annie's beau during her university days? What was the name of the Saskatchewan town where Annie had her first teaching position? Was this

Annie's way of telling us that only events and their effects were of importance in a person's life? Why was she forthcoming about some elements in her life and not others?

In spite of my fascination with Mrs. Garland Foster, my life commitments intervened, and Annie and her papers were relegated to the back of my file cabinet for several years. Nonetheless, the spell this woman had cast on me remained. The roadblocks I encountered merely heightened my resolve to delve further and learn what made this woman tick. Our unbidden friendship survived six or seven years of neglect but the pieces of Annie's puzzle, which had become my puzzle as well, slowly presented themselves for consideration.

In 2000, with the help of a researcher friend, the complete court and administrative records and correspondence regarding the 1925–1926 murder were obtained from Library and Archives Canada. The "Case of the Missing Pages" had been re-opened and official documents revealed Annie's role in the case.

In August 2002, my "research assistant" Ron and I visited Annie's Fredericton and Woodstock in New Brunswick. We walked the streets of the old towns, noting and photographing addresses and landmarks gleaned from directories and hints from Annie's memoirs. At the Harriet Irving Library at the University of New Brunswick, we introduced ourselves to the keepers of Annie's fonds and learned as much as we possibly could from first-hand scrutiny of the manuscripts and materials held there. May 2005 saw us at the White Rock Museum and Archives examining Annie's scrapbook of newspaper clippings.

Annie had spent most of her senior years in the pleasant, seaside community of White Rock, located south of Vancouver. There she championed women's groups and campaigned for a local hospital, but her community involvement in White Rock was not nearly as spectacular as her much earlier roles in the new City of Nelson had been. Her causes and activism in White Rock were now of a more private nature, but her profile in the community was positive and she was greatly respected.

White Rock archivists recognized Annie's contributions to their community, and cared for a small file on the woman White Rock and neighbouring Surrey residents revered as Mrs. Ann Hanley. Here, hidden among the clippings, was a simple stenographer's notebook containing a diary of the time Annie spent in Britain during the Great War. The diary was a thrilling discovery! Away from home and hearth, and possibly with a sense of immediacy, she candidly wrote about her most meaningful, rather than mundane day-to-day, experiences in and about London. In this diary, she named names and placed people in their proper time and context.

I was starting to put Annie's life in order. As I slowly re-assembled the days and careers of her life, I sat down to write. The devil was in the details, tracing and reading the myriad articles she wrote (or purported to have written), looking for bits of Annie to be revealed. Always I was on the lookout for evidence that Annie had shown an interest in seeing "Passing Through" published or shared with associates or family—but no indication was found. Except to excise the six pages, Annie never referred to or returned to her 1939 memoir manuscript to revise, continue, explain or comment. She closed the book on her life at age sixty-three. But I have endeavoured to open that book for my purposes as well as for my friend Annie's benefit.

It was simple curiosity about this determined, resourceful woman that initially motivated my quest to unravel and reveal the story of Annie Garland Foster. However, my interest was furthered or even abetted by the recognition that Annie represented a certain time period in the small developing city whose history and life I have grown to love and enjoy. Annie's feistiness coupled with her search for justice, her varied talents and broad interests are evidenced today in the women and newcomers who still seek opportunities and a living in Nelson and the towns of the West Kootenay of British Columbia.

I invite the reader to meet and question Annie—young lady, mature woman, and dogged senior citizen. Why did she make the choices she did? What gave her the determination and sagacity to single-handedly take on issues of considerable magnitude? One of the most interesting people to have called Nelson home was Annie Harvie Ross Garland Foster Hanley (1875–1974). Here is her story.

August 2011
Frances J. Welwood

Annie Garland Foster, writer and social and health advocate, c. 1926. Photo courtesy of the University of New Brunswick Archives, MG L7, Series 3, File 1, #3.

THE STUDIO

*I*t was a grey West Coast morning in 1938 when Annie Harvie Ross Foster sat down purposefully in front of her sturdy 1911 Underwood typewriter to begin her story. Annie had written many articles and essays, but for the first time she set out to write about herself. The distant waters of Semiahmoo Bay were barely visible from the window of her studio. Many tides would ebb and flow across the sandy beach that defined the cottage community of White Rock, British Columbia, before her story was finally told.

Annie was sixty-three years old, and she felt it was time. In her estimation, her life had been a "simple tale"; nonetheless, she felt an inexplicable need—a duty, in fact—to record the events and observations of her life. "Future psychologists," she would write in her memoir, "would welcome how a person such as me has reacted to life."[1]

Although Annie began her memoir as a retrospective of her life, she would live another thirty-six years. The memoir would thus tell only two-thirds of her story; throughout her remaining senior years, however, she would continue to dedicate herself to the written word.

Annie, who preferred to be known as the widowed Mrs. W. Garland Foster, was a very busy woman. She had recently served as president of the Vancouver and Mainland Branch of the Canadian Authors Association (CAA) and she had travelled British Columbia (as much as time and money allowed) speaking to other branches of the CAA, Women's Institutes and Canadian Clubs. The formidable Mrs. Garland Foster promoted Canadian authors, characters and adventurers from Canada's rich history, as well as women's and health causes.

Seaside, East Marine Drive, White Rock, British Columbia, c. 1927. Vin Coyne Collection. Photo courtesy of Surrey History.

Now, at age sixty-three, she could step back from these serious, vital activities and devote her attention to this more personal calling.

Writing, research, inquiry, causes and controversy had been her lifeline and her livelihood for the past two decades, yet when it came time to take up the task of confronting her own story, she had deep reservations: "This being the product of my private garden my reluctance can easily be understood...."[2] In the hundreds of publicly available articles, papers and commentaries Annie composed as teacher, healer, critic and researcher, nowhere did she relate incidents from or insights into her personal life. She wrote always in the third person; her daily life was not part of the work of writing.

For 248 pages, Annie typed away at her story, which she entitled "Passing Through." The manuscript now resides, unpublished, in the archives of her alma mater, the University of New Brunswick, and it reveals a life far from "simple." Annie's adult life was one characterized by deep sorrows, profound convictions and firm dedication. While much of "Passing Through" recalls her early childhood impressions and the foibles and charms of her many Ross and Doak relatives, this autobiographical exercise is not an open book. One entire compelling episode from her adult story was omitted (or removed) completely. Annie's association with the murder trial (and its chief protagonist) held in Nelson in 1926 is not mentioned in the chronological unfolding of her life story.

This intriguing episode, uncovered through other research methods, gives added significance to many curious references and musings in "Passing Through."

In 1939, when Annie had completed the manuscript, the mysterious tale behind the missing pages was far from resolved. The plot would eventually play itself out, but Annie found no reason in the following years to return to the manuscript or to neatly rearrange her life story with a proper Introduction, Middle, Climax and Conclusion. In the peaceful presence of Peter, her canine companion, her cherished tangled garden and the seaside village, Annie had recorded her life and thoughts in her own inimitable style. "Passing Through" captured her story to a particular time. Annie would share only those parts of her life that she considered relevant to "future psychologists"—and possibly to scholars or social historians. However, by her deliberate omission from her memoir of a critical incident in her fascinating life, Annie created an opportunity for an inquisitive admirer six decades later to follow this woman across Canada. Her biographer would share and investigate elements of the Great War, the politics of a vigorous small city in the interior of British Columbia, social welfare causes and journalistic diligence, and uncover the missing chapter in the life of Annie Harvie Ross Garland Foster.

"SCOTSMEN ALL"

Ann Harvie Ross was born on February 15, 1875, in Fredericton, New Brunswick, to Christine Doak Ross and Robert Fulton Ross. The child, Annie, was intelligent and inquisitive with an incredible ability to gather and retain family and local anecdotes. The adult, Annie Harvie Ross Garland Foster, was a serious-minded woman with a great desire to set things right and see justice done … and quickly. In later years, she admitted to have taken life much too seriously and regretted the quickness with which she pursued solutions to problems, leaving little time for sociability. All these traits she attributed to, even blamed upon, her Scottish forebears: those "dour" Ayrshire folk who dared leave the homeland to which they were deeply attached. Those dour Ayrshire folk included McDonalds, Doaks and Rosses—"Scotsmen all"—who were bound for New Brunswick in the late eighteenth and early nineteenth centuries.

ANNIE'S MATERNAL ANCESTORS: THE MCDONALDS, STORYS AND DOAKS

Donald McDonald (1750–1854), Annie's great-great-grandfather was born in Ayrshire in 1750. He joined the 42nd Royal Highland Regiment of the famed and gallant Black Watch and the most senior of all the Highland regiments. On May 1, 1776, with war threatening in the American colonies, a convoy of ships bearing the "42nd Foot," Sergeant Donald McDonald among them, left from the port of Greenock, near Glasgow, for America. The Black Watch fought as a unit on the British side throughout the American Revolutionary War. When this long and contentious war came to an end in 1783, many members of the 42nd Royal Highland Regiment, who had acted as guards while the United

Homestead of Squire Doak and Annie Ross's maternal family, the Doaks. Doaktown Provincial Historic Site Village, Doaktown, New Brunswick. Photo courtesy of the New Brunswick Department of Tourism and Parks. Image Bunk #530.

Empire Loyalists were relocated to the northern British colonies, elected to take their discharge and stay in British North America. Donald McDonald of Ayrshire was with those Loyalists who set their stakes in the British colony of Nova Scotia (which included the future province of New Brunswick).

However, McDonald was not a man to settle down easily. When the northern British colonies were again threatened by war, this time by France in 1793, and the redoubtable Highlanders' commander Dugald Campbell and Governor Thomas Carleton were recruiting veterans of the American conflict and organizing the King's New Brunswick Regiment for the defence of the colony, Donald McDonald immediately joined the home guard regiment. His military fervour was recorded in the King's New Brunswick Regiment History (1793–1802).

In 1800, when this latest military threat had ended and his Highland companions were now long settled along the Nashwaak River, Donald McDonald, somewhat reluctantly, took up his land. At the age of fifty, he was apparently the last of the 42nd Highlanders to do so. With equal reluctance, McDonald acquired a wife. Hanna Crane of the nearby settlement of Penniac was of Native blood, "but all concede that she made him an excellent wife"[1] and was much respected in the community. Indeed, Hanna and Donald raised a family of eight children. The eldest was to be Annie Ross's great-grandmother.

Donald McDonald of Nashwaak, New Brunswick, the longest surviving member of the original band of Loyalist Highlanders, was renowned for his longevity. Christine Doak (1847–1935), Annie Harvie Ross's mother, told her daughter of meeting Annie's great-great-grandfather McDonald when he was about one hundred—five years prior to his death. She related an anecdote telling how McDonald had given the plumes from his regimental headwear to a Doak relative who subsequently used them as a duster. This did not sit well with the venerable gentleman, who, although by then shrunken in stature, remained upright in defence of the regiment and its regalia.

In 1823, Christine McDonald (c. 1801–18??), eldest child of Donald and Hanna Crane McDonald, married Joseph Story. Joseph was the son of a New England or English sailor who had landed unannounced on the bank of the Miramichi River in the late eighteenth century. Christine and Joseph Story homesteaded well up the Miramichi in a community eventually named

ROYAL HIGHLANDERS SETTLE IN FUTURE NEW BRUNSWICK

In late 1783, a detachment of approximately a hundred weary Royal Highlanders fled north with the British fleet from the new American states to the colony of Nova Scotia, which then included what would become New Brunswick. Under the command of Lieutenant Dugald Campbell, the "lads" disbanded at Parrtown, where thirty-nine of them were granted heavily timbered, city-sized lots. This arduously cleared settlement would later become the port and city of Saint John. Along with the former soldiers, 14,000 Americans loyal to the British Crown also settled in present-day New Brunswick. This immigration greatly altered the character and economy of a colony that had welcomed many newcomers and governors from Scotland, Wales, France and New France, but never in such numbers. The Saint John River Valley was one of the major settlement areas for United Empire Loyalists.

In April 1784, Dugald Campbell was once again commissioned to lead his band of Royal Highlanders further into the Canadian wilderness. A devastating fire at the new settlement at Parrtown, followed by an extremely difficult winter, had forced the soldiers to accept new allotments about 125 kilometres further up the Saint John River in a wilderness called Nashwaak. The Highlanders' settlement was twenty-five kilometres beyond the settlement of Ste. Anne's Point on the Saint John River, in the parish of St. Mary's, on both sides of the Nashwaak River. Campbell surveyed the land and divided it into 185 lots. The Highlanders finally had home plots of their own.

Storytown. Like so many tales from northern New Brunswick, the Story family's future history was measured from the time of the cataclysmic Great Miramichi Fire of 1825.

On October 7, 1825, following an unusually hot summer and industrious efforts to clear land and settle in wood supplies, a mighty conflagration destroyed the town of Newcastle (pop. 1,000) and all the communities along the Miramichi River and its many tributaries. The fire burned almost 16,000 square kilometres or about one-fifth of New Brunswick's forests. Flames funneled up the valleys and riverbanks 240 kilometres to the capital of Fredericton itself, where one-third of the dwellings were destroyed.

When the fire overtook the Story homestead on the north bank of the Miramichi, Christine, with her eldest child Benjamin in her arms and pregnant with her second child, waded into the river to escape the blaze. Amid the roaring of the fire, the heat and the smoke, the women, children and the elderly watched in horror as their homes and possessions burned. Wildlife joined the desperate people in the life-saving river. At least 160 lost their lives in the fire.

In time, the countryside recovered. Joseph Story's land was exceptionally rich and arable; in addition, in 1837 he acquired 100 acres at Blissfield in a New Brunswick Land Grant. Story, however, never prospered as he ought, due to a not uncommon addiction to the drink. His great-granddaughter Annie Harvie Ross reports,

> Too late to recoup his fortunes entirely, he was cured by his wife Hannah [*sic* Christine]. Having made her arrangements with the bartender to sell her a bottle of whiskey filled with cold tea during one of her husband's [saloon] visits she was ready for her coup. There she stood at the bar purchased her bottle of whisky and stood drinking it with the rest of the topers.... In those days it was an unheard of thing for women to so demean themselves. Women who did so ran great risk of being considered unsexed creatures.... But great grandmother Christine Story was too well known and too popular to run much risk.... Her ruse worked, for her husband over-come with shame that his wife should openly drink in a common bar with men, took a solemn vow never to drink alcoholic preparations again.[2]

Christine and Joseph Story had six children. In 1844, Susannah, their eldest daughter married James A. Doak, whose family had settled on the southwest Miramichi River opposite Storytown.

Susannah Story Doak (1827–?), Annie's maternal grandmother. Photo courtesy of the University of New Brunswick Archives, MG L7, Series 3, File 1, #10.

The first Doaks in the Miramichi region were also Ayrshire Scots. In 1820, three Doak brothers were established by their father on an acreage on the Miramichi River. Andrew Robert, the eldest and reputedly the most influential and entrepreneurial man in the area, became known as "The Squire." The Doak Historic Site at Doaktown, established in 1989 as a provincial historic property, incorporates his family home and celebrates the family lumber, carding, and oat grist mills. The Doak homestead on the post-road linking Fredericton with Newcastle at the mouth of the Miramichi River and the Gulf of St. Lawrence was a prosperous, healthy farm.

The Squire's brother, James, was a schoolteacher with a wife possessed of the

James A. Doak, born mid-Atlantic (1820–c. 1901), was Annie's maternal grandfather. Photo courtesy of the University of New Brunswick Archives, MG L7, Series 3, File 1, #9.

most dour and sternest nature encountered anywhere in the new world. Mary (Miriam) Symington Doak prided herself on never having kissed any of her children. Her grandchildren declared that a dim daguerreotype of the woman confirmed this description. Like Annie's great-great-grandfather, Donald McDonald, she contributed to the family longevity pool, and lived to the age of 101. Annie enjoyed recording in her memoir anecdotes such as this tale of the unaffectionate mother. She learned family lore from her own mother and delighted in retelling the stories.

James A. Doak, Annie's grandfather, had been born in the mid-Atlantic in 1820 when his parents were on their way to New Brunswick. He was the son of the schoolteacher James Doak and Mary Doak, and was always referred to as James A. It was James A. who in 1844 married Susannah Story from across the Miramichi.

Officers' Quarters on Officers' Square, Fredericton, New Brunswick. Site of James Ross's smithy in the mid-nineteenth century. Photo by Ron Welwood, 2002.

Christine, Annie's mother and the second of James A. and Susannah's ten children, was born in 1847. She was a delightful, hard-working youngster who was sent to help the elderly squire, her great-uncle Robert Doak, when that gentleman was ailing. The Squire's son (the "young Squire" of the Doaktown homestead) and his capable, welcoming wife, Aunt Ann (née Herve or Harvie) became second parents to Christine. In 1873, Christine married Robert Fulton Ross. Both Christine and her children had a special affection for Aunt Ann, evident in the name Christine and Robert gave their eldest daughter—Ann Harvie Ross.

ANNIE'S PATERNAL ANCESTORS: THE ROSSES

By the early nineteenth century, nearly as many Rosses as McDonalds had found their way to New Brunswick. A goodly number were named James, and some were Ayrshire folk. James Ross (1800–1885) of Muirkirk, Ayrshire, Annie's grandfather, sailed for Saint John, New Brunswick, in 1820. Despite having acquired valuable land in Saint John's "Indian Town," James soon returned to the dark confines of Glasgow in Scotland to learn the blacksmith's trade.

By 1831, he had married Margaret Kelsie Elphinstone and, together with their infant daughter, Margaret, they sailed aboard the *Trial* from Londonderry, Ireland, for Saint John. Margaret Elphinstone Ross seemed an unlikely immigrant. She was of stern, proud heritage, not given to merriment or smiling. Her father was another "dour Scottish" relative. Margaret, who became the mother of nine New Brunswick-born children, considered photographs "… graven images and would never have one taken. After her death in 1874, her family, wishing to have some record of her had her photographed."[3] Her son Robert, Annie's father, kept his copy hidden, as he considered a dishonourable advantage had been taken of his mother.

The James Ross family partnered with several Ross brothers—including Malcolm—and took up land in Maugerville, just east of Fredericton on the

Saint John River. Malcolm proved most unreliable. Sent to Fredericton to discharge payment on taxes, he somehow neglected his purpose and squandered the family money. About 1840, James moved his family to Fredericton and took up the mechanical and blacksmithing trades. Malcolm relocated, amid familial disapproval, to Acton Settlement in the Parish of Manners Sutton, southwest of Fredericton.

The bustle and sociability of Fredericton suited James's temperament much better than the rural life at Maugerville had done. From 1785 until 1869, Fredericton was a significant and popular British military garrison. James Ross's house and smithy were located in the lower level of the stone, fortress-like Officers' Quarters Barracks on the bank of the Saint John River. Hutchinson's City Directories 1865–1868 place James Ross, blacksmith, on Queen Street, while his son Robert (b. 1840) was listed as a "fireman County Court House, Queen St." The directory for 1871, following the closure of the Officers' Barracks, located the Ross enterprise on Market Square.

The military location opened directly onto the Parade Ground—the perfect winter and summer sports venue: "How James Ross got any work done in the [winter] season is a mystery for he was always in demand when an expert curler was needed. As his boys grew up they could always fill in at the shop."[4] Good-time "Jamie" would grab his besom (twig-bundle broom) and join the lads on the frozen Parade Ground at a moment's notice. For the Ross children, life with Father was rarely dull. There was no dourness in James. There were games, sleigh rides, and gatherings Annie referred to as "pow-wows" with Native people and the Lieutenant-Governor of the colony in a field in the midst of winter. One can imagine the disapproving words or glances from his wife Margaret in response to all this gadding about.

James was also a popular entertainer at St. Andrew's Day banquets and Robbie Burns Day recitals and storytellings. His rich baritone was heard regularly at St. Paul's Presbyterian Church until the week before his death in 1885 at age 84. A legacy of this man is a scrolled, wrought iron grillwork on the front doors of St. Anne's church at George and Westmorland Streets in

551 Charlotte Street (between Regent and Carleton streets), Fredericton, quite possibly home to the James Ross family 1870s and 1880s. Photo by Ron Welwood, 2002.

Fredericton. The James Ross family itself was also his legacy—ten children were raised and educated, and, in several instances, became successful in business and married well.

Robert Fulton Ross (1840–1921), the fourth child and second son of Margaret and James, was born in Maugerville in 1840, just before the family moved to Fredericton. He was a responsible lad, employed or described variously as fireman, stationary engineer, or foundry-worker. Robert married Christine Doak (Christina, according to the 1873 marriage record).

And so it was that on February 15, 1875, Ann Harvie Ross was born to Christine and Robert on Charlotte Street in the City of Fredericton, New Brunswick, in the eighth year of the Canadian Confederation.

HOMESTEAD AT MANNERS SUTTON

nn Harvie Ross believed passionately that beginnings and childhood first impressions were very important. Her memoir, therefore, is a series of pictures, sensory images and insights from her earliest days. As her life on paper reveals, these pictures remained vivid, albeit idealized, for many, many years. To Annie, the chronology of events was of little importance; geographical locations were seldom defined and few individuals from her adult life were clearly depicted. But early memories, which she strove to record in detail and with delight, were cherished and analyzed. What was the meaning or significance of a memorable childhood incident? What did a childhood anecdote or observation reveal to her about herself?

For example, her earliest recollections include Robert Fulton Ross's gun standing at the cellar-way, a very small Annie's near-asphyxiation of her baby brother, wanderings about the neighbourhood beyond the well-latched front gate, and a proclivity for eating buttons from her mother's button bag—all incidents from when she was barely two years old. These recollections and observations obviously weren't described for public consumption or publication, but were an exercise in reviewing her earliest memories of a time when names, places and dates didn't matter. It was her chronology—of her life—for her own reflection.

The Ross family home on Charlotte Street was in a well-established, comfortable neighbourhood of Fredericton. Churches, schools, markets, businesses and professional offices were within four or five blocks. Annie was much taken with the grand picket-fenced property on the nearby corner of Regent and Charlotte Streets. In 1878, this imposing house with the sumptuous garden was the home of Edward H. Wilmot, a half-brother to Lemuel Allan Wilmot, a former Lieutenant-Governor (1868–1873) of the province of New Brunswick. Annie mistakenly identified this house as being the home of a Father of Confederation, a distinction which neither Wilmot held. Their cousin, however, the Hon. Robert Duncan Wilmot, was indeed a Father of Confederation, and, like Lemuel, also served as Lieutenant-Governor of New Brunswick. But that was in the future (1880–1885) and it did not suit the small girl's fantasy that the house was actually occupied by an elderly Wilmot who, while not a Father of Confederation, occupied his own place in history as the registrar of the University of New Brunswick in the 1870s. At some point in writing of this Wilmot family confusion, I realized that there may have been a thread of opportunism in Annie's character, in her stories, in her memoir. It seems that she may have stretched the truth to better the story and included bits of information and gossip that made her life story a little more interesting. Did she include these embellishments to interest readers or were they intended to intrigue those "future psychologists"?

Annie's father, Robert, was employed as a stationary engineer (a mechanic of fixed machinery) but before long, unspoken family matters obliged him to consider the rural life—just as his own mechanic father had abandoned rural life and moved to the bustle of Fredericton decades earlier. In January 1877, Christine and Robert's only son, James Loggie Ross, was born at the Charlotte Street home. Christine's delicate health after the birth also encouraged the family's relocation to the farming settlement of Acton, in the Parish of Manners Sutton.

Uncle Malcolm Ross, the fellow who had earlier misappropriated the family's tax funds, had acquired property and a lumber mill at a settlement fifty kilometres southwest of Fredericton. Now Malcolm was heading to California and his nephew Robert bought his uncle's several hundred acres of property. Interestingly enough, according to the 1878 *Atlas of York County*, this property was registered in the name of J. Ross, Robert's father—another family puzzle.

Country life with all its attractions and distractions was a new and wonderful world to Annie. The two-storey colonial farmhouse had a parlour in which no one sat. Annie considered the wallpaper of a pale green hue with large pink roses and Paris green leaves "poisonous," while a large oval table draped in a cloth was a secret hideaway for young James and Annie. A trundle bed, a "settle" seat in the kitchen, and the classic high-backed mother-love rocking chair provided the familiar early Canadian home setting. Six decades and a continent-width later, Annie recalled with extreme fondness household items such as the cooking stove, an ancient three-legged kettle, the copper canning kettle and a precious tall china teapot with gold bands and golden sprays. All the props for a mid-Victorian stage setting were in place and vividly remembered.

The outdoors and outbuildings called continuously. Piles of maple sawdust from Uncle Malcolm's old mill hid empty old bottles that Annie imagined to have contained rum from exotic Jamaica and coloured flasks from across the seas. Fields beyond the house, the cow barn and its occupants, the vegetable garden, and the mature orchard supplied a never-ending playground for adventure and inadvertent mischief. Trees were draped with blossoms or apples. The meadow lived seasonally with buttercups, daisies and poppies.

A frightening encounter took place when Annie thumped bees one by one with a hammer as they exited their orchard hive. In spite of a dash for the house to her mother's arms, this misadventure resulted in nasty stings. The terrifying bee mishap was of great interest to Annie because she did *not* remember the event and yet felt that it must be analyzed: "It is curious that of the many pictures I acquired at this time that I have no recollection of this adventure—perhaps because for some time after I could not get outside myself and look on it as a picture."[1] One of Annie Ross's fascinating characteristics was her remarkable ability to peruse her life from above as if she was living it from two places—simultaneously as a participant and as an observer. Although outwardly a dispassionate observer of events and foibles, Annie, as her life story will reveal, ultimately applied the practical lessons of her childhood to events of great consequence.

Meanwhile, in this verdant and rural domestic world, the children's father, Robert Ross, emerges as loving, playful and knowledgeable—a parent brave and strong, full of stories. He carried the children on his shoulders across the millstream that was the home of hideous leeches. He explained why snakes swallowed frogs. He knew where and how to pick berries. In the long winter nights, he fashioned axe handles with admirable skill. The whittling and shaping of ash sections into strong, smooth axe handles held a special fascination for Annie. She watched thin, white shavings curl away from hardened wood. The handle was then smoothed and polished with a piece of glass. With blacksmithing skills acquired at his father's forge in Fredericton, Robert manufactured tools, sledges and all manner of machinery. Snowshoes and moccasins were produced as practical wear but their making was accompanied by stories of hunting and Native lore. Like other men of the times, Robert Ross, with a full and lengthy dark beard, gave the impression of a "walking tree." For a lark, one day he appeared clean-shaven and greatly astonished his wife and family.

Annie's mother, Christine Ross, was as much loved and loving as her husband. It appeared Mother always knew best. She possessed all the essential rural domestic talents from milking cows to knitting underwear, bottling vegetables, and administering first aid for the many knocks and bruises suffered by her children. She entertained all manner of visitors and travellers with equal grace and provisions. Her curious elder daughter observed and overheard conversations with gentlemen who came to hunt in the country, clergymen, "tramps" and especially relatives.

Childbirth is a scene seldom excluded from any life story of these times. A home birth was accompanied by an elevated sense of urgency and secrecy, unfamiliar women scuttling about the house, and general fuss and bother. This was demonstrated when Margaret (soon to be Madge) Stevens Ross arrived at the Rosses of Manners Sutton colonial farm on October 26, 1880. Jamie and Annie initially were not impressed, but soon came to the realization that three children was the perfect number for a family.

In "Passing Through," Annie related an anecdote on a subject somewhat uncustomary in a recollection of this nature. She described the dilemma in which her father and grandfather Ross found themselves when Christine had gone to Harvey Station village, leaving in their care one–year-old Margaret, who had not yet been successfully weaned. The men had a thoroughly frustrating time with the howling child but, upon her return, Christine had little sympathy for their plight. Grandfather, who had brought up nine children of his own, should surely have understood something of how babies were weaned. The Ross family's allopathic remedy was to have the mother apply bitter aloes to her breast in an effort to discourage the child. In fact, this method was employed and Margaret eventually accepted cow's milk!

Toys were another ingredient of childhood memory. Of these there were few. It is no wonder so many late-Victorian dolls survived into the twentieth and twenty-first centuries. Elegantly dressed, these wax-faced darlings were loved from afar. Annie's precious doll was one of these beautiful, untouchable creatures. Jumping-jack marionette-like dolls created by Father were much more fun. Amusements, however, were often of the educational order: a stereopticon (magic lantern), a collection of intricately decorated Christmas cards, a sewing basket of colourful silken scraps and later, books, newspapers and magazines left behind by visitors inspired creative play and imaginative education.

Animals were family members. At the Ross homestead, calves lost when the meadows flooded in the spring and sheep attacked by wild dogs or ravaged by a bear were seriously mourned by Robert and his family. Their old work horse was Frank, and the small carriage mare was Dixie. A gentle, large yellow dog named Dan watched over the three children and more than once retrieved

*A formality: the children of Christine and Robert Fulton Ross of Fredericton, c. 1885.
Margaret Stevens, James Loggie and Annie Harvie. Courtesy of the University of New
Brunswick Archives, MG L7, Series 3, File 1, #5.*

one from a dangerous situation. An unhygienic cat was not so valued and was refused admission to Annie's lonely upstairs bedroom. ·

The darkened, chilly upstairs was also the storeroom for articles from Christine and Robert's earlier life. These cast-offs were a comfort and imaginative treasure for their curious daughter. Mother's silk "appearing out dress" (for visiting following one's marriage), a black velvet coat with a fringe that shed beads, hoop skirts from the late 1860s and an antique grey moiré gown dotted with bow-knots kept Annie enthralled on cold winter nights. Most delightful of all was Mother's wedding bonnet, adorned with tiny lilies-of-the valley, forget-me-nots and miniature pink posies. The tactility and sensual detail in Annie's memoir are astonishingly realistic, and made me wonder whether Annie saw herself as a social historian or whether she was interested in the psychological effect of these images. Was she reliving the comfort and security of her childhood or was this descriptive detail simply a stylistic carry-over from the magazine articles she had been writing most recently?

In September 1879, at four years of age, Annie Harvie Ross started along the exciting road of education. Sometimes her father drove his daughter and her rural companions in the hayrick to the little school at Harvey Station. On other occasions, Annie and a collection of Halford, Rosborough, Sullivan and Moody children—all from large Irish families—jostled and teased each other down the long, dusty road. It was over six kilometres to the schoolhouse, and the Ross children often stopped to rest at the home of one of their mother's friends about two-thirds of the way along the route.

This pretty rural picture changed significantly when Robert Ross decided to take up his old job at a lumber mill near Fredericton. (Fredericton was "town" or sometimes "the city" in Annie's memoir.) Farming had not proven profitable, and a cash income was needed. Robert had frequently walked the forty kilometres to the mill and returned to the Manners Sutton farm only at week's end. Although there was a rail line from Fredericton to Harvey Station, the fare would have been too much to justify. The idyllic rural family setting was showing some practical flaws. Although the census-taker who travelled the back roads of New Brunswick recorded on April 4, 1881, the names and ages of the five occupants of the Robert F. Ross family at Manners Sutton, he noted Robert's occupation as engineer rather than farmer. Before the year was out, the family would decide to move to the mill town much closer to Fredericton, so that Father might stick to city work.

In addition to not following chronological order and omitting people's names, Annie also did not record the location of the family's various homes. These omissions led me on searches through censuses and directories, and had me measuring distances and scrutinizing landmarks. Since the memoir was written nearly sixty years after many of the events had taken place, and the manuscript had been secreted away in a university archive, protection of privacy or sensitivity to making family history public seem unlikely reasons for leaving out information such as dates and places. Annie's rationale remains a mystery. Curious.

MILL TOWN

By mid-1881, the Ross homestead at Manners Sutton had been leased or transferred to Christine's younger sister and brother-in-law, Ruth and Cook (or Coke) Price. The Price family was not popular with Annie, although there were girl cousins of her own age with whom she might share games and chatter. Annie had witnessed an exchange of words or a disagreement between Aunt Ruth and Christine. She displayed an intense loyalty to her mother and could not sanction her aunt's disturbing "tongue lashing": "My sense of justice which has often been a torturing concept to me was outraged. I knew my aunt had not been fair and I never wished to see her again. In fact in later life I never did take much interest in her, although she was apparently forgiven by my mother."[1] Ironically, Aunt Ruth was described as a "thin, tall, dark woman"—a description that could have been used to identify Annie herself as a mature woman. But there the similarity ceased.

The mill town or mill village to which the Ross family moved was in the Kings Ward of the City of Fredericton, a very short distance down the Saint John River from the city centre. Contemporary panoramic photos taken from the hills south of the city centre show signs of the earlier lumbering and shipping industry along the river's eastern curve. Although over 125 kilometres to the river's outlet at the Bay of Fundy, the river here was broad and slow-moving, leaving dangerous and unattractive muddy tidal flats. This industrial, hard-working area has been known variously throughout its 200-year history as "Salamanca," "Lincoln Road" and "Forest Hill"—each name having historical significance.

View of the Saint John River and Lower Fredericton looking northwest from Forest Hill, c. 1885–1890. Photo courtesy of Stephen White Gallery of Photography Collection. LAC/PA 165624 Box 0235.

In 1839, the British Regiment stationed at Fredericton staged a re-enactment of the 1812 Battle of Salamanca at which the 36th Regiment had claimed victory over Napoleon in Spain. The mock battle was held below Fredericton on the flats (less than a kilometre from the present Princess Margaret Bridge). The area, including the railway station, became known as Salamanca as a result of this patriotic revelry. Lincoln Road, as it is still known, parallelled the Saint John River and ran directly through the mill village, extending to farmland beyond the city. The large number of former American slaves who lived in the village in the 1880s no doubt identified with the name "Lincoln"—although the name was brought from Lincoln, Massachusetts, by the United Empire Loyalists. Forest Hill aptly describes this prosperous twentieth-century residential area.

The first ethnic "Africans," so described in the 1881 census, had arrived in Canada along with the United Empire Loyalists in 1781 or had gained their right to passage through having fought on Britain's side in the Revolutionary War or in the War of 1812. By the mid-nineteenth century, several Underground Railway stations along the border with Maine provided access to New Brunswick for escaped slaves. The Black people who settled in the Lincoln Road area were primarily labourers and members of the Church of England, and their families were an integral part of the community. They represented up to a quarter of the local population, with thirty to forty members in the Diamond or Dimond family alone. Annie Ross was fascinated by the historical Christian names of some of the Black children, such as Sebastopol and Augustus. Some children had five or six such exotic names.

Forest Hill Cemetery, where other Loyalist families and notable New Brunswickers are interred, rose above Annie's mill village, bordering the more respectable neighbourhoods of the capital. The cemetery provided a green and pleasant park where the Ross family would wander on Sunday afternoons.

Two major steam-driven sawmills operated along the river and Robert Ross could have been employed in the machine shop of either John A. Morrison's steam mill or the mill owned by Guy Stewart. Lumber mills had been on these sites since the beginning of English settlement and a village, complete with shops, churches and a school had grown up between the flats at water's edge and the railroad line which parallelled the river. The "mill people" lived in cottages along the main street. It was a very different place than Annie's very early childhood neighbourhood and home on Charlotte Street in Fredericton proper. The mill manager and his family lived in a house with a wild and wonderful garden, across the street from the Ross family. The manager's house "... had a high fence all around the grounds, designed no doubt to shut out the scene from which their wealth came."[2] The tangled garden was of greater interest than the residents of the grand house, and it reminded Annie and James of their rural home and the freedom of invention and adventure to which they were accustomed. The schoolhouse was across the railway tracks and up the hill. A wonderful teacher, who enjoyed her lunchtime at Christine Ross's table, taught numbers with the aid of an abacus, but was strict in matters of recitations. She was unimpressed with youngsters, like little sister Madge, who cleaned their slates with a spit-upon rag, rather than the water bottle provided!

Groves of firs and pines surrounded the little schoolhouse and hid springtime carpets of moss and violets. Learning and playtime were as enjoyable and imaginative as ever, but the children of the mill families were unlike other children Annie, James and Madge had previously met. The Ross children were intrigued by their Black playmates and their families. There was something about their chum little Nat that seemed to bother the elders: "The only way we could work it out was that his grandfather was also his father, a relationship that was beyond us, so we did not try to understand it."[3]

"The Rectory," 734 George Street, Fredericton, home of Canon Roberts and the noted Canadian literary family of Confederation Poet Sir Charles G.D. Roberts. Photo by Ron Welwood, 2002.

Although she wasted no time trying to account for the differences in the shades of colour, Annie's awareness of the intricacies of the personal troubles and foibles of the adult world was growing rapidly. Lucy, who had no mother, was neglected by her father; the little girls above the store had no playmates. Annie's mother cared for an elderly Scottish woman next door who was pain-fully dying from cancer, while another woman was merely destitute. Childhood diseases struck. All three Ross children contracted scarlet fever, "diptherictic" throat and jaundice. After the illnesses, the popular schoolteacher no longer came to visit, but merely delivered honour cards and other such educational matters to the front door. The early witnessing of preventable diseases and the neglect of children would have a profound effect on seven-year-old Annie Ross. These images returned to her many times in years to come and influenced several courses of her life.

One family from the lower quarters of the mill town, whom Annie's fam-ily was known to visit, sought solace in the popular, but mysterious religious movement of spiritualism. Adherents to mid-nineteenth century spiritualism believed in the possibility of communication between the living and the dead. This interchange was usually carried out through the use of mediums, séances and other dark techniques. In the case of the mill town family, it was told that upon the death of her parents, the only daughter, on one lonely night, tragically followed her parents' image over the end of the wharf. Such an event drove the community's belief in spiritualism into disrepute.

Like most residents of the mill town, the Rosses were God-fearing church-goers, with no use for such odd beliefs or behaviour. Annie had been baptized in her grandfather's Presbyterian church in Fredericton and the census of 1881 records the family's adherence to that traditionally Scottish faith. However, the Anglican clergy of the extended Cathedral parish of Fredericton considered the mill town a mission area, and in 1870 founded St. Margaret's Church in an old village schoolhouse.

It was at St. Margaret's that Annie, without realizing the singularity of the occasion, met a woman she was to greatly admire for a very long while. Mrs. Emma Roberts, wife of the Reverend George Goodridge Roberts, rector of St. Anne's (now Christ Church Cathedral) and mother of a poet of rising fame, (Sir) Charles G.D. Roberts, conducted sewing classes at St. Margaret's. Annie was at first impressed with Mrs. Roberts's ability with embroidery threads, but she came to genuinely appreciate the gracious and friendly but dignified bear-ing that characterized the matron of one of Canada's first truly literary fami-lies. Christine and Robert Ross were no doubt delighted with their daughter's admiration for Mrs. Roberts. The Robertses and the Rosses had been, after all, nearly neighbours in their city days and dwellings. In 1874, the Reverend George Roberts had been appointed canon of St. Anne's Parish Church, for which Annie's Ross grandfather had created the intricate iron gate. Also, the solid red brick St. Anne's rectory, built in 1829 at 734 George Street and the home of the Roberts family, was just around the corner and down the street from the Ross home. "The Rectory" was a gathering spot for the educated and literary sector of Fredericton society. The Rosses, Wilmots, Phairs and many other families of solid Loyalist and British heritage took pride in the proximity of this now-historic family.

All the while the Rosses lived in the mill town they were familiar with the occupants of some of the grander homes just beyond the formal limits of the city. Annie recalled visiting a large house with a gatehouse. Could that home have been Elmcroft, a still-elegant Georgian manor that was the home of railway construction engineer H.G. Ketchum? Was "the old lady who was the sister of one of the first families in the town and of Loyalist stock…"[4] living on Cemetery Hill, and whom the Ross family called on to chat, a member of the politically and socially influential Fisher family? How was it that a little girl and her littler brother from the mill town were invited to a birthday party for the daughter of the principal of the Fredericton Institute for the Deaf? Mr. Woodbridge was the first principal of the institute that quickly became a landmark of pride and architectural distinction in the city.

In the minds of their parents, the mill town presented an increasingly dangerous and inappropriate environment for the Ross children. The tidal flats and wharfs, the railroad tracks and shunting trains, combined with "… the naughty habits of the children of the mill neighbourhood and the risks of contagious diseases… proved too much for my mother. We soon moved to the city again."[5]

FREDERICTON SCHOOL AND FAMILY

By 1883, with the family once more situated back in Fredericton, Christine could rest a little easier. Grandfather Ross had retained the family home on Charlotte Street where her two eldest children had been born. An uncle and two or three unidentified aunts also lived in the ancestral home with Grandfather. Although there were more relatives and cousins within blocks, a long-standing feud among the adults prevented the young cousins from becoming friends.

The Robert Ross family settled into a rented house in the familiar neighbourhood "just around the corner" from Grandfather. Who needed cousins! Previous occupants of the rented home had left behind a treasure trove of items that excited Annie and her brother's experienced imaginations. An earlier resident had been Thomas Hogg, a printer who, Annie tells us, had left pots of red ink, a Wedgwood jug, a generously proportioned pepper shaker in the figure of Napoleon and a copy of the British literary news journal, *The Spectator*, containing the first published version of Robert Browning's classic poem "My Last Duchess" (c. 1842). From 1866 until 1876, Hogg had been the editor and publisher of *The New Brunswick Report and Fredericton Advertiser*, at the time the most successful weekly newspaper in the province.

Thomas Hogg had lived at 725 George Street, across the street from the family of future Confederation poet, Charles G.D. Roberts. As noted, the Roberts home (The Rectory) was just two blocks from Annie and James's grandfather's house. Hogg might well have left behind in this attic some clues to his profession. His father, James, had founded the Fredericton paper in 1844 and through its pages fought for Reformist principles and non-sectarian schools. Hogg Sr.

went on to support Leonard Tilley in advocating Confederation with Upper and Lower Canada, but died in 1866 before the union came to pass. The Ross children never knew their playthings were most probably the discarded possessions of two very significant New Brunswick political and literary figures. Annie attributed contact with these abandoned artifacts as her first introduction to antiques, and her realization that her grandfather Ross's grandfather clock, a violet-printed copy of the poetry of Robbie Burns brought from Scotland in 1820, and bits and pieces of her aunts' jewellery and china were part of her history.

As in the mill town, school must be attended. Brother and sister walked to York Street School, a statuesque three-storey brick building, formerly the New Brunswick Baptist Seminary. Following the establishment of the public school system in the province in 1872, the facility became York Street Elementary School. A late-twentieth-century plaque notes the seminary's historical significance: "The first institute in Canada to admit men and women on equal footing. The first institution with no admission on religious basis." The seminary was thus liberal in its inclusion of women and admission of those with varied religious beliefs.

Had the Rosses returned to Fredericton in 1882 rather than 1883, they would have had the distinction of advising later family and friends that Sir Charles G.D. Roberts was their principal at York Street School. Quite surprisingly, Annie did not make this observation in "Passing Through." This is the type of aside she would have enjoyed.

The poet's career at the York Street School was brief. In February 1882, following a two-year stint as headmaster at the Chatham, New Brunswick, Grammar School, the 22-year-old Roberts and his young wife returned to Fredericton and the family shelter of "The Rectory" on George Street. Like the Ross children,

York Street Elementary School, Fredericton, which Annie and her brother James attended from 1883 to 1885. Photo by Ron Welwood, 2002.

Left: Fredericton's "Old Burial Ground" (established 1784), where Ross family members are interred. Ross children walked through the historic site en route to school. Photo by Ron Welwood, 2002. Right: Ross and Fulton family memorial marker in the "Old Burial Ground," Fredericton. Photo by Ron Welwood, 2002.

Roberts daily trudged the several blocks from the George Street house to York Street School. By May 1883, Roberts was granted a leave from the Fredericton school. He accepted his severance in 1884, never to return to a grammar or high school classroom. He was off to Toronto to try his hand at editing a newspaper and to follow his literary muse to the United States and Europe.

Annie was so imprecise about certain details in her 1939 memoir that it is difficult to identify York Street School as the school she and James attended. Annie writes only that the "… school we attended was about six blocks away, but there was a short cut through the old cemetery where the family plot was located. If it was not a short cut, we liked to think it was and often went that way."[1] Both the York Street School and the Model School at the Provincial Normal School on Queen Street in the commercial centre of Fredericton fell within the geographical range Annie offers. The Model School was an imposing brick structure (largely reconstructed after a 1929 fire) that later became and remains the city's Justice Building. A quality education and the care by New Brunswick's future enthusiastic teachers and mentors would have been assured the Ross children at the Model School, but the local public school was also deemed an acceptable educational institution. Annie remained more interested in making friends and observing the quirks, manners and matters of neighbours and relatives. Many friendships made during her New Brunswick childhood would amazingly be rekindled years later in the small town of Nelson, British Columbia. In 1884, Nelson was but an unnamed collection of miners' tents and log cabins.

The "Old Burial Ground" on the route to school was everything a cemetery should be. There were large shady elms, grassy paths, iron gates, monuments of various sizes, and elegance and an aura of mystery. Annie and James whispered between themselves and paused beside the grave of Aunt Kathryn Ross, who had died at age 24, and the graves of little cousins Bernice and Kate Harding.

There was also the small, but revered, Ross family plot near the corner of Sunbury and Regent Streets, purchased by James Ross in 1870. Prior to Grandfather Ross's death in 1885, Grandmother (the severe Margaret Elphinstone Ross) had rested there since her death in 1874. She shared this space with her somewhat questionable Ayrshire-born cousin, Robert Fulton (after whom she named her second son). Fulton had been chief clerk to the New Brunswick Provincial Secretary in Fredericton from 1823 until his

Fredericton Model School and Provincial Normal School (opened 1876, replaced 1930), now the city's Justice Building. Photo by Ron Welwood, 2002.

death—allegedly from drunkenness—in 1867. James Ross generously had Fulton's remains relocated and laid alongside his cousin and Ross's wife Margaret E., where a simple inscribed white stone was laid over both graves.

In 1884, at the time of James's and Annie's visits, all was peaceful—on the surface—in the Old Burial Ground. Fulton's 1867 will, however, had been varied on the application of James Ross, and Fulton's properties were divided among the deceased's cousins in Scotland. Rumour had long held that Fulton had had a romantic relationship with a Mrs. Beverly of Fredericton and in his will, Robert Fulton assigned properties to the Beverly family. Little can be learned of this liaison, but the 1881 census records a gentleman named Fulton Beverley (Beverly?) born in 1849 residing in Saint John, New Brunswick.

Associations between the Beverly and Ross families were severely strained for many years. Eventually, a very elderly Beverly relative convinced the Fredericton Improvement Society to eradicate the inscriptions of both Robert Fulton and Margaret E. Ross from the simple stone overlaying their graves. The Ross family, however, had not been consulted in this matter and was most incensed at the desecration. How the Beverly relatives managed this alteration remains a matter of conjecture. The provincial government then erected a rather elaborate white marble monument (on the Ross family plot) for Robert Fulton marking his years of service (1823–1867) with the government of New Brunswick. The Rosses were not remembered on this monument.

Annie's companionable brother, James Loggie Ross, struggled with the serious matter of the erased inscription until the 1950s. He had secured a legal affidavit outlining the historical facts signed by his father's sister Jean (who died in 1941). Before his death in 1953, James Loggie decided that the family should finally lay a small stone over the graves of the grandparents who had passed away over sixty years previously. The Rosses were finally allowed to lie in peace and recognition in the Old Burial Ground, where they share history with governors, clergy, judges and grand old families.

THE DOAKS OF DOAKTOWN

The Robert Fulton Ross family, although separated by miles of dusty or muddy roads, forest track and seasonal river routes, retained close ties (with a few unmentionable exceptions) with family members. This arrangement was most satisfactory for a young girl of Annie's curious nature. Her interest in the lives of others was more than a passing occupation. Close family ties allowed her the intimacy to observe and absorb stories and issues as they developed over the years. Annie was particularly aware of the roles—both humorous and human—that women played in most compelling situations. The Doak and Ross women provided her opportunities to examine immensely strong and capable figures.

It was the seemingly minor events and instances of old-fashioned womanly ways that impressed Annie. She would often, in later life, refer to these visual memories and apply the frivolous or frightening lessons learned as a result. The only visit paid by Grandmother Susannah Doak (whose mother had braved the Miramichi Fire) to her daughter Christine Ross in Fredericton, prompted an interest in women's underclothing and the impracticality of the garments. Grandmother wore woollen bloomers to ward off the winter cold, but preferred the layers of heavy quilted underskirts of a much earlier Victorian era. Pantalets—frilly wide-legged drawers that hung well below a little girl's voluminous skirt—were going out of style in the 1880s and Annie felt terribly sorry for any youngster with the misfortune to be forced to wear pantalets. She detested a tartan dress her mother had sewn from an old shawl because a male cousin had criticized it unfairly. An encounter at Aunt Ann's home at Doaktown with an extremely outdated senior lady, wafting in antebellum style through

G. A. BURKHARDT, FREDERICTON, N. B.

Ann Harvie [Herve] Doak of Doaktown, Annie's favourite aunt and mentor. Photo courtesy of the University of New Brunswick Archives, MG L7, Series 3, File 1, #11.

doorways and sinking/floating into a soft chair due to her monstrous hoop skirt, was a sight to remember. Aunt Ann herself wore puce and lilac, reserving black for ceremonial occasions and disdaining to wear a widow's cap. All these fashion notes Annie accurately recorded in her memoir half a century later.

One memorable Christmas, Annie and her family travelled on a sled drawn by the faithful pair Gypsy and Frank, from Manners Sutton, to the Doak grandparents' home near Doaktown, a distance of nearly 115 kilometres. This was an adventure from a Currier and Ives print, set to the tune of "Over the river and through the woods, to Grandfather's house we go." There were blankets, hot stone bottles, a night on the road for added excitement, and a cozy welcome from Grandmother and numerous relatives.

Annie's mother, Christine Doak Ross, had spent a good part of her youth at the Doaktown homestead on the Miramichi River helping the "young Squire," Robert Doak, and his wife Ann Herve (or Harvie) Doak. This young Squire was Christine's father's first cousin and the son of the founding "old Squire." His charming wife Ann was known as Aunt Ann to all Doak relatives, regardless of generation or familial connections. In the summer of 1884, Christine sent her nine-year-old Annie on the stage from Fredericton on her "first great adventure alone," to visit Aunt Ann. The Doak homestead was the centre of activity for the extended family and the community. Grandmother Susannah Story Doak still lived in the spartan, well-worn, and well-loved house where she had raised ten children about one section away from Aunt Ann.

When Annie came to write "Passing Through" in 1939, she mentally relocated herself to times and places she deeply cherished. Annie vividly revisited every house, outbuilding, pasture, garden, stream and domestic animal she had encountered as a young girl. Her first impressions had lasted a lifetime and she exuded confidence in the way she described things and people just as they were.

The large acreage on the Miramichi River had been acquired by Annie's
great-great-grandfather Doak. This first Doak settler quickly established a mill
on the stream ("the race") that traversed his property. The Doak family had
brought from Scotland the complete equipage for lumber, wool and grist mills.
The flour or grist mill was managed in the 1880s by an uncle, Horace Austin,
who existed in a cloud of light grey dust. Below the flour mill, the saws of the
lumber mill screamed through the wet logs. Annie was familiar with the huge
sawmills at Fredericton and was unimpressed with this operation. However, the
woollen mill with its massive grey bundles and soft curls of fleece smelling of
lanolin and warmth was "dearest to us children." Annie recalled that "about the
mill there was a sort of triple fascination that no other place even the great yard
where the cows collected to be milked in the evening held so much interest."[1]

For Annie and assorted Doaktown children, raspberry and blueberry pick-
ing was both enjoyable and productive. Bothering the trout in the millpond
was entertaining. But nothing was as exciting as hunting Atlantic salmon in the
depths of night with teenage uncles Peter and Miles. The two lads lured the fish
to the surface of the water by means of a brazier of coals perched precariously
low on the bow of the skiff: "As the great salmon of the Miramichi saw the light
they clustered around. The spearman picked his choice and swiftly and unerr-
ingly drove his three-pronged trident downward and held the struggling fish
which was soon in the boat."[2] This method of fishing was used by the Native
people of the area as well.

From the farm at Manners Sutton to the tangled garden of the manager's
house at "the mill town," Annie delighted in any manifestation of vegetation
and woodlot. The Doaktown homestead's massive vegetable and flower garden
produced a bounty of wild herbs, blossoms, branches and seeded vegetables.
Vines and morning glories tumbled over each other. Cultivated roses and gera-
niums served double-duty for jellies and beauty. A trademark double white
geranium graced an interior windowsill. All these became vivid, lasting pictures
in her memory book.

Details of the main house, including the precise configuration of the rooms
as well as the simple furnishings, were deeply implanted in Annie's mind's eye.
Each room was a tribute to the decorating and handiwork skills of numerous
female contributors. Homemade carpets of bright Roman stripes, woven car-
pets in bedrooms, lemon soap at the washstand and gleaming jars of colourful
jams and preserves gave evidence of both competence and hard work.

The practical skill of knitting was not to be overlooked. It was a constant
struggle for women and young girls to produce enough woollen socks, mittens,

caps and underwear to keep a horde of hard-working and hard-playing men and boys warm (and perhaps clean) during the long and desperately cold winters. Clothing was re-cut and re-fashioned into various garments until there was no goodness in them, except as mats and throws. Spinning wheels of several nationalities and sizes were part of everyday life. Children were charged with collecting plants, such as a sweetly aromatic fern, *Myrica comptonia,* which grew in companionship with the blueberries. The plant produced a vivid yellow dye, much favoured by Grandmother. Old rags were dyed a deep blue from a fixative of logwood, then hooked or braided as rugs. Prompted by the output of the Doak woollen mill, the weaving of blankets and cloth on heavy looms was done in private homesteads as a regular occupation. Annie's grandfather, the irascible James A. Doak, was content only when wearing a shirt of tough, grey home-woven cloth. The shirts wore so well they were likened to rock maple.

Annie's mother, Christine Doak Ross (1847–1935), c. 1900. Photo courtesy of the University of New Brunswick Archives, MG L7, Series 3, File 1, #12.

Aunt Ann had been widowed in early middle age and yet had run farm, mills, hay fields and hog farm, and all in such a manner that her children's well-being was ensured. She was the matron and confident in manners of money, life, and love—an example of what a lone woman could often accomplish. In describing Aunt Ann and her own grandmother Susannah, Annie recorded, "They were both towers of strength in a weary land, but a great contrast to each other…"[3] in personality and presence.

Susannah Story Doak had a considerable knowledge of the "healing arts" learned from her grandmothers and the mysterious Native women in the Story family's past. A gentle, unprepossessing woman, Susannah quietly delivered babies in the middle of the night and made house calls, regardless of her own health and safety. She possessed an innate understanding of "asepsis" and the necessity of cleanliness. Through a mixture of folk healing and old wives' tales, Grandmother believed that children could be marked by prenatal occurrences.

Annie's father, Robert Fulton Ross (1840–1921), c. 1900. Photo courtesy of the University of New Brunswick Archives, MG L7, Series 3, File 1, #13.

One of her own children was pecked on the nose by an unfriendly gobbler, inflicting a distracting wound. As a result, that child as well as the child in her womb (Annie's mother, Christine) were afflicted with crossed eyes!

For some ailments and occurrences of life, there were no ready treatments and little understanding or diagnosis. More mature reflection tempered Annie's blissful observations of life at the Doaktown settlement. Aunt Caroline Austin, the tall "Indian-like" wife of the dusty miller, Uncle Horace, and a Story family member, had an addiction of some manner. Yet the addiction was in response to "terrible headaches for which she consumed quarts of patent medicines... [and] most of the time she went about with her head bound up in a bandana handkerchief."[4] Uncle Horace's penchant for alcohol did not make her situation any happier. "The drink" was indeed a matter of concern, especially in lumbering and hard-working communities such as those along the Miramichi.

In 1878, the Canada Temperance Act (Scott Act) permitted any county or municipality to prohibit the retail sale of liquor as determined by popular vote. This "local option" to prohibit alcohol did not apply in the Doaktown area. Halfway between Aunt Ann's home and Grandmother Doak's were the post office and general store where loggers and millworkers could find their "favourite liquid." On Saturday nights, fisticuffs resulting from the trade in and consumption of libations frequently occurred. When Annie's young Uncle Peter Doak became a participant in the business of "broken heads," he was frequently called before the magistrate, but with humour and guile worthy of an Irishman, he managed to entertain the court. He would argue his own case with "vituperative remarks" aimed at his opponents but enjoyed by the court watchers. Geordie Bowman, a gnarled and elderly hunter and woodsman, was also the victim of the drink. Aware of his strong weakness for spending his hard-earned money, Geordie decided on one occasion to hide his pay packet in a hollow tree. Following his next debauchery, he could not recall the location of the rich hollowed tree and thenceforth brought all his money to town and spent it as quickly as possible.

Social ills of a more serious nature also presented themselves in this idyllic community. One of Grandmother's resident brothers was of necessity taken away for institutional care after developing a "religious mania." His family was dispersed and for a while a troubled young cousin was sent to live with Annie's family. The lad, who had a lisp, exhibited unusual behaviour and was not set right until his poor mother could find work and re-settle her family.

A sad and sentimental story was being enacted during Annie's last summer visit to the homestead and Grandmother Doak's. Pretty and vivacious Aunt Susie (Christine's youngest sister) had married and had just given birth to a lovely baby. Annie related the gothic Victorian tale. Upon arrival "… I was not prepared to see two [babies], nor for the sadness of my aunt who had been a merry sort of person. But even I, young as I was, could understand that there was some thing[s] not to be borne. A few days after her own baby arrived another was left at her door, with a note to say that it also belonged to her husband! No doubt she had the sporting instincts of the family, for she attempted to care for both, but such a thing proved too much or too sudden even for her generosity and she died of a decline. I do not think that either child survived."[5] Although Annie did not express immediate outrage at the revelation of such personal incidents, she experienced great sorrow for the people involved. She held these stories closely in her heart and memory. They would provide motivation for action and expression in future years.

Alas, the summers and chapters of pleasures and discovery were over and the Robert Fulton Ross family prepared for another home, another town.

WOODSTOCK HOME

*A*nnie's father, Robert Fulton Ross, had left the Fredericton "mill village" lumber mill while Annie and the rest of the family were still settled in to home and school in the city. He had taken up employment in Woodstock, commuting by steamer to Fredericton on weekends. This was an unsatisfactory arrangement and upon the death of Grandfather Ross in 1885, the family was reunited in Woodstock. Woodstock was to be truly "home" for generations to come.

Curiously enough, Annie's memoir does not ever use the name Woodstock. Chapter five of "Passing Through," called "Growing Up," is twenty-two pages long, yet there is nary a mention by name of the town so affectionately known thereafter as "home" or "our town." It was through reference books such as the 1936 *Who's Who in Canada*, alumni records, newspaper articles and obituaries that Woodstock, New Brunswick, was identified as the home of the R.F. Ross family after 1885. Thus, with a few exceptions accorded to members of the Doak family, Annie consistently kept to her pattern of secrecy. Ross neighbours were identified by location, occupation, or personal quirk. Playmates were recognized by first names or nicknames, teachers by personal traits or a grade taught. Other than indicating names, the details of their lives and the games they played were described with honesty and credibility.

Both parents were close at hand. Life, although far from affluent, was generally secure and free from serious cares. The Union Foundry, founded in 1865 by tinsmith A.J. Small and John Fisher, Jr. and where Robert Ross worked, was one of three such operations in the town. John Fisher, Jr. had been granted his own patent in 1872 but had sold the foundry located near the town centre on

Robert F. Ross instructing his son James Loggie in the art of blacksmithing. Woodstock, New Brunswick, 1888. Photo courtesy of Andrew and Charles Gordon Ross.

WOODSTOCK, NEW BRUNSWICK

Queen Square in Woodstock, New Brunswick, the town Annie would always call 'home,' 1881. Photo courtesy of Carleton County Historical Society.

Woodstock, at the junction of the Saint John and the Meduxnekeag Rivers—like the grander City of Fredericton nearly a hundred kilometres downstream—owes a good part of its heritage and history to Loyalist settlers and veterans of the American War of Independence. Did it take its name from a charming village near Oxford, England, as suggested by the 1985 *Canadian Encyclopedia*? A more practical suggestion from a local perspective was put forth by William O. Raymond in July 1895:

> There seems to have been no connection between the name "Woodstock" and that of the former residence of any of the first settlers, nor was there any English statesman or notable public character in honor of whom the new settlement might have been named whose title was in any way connected with "Woodstock." The only theory therefore that can be advanced is that the unbroken forest surroundings suggested to the founders of Woodstock the name by which their settlement should henceforth be known.[1]

By 1885, Woodstock had become a river town dependent upon lumber mills, foundries, transport up and down the rivers and its proximity to the state of Maine. The town, the first incorporated in New Brunswick in 1856, had survived a major fire in 1881 that destroyed many wooden structures.

upper Main Street in 1882. The plant employed thirty-five men and manufactured rotary sawmills and machines, shingle machines, stoves, hot air furnaces and gigantic farm machinery. The variety of manufactured items was of greater interest and challenge to Ross than his previous job at the sawmill had been.

Now that Annie was settled nicely in the new town, she set out to do one of the things she did best—get to know the neighbourhood and make friends. A twelve-year-old lad from a very large family down the hill took a shine to Annie and would shyly slip her an apple on the way to Sunday school. On occasions like this it was a chore to have five-year-old sister Madge trailing at her apron. A new friend, Emma, introduced Annie to vividly gruesome storybooks about the Wild West; with Ella, she mastered the handicraft of crochet work; Louise told hilarious stories and passed on intriguing gossip; a neighbour woman with a continual nest of kittens and a host of patience imparted housekeeping and needlework skills.

Pleasing as Annie's life appeared, she was extremely bothered by (one might even say resentful of) the adventures in which her brother and his friends engaged. James belonged to a real "gang." The acknowledged leader of this gang, Garvie, was the teenaged son of the Anglican minister. He had lost an eye in a

Looking up the roughly hewn Main Street of Woodstock, New Brunswick, 1881. Photo courtesy of Carleton County Historical Society.

Three generations of the Ross men of Woodstock, New Brunswick, c. 1921. James Robert (son of James Loggie), Robert Fulton and James Loggie Ross. Photo courtesy of Andrew and Charles Gordon Ross.

self-conducted experiment concerning the way a certain powder explodes in a bottle and posed no end of trouble to his parents. James's mother "… was sure he was leading her boy astray…. Years after we learned that Garvie's mother was just as sure that our brother was leading her boy astray…."[2] One thing for certain, no girls were ever involved in any of the gang's undertakings: "No Quaker meeting house was any more firm on the segregation of the sexes than these gang youths."[3] "Croak" (James's gang name) and the boys camped and cooked along the riverbanks. One summer Ernest, a lad overburdened with older sisters, took adventuring to an extreme and solo-rafted all the way to Fredericton. Ernest's family was rather religious and Ernest was much taken with the idea of walking on water. Engaging Croak's mechanical ability, the two constructed a set of early water wings. Not satisfied with wearing the device under his arms, Ernest endeavoured to attach the "wings" to his feet so that he might walk upon the waters of the Saint John River. Needless to say, the wings floated, but the walker sunk headfirst and required rescuing by his companion.

There was a no-girl rule in a basement theatrical group as well. How aggravating to pay admission to see one's own brother dressed up for the feminine roles! Girls contented themselves with hopscotch and marbles, highlighted by group tag-type games like Prisoner's Base.

The more solitary side of Annie's personality was satisfied by her growing passion for reading. Later, when she became a teacher, she deplored the depressing collection of stories, such as *Babes in the Woods* and *Little Jim,* included in the readers and curriculum of the late 1880s. There was little or no opportunity to learn useful information in geography, nature and science. Annie, furnished with only the Sunday school library and later the high school library, would seek out and read anything that came her way. Given the book selection parameters of school and church, most novels available had a strong historical flavour and were suffused with morality lessons.

Annie recorded the titles and authors of every book she read as a teenager. She recalled that "generally books were divided into two classes, those with board and those with paper covers. This was not such a poor division as books which were to endure were rarely bound in paper covers. Popular novels and such sentimental publications as were known to that day were always in paper covers."[4] Isabella Macdonald Alden, writing as "Pansy" from 1865 to 1929, produced approximately a hundred books and many more serialized stories for magazines. Pansy's *Chautauqua Girl* series, along with the numerous stories of Edward Payson Roe were of the acceptable board cover variety. Roe (1838–1888), so little known in the twentieth or twenty-first century, was the most popular American novelist of his time and sold more copies than Mark Twain. His Christian message was delivered through fictional stories inspired by current news items and historical incidents. *Without a Home* dealt with "… the pernicious results of the morphia habit… portraying its influence to wither and destroy manhood and to wreck the happiness of the family."[5] This was rather vivid subject matter, but the impact of his novels was undeniable. Lew Wallace, creator of *Ben Hur*, and Silas Hocking, the first author to sell one million of his books in his own lifetime, were also acceptable authors. The likes of Mary Elizabeth Braddon's *Lady Audley's Secret* was questionable, while the "dime novel" works of Charlotte M. Braeme were taboo. Sir Walter Scott was her father's choice but James's choice (with Annie surreptitiously reading on the side) was the blood and thunder of *Boy's Annual* and the Ballantyne books. All this attraction with life through and on the written page is a powerful indication that books, literature, journalism and organizing stories and knowledge were to be consistent defining factors for the rest of Annie's very long life.

Most of the Ross children's reading was guided neither by curriculum nor by teachers. Teachers were not distinguished for what they taught but for the popularity or affection they engendered in the pupils. Miss Grace was a mere ten years older than her students and was considered a friend as much as a teacher. Changes in

Annie and her siblings c. 1895. James Loggie, Margaret Stevens and Annie Harvie Ross of Woodstock, New Brunswick. Photo courtesy of the University of New Brunswick Archives, MG L7 Series 3, File 1, #6.

homes, grades and pupil numbers resulted in the Rosses attending three or four different Woodstock schools and encountering an increasing number of teachers and administrators. A very young Robert Landells made such an impression as principal of one school that his full name was registered in Annie's memoir: "We youngsters thought him a wonderful person and used to gaze at him in admiration of his glowing health."[6] Landells's departure for a teaching position in British Columbia was deeply regretted by the community—but later fondly recalled by one of his most admiring female students, who also found her way to teaching in rural British Columbia.

The headmaster of the next school Annie attended was occasionally stricken with epileptic seizures. The boys in the class coolly learned how to deal with the situation. There were signs that maturity was being achieved. A tolerance for "sub-standard people wandering about" became more evident. Tramps such as Angus Burr, who wound his way from community to community, even as far as Aunt Ann's in Doaktown, were no longer made fun of, nor was his mother, who picked up feathers to put in her hat, or the rocking-chair granny who smoked a pipe. Gardening and the scientific application of planting schedules and development of varieties of fruit, along with an awareness that sand plums and unique indigenous turtles were seen less often, showed a broadening of intellectual horizons.

Unlikely as it may seem, Annie's senior grades at high school passed without major recorded incident. One nameless principal was destined to become a powerful person in provincial education circles. Under the guidance of the English literature teacher, Annie and companions gave up outdoor games and engaged in parsing Greek and Latin verbs and memorizing lines of English poetry instead. Only as an aside did Annie mention that there were "but few boyfriends" in her life. This was attributed to having a brother who was a terrible tease.

Annie quite bluntly states, "finishing with school was the event of the year 1892. Bracketed for two medals and having won another, I felt generous giving up the others. But I did wish I might have had the essay medal."[7] This brief revelation greatly understates the significance of the awards Annie collected. Did she win other awards that she was asked or volunteered to refuse or pass over to another graduate? The L.P. Fisher award for "regularity of attendance" was meagre recognition of the young woman's academic prowess. How proud (and possibly bemused) her parents must have been when their eldest daughter received the more prestigious and practical Carleton County Scholarship that would admit her to the University of New Brunswick in Fredericton in September 1892. Her prize as leader of the graduating class also included a copy of Macauley's *History of England*. We can surmise that Annie was pleased enough to simply collect her rewards and move on to Fredericton. The inquisitive daughter of a New Brunswick blacksmith and a farm-reared mother would attend Canada's oldest English-speaking institution of higher learning, founded in 1785.

THE UNIVERSITY OF NEW BRUNSWICK

*T*here was an enthusiastic flourish of crisp typing paper when Annie Garland Foster, late in 1939, came to the point in her memoir where her thoughts were carried back to Fredericton of 1892 and up the hill to the University of New Brunswick (UNB). This was where and when her new life really began.

It is highly probable that Nan Ross (as Annie would be known by her colleagues and classmates) kept a journal during her four years as a co-ed at UNB and that this journal formed the reference point from which Annie, the writer and autobiographer, looked back on the happiest years of her life. Sadly, such a journal (if indeed it was created) no longer exists; but recollections of scents, surroundings, and people were so vividly revealed in "Passing Through," they most surely were copied from notations made by a perceptive young woman.

Nan's reverent descriptions of the campus of the mid-1890s were as credible and inspired as any other recorded contemporary observation—or any commentary since. On her autumnal walks to the halls of learning, the seventeen-year-old "lady student" found that "… the pathway traversed the beech grove, wound its way between scarlet maples and an occasional evergreen, to a terrace upon which reposed an old gray building…. The many windows with small panes [of the Old Arts Building] revealed no sign of life. The pathway was a short-cut which just below the terrace crossed a driveway that wound around the hill and disappeared among the buildings beyond the central hall."[1] Nan spoke of "… the smell of frost, the pungent odor of the fading fern … and the pathway of mosaic woven of green and gold fading leaf…."[2] and the violets that tumbled over the terrace wall welcoming the spring! These delicate blossoms were recalled in all three reminiscences Annie was to write about UNB.

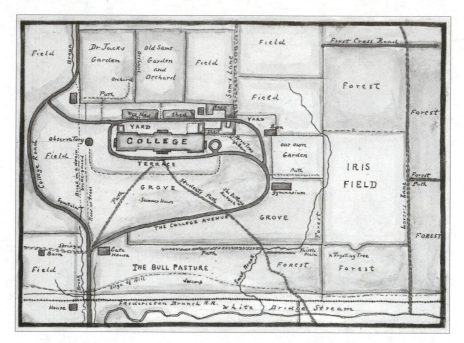

Popular hand-drawn map of the campus of the University of New Brunswick, created by Joseph Bailey in the 1880s. Image courtesy of the University of New Brunswick Archives, MG H1 MS5.3.11.

The Old Arts Building, UNB, Fredericton, 1930. Photo courtesy of Madge Smith and Shirley Miller.

FOUNDING UNB

A college, which later became the University of New Brunswick, had graced the northern slope above the provincial capital all the years the Rosses had lived in and out of Fredericton. Now Annie would be part of that small citadel of knowledge from which so many familiar political luminaries, educators, literary masters, and scholars progressed onto the local scene, often en route to wider national and even international fame.

Every historical background piece written about the University of New Brunswick acknowledges its unlikely beginnings. In 1785, fast upon the first sitting of the future province's legislature, Mrs. Paine, a Loyalist living in Charlotte County near the Maine border, urged her husband, a recently elected member of the legislature, to gather a petition to Governor Thomas Carleton. Dr. William Paine and six other gentlemen of distinction requested the formation of an academy or college and two years later, in 1787, the Provincial Academy of Arts and Sciences, professing the aims and objectives of the Church of England, was established and offered classes in Fredericton. A charter was granted in 1800 and the school renamed the College of New Brunswick, but it was not until 1828 that three students were awarded Bachelor of Arts degrees. These three were the first and only graduates of the College of New Brunswick. Funds and students were always in short supply. The generally rough living conditions, the exclusivity of the governing Church of England, and the rigid classical curriculum hindered the college's immediate success. By 1829, the College of New Brunswick had ceased to exist. It was succeeded by Fredericton's King's College, which was promptly granted a Royal Charter to grant degrees.

As early as 1826, Lieutenant-Governor Sir Howard Douglas had selected the hillside building site, and the cornerstone for a large, solid granite building was laid. The structure would come to represent the future university to the academic world. The "Old Arts Building" stood centrestage on the hillside campus of nearly 2,000 acres. The institution was re-constituted in 1860 as the University of New Brunswick and the campus slowly began to develop a distinctive and impressive character. However, the granite-stoned Old Arts Building stood as the lone sentinel to learning until 1900 when a far less grand edifice to house the School of Engineering was erected on the campus.

The Ladies Reading Room in the Old Arts Building, UNB, 1900. Photo courtesy of the University of New Brunswick Archives, UA PC 9 no. 7.

The interior of the Old Arts Building did not merit the poetic attendance given its exterior and setting. In 1891, students called for a steam or hot air heating apparatus. A correspondent in the March 1891 *University Monthly* explained: "A system of heating, such as is in use in nearly all our public buildings, would not only save labour and money, but would greatly benefit the health of both Professors and Students."[3] A telephone was also recommended, for its very obvious advantages. When Nan Ross entered the university in 1892, the few women students were afforded two modest sitting rooms on the second floor that they could call their own. The Ladies Reading Room overlooked the violet-strewn terrace and the pastoral slope leading to the city and the Saint John River. It was Spartan, but comfortable. The fall 1896 issue of the *University Monthly* observed that the brilliant, cheerful conversation of recent graduate Nan Ross would be missed in the little Ladies Reading Room. Nan was known to have punctuated her comments with the vigorous clatter of a poker as she prodded the meagre fire in the room's tiny grate. There were no housing residences for students and the serious-looking lecture halls were for formal lecturing.

The majority of UNB's students of the 1890s were bright, eager young people raised and schooled in the Maritime provinces. Like Nan, they were inexperienced in travel, culture or the ways of the world. They had no basis for comparing the simple Fredericton campus or its faculty with the renowned and sophisticated Ivy League institutions of New England or the universities of Upper Canada. And yet UNB, in setting and style, was a surprising miniature of these more prestigious institutions. The sense of discovery and expectation experienced by UNB's undergraduates was as genuine as those permeating the air at Cambridge or Yale.

Annie Harvie Ross, BA Graduate, UNB, 1896. Photo courtesy of the University of New Brunswick Archives. Graduates. Composites. Encaenia. 1896.

Nan Ross showed no reluctance or even hesitancy in approaching the Old Arts Building in September 1892. Her family, her teachers and, no doubt, the entire community of Woodstock assumed Ann Ross would continue studies following matriculation from high school and now, bolstered by the Carleton County Scholarship, she would follow that destiny. In August 2002, I followed Nan Ross's footsteps past the Old Arts Building (Sir Howard Douglas Hall) with considerably less confidence and elan than she had exhibited as a first-year student. It was in the solid grey building before me that Nan had studied Greek, history, science and literature. She would never have imagined that her self-appointed biographer would, more than a hundred years later, visit UNB to pry into her life and her thoughts now so securely archived at the university's modern Harriet Irving Library.

In the 1880s, admission of women as students and faculty was being debated at UNB, but with somewhat less political passion than elsewhere. Nonetheless, the topic was of very recent and ongoing interest and the universities of the Maritime provinces were leading the way in accepting women ("the ladies") as students. Mount Allison College in Sackville, New Brunswick, admitted women in 1862, and in 1875 (the year of Annie's birth), Miss Grace Annie Lockhart of Mount Allison became the first woman in the British Empire, and

UNB'S FIRST CO-ED

In 1884, Mary Kingsley Tibbits of Fredericton, aged fifteen, passed the New Brunswick matriculation examinations. Mary and her mother were determined that Mary should attend a university, but Harvard Annex (later Radcliffe), Wellesley College and Boston University told Mary she was too young.

While passing the time of day, Mary read the *Statutes of New Brunswick*, particularly the University Act. Here she learned that any *person* who had passed matriculation exams and paid the fee might enter the university and obtain a degree. Mary, her mother and their lawyer, William Nelson, realized that Mary was indeed a person. A request for admission was directed to UNB President Thomas Harrison. The University Senate refused Mary's application: "During the ensuing session of the Legislature [1885] the grant for the University came up for discussion. Mr. John Valentine Ellis, member for Saint John and future Canadian Senator, opposed the grant, because the University had refused admission to a duly qualified student... one Mary K. Tibbits."[4] Upon considering the financial repercussions of refusing this *person's* application, the Senate reconvened and informed Miss Tibbits of her admission. And so it was that UNB's first woman student enrolled in September 1886.

As Mary was researching and planning her route to academic recognition and the University Senate and provincial legislature pondered post-secondary co-education, the students at UNB debated the principle in print and forum. The *University Monthly* editorialized in November 1885: "We believe the subject will receive the grave consideration its importance demands. Ladies contend that they should have equal rights with men, as far as education goes anyway and no one, we fancy, would presume to deny them this."[5] Such simple sentiment was not unanimous. The benefits of co-education could be recognized, but was it beneficial in "our own University"? Three valiant co-eds registered in 1887. Mary Tibbits graduated in 1889 with honours in English and was awarded the Stanley Gold Medal (named for the Governor General of the day). In 1892, when Nan Ross enrolled, there were an equal number of women and men in the freshman year. This was a significant change in student demographics.

Here the matter of the prophetic use of the term "person" should be examined. If Mary was recognized as a person by the University of New

Coeds of UNB, c. 1896, pose on the north portico of the Old Arts Building. Student at 3 o'clock, wearing a white blouse and dark sweater, is thought to be Annie Ross. Photo courtesy of the University of New Brunswick Archives, UA PC 16 no. 101.

Brunswick in 1886 and admitted to its ranks on this basis, why did the Supreme Court of Canada rule in 1927 in the famous Persons Case that person status did not apply to women? Why did UNB (and other postsecondary educational institutions) admit women if, under the Canadian constitution, the word "person" did not apply to women? Were the universities in contravention of Canada's constitution of 1867? Or were the government of New Brunswick and the University of New Brunswick more enlightened in this regard than other agencies? It was not until 1929 that a Judicial Committee of the Privy Council in London stipulated that "person" was in itself ambiguous and that women were legally persons. Surely Mary Tibbits, the first woman school principal in New Brunswick, chuckled when the Famous Five women who championed the Persons Case achieved their moral victory.

hence in Canada, to be awarded a bachelor's degree. Her degree was an unfeminine Bachelor of Science. Harriet Starr Stewart accepted the first Bachelor of Arts degree bestowed upon a woman in Canada from the same college in 1882. An Ontario university, Queen's at Kingston, granted its first degree to a woman in 1884.

Girls graduating from New Brunswick high schools had on occasion written the provincial matriculation examinations. In 1880, UNB began offering certificates to girls who scored well on the examination, but this certificate was not an entrance ticket to the university. Matriculation examination proficiency was, however, helpful in securing further training at a Normal School or nursing college. Nan and her freshman classmates of 1892 would be very familiar with the breakthrough of women into the halls of learning, a feat accomplished by Mary Tibbits in 1886.

Nan's views on the issue of women as equals were less profound and of less consequence than those held by Mary Tibbits or the Senate of the university when Mary was welcomed as the first female student at UNB. Nan had experienced childhood instances of resentment against the physical activities and freedoms enjoyed by her brother and his friends. As a youngster, the lot of less privileged women had not escaped her notice but such observations did not seem to have any direct application to her scholarly or social life. Like any co-ed of the day, she encountered the sentiments of "anti-feminist" men in social or informal educational settings. Her reaction to such situations was usually one of indignation rather than moral conviction.

The women of the freshman class of 1892 regarded themselves, in an academic sense, as "better men than they," and set out to prove it in the examination hall. They took pride in asserting themselves in the presence of the young men. In her memoir, Nan recounts a true but novel-like conversation with an acquaintance named Charles, which she felt showed her in the role of a confident young woman dealing with an aspiring young beau who was threatened by the notion of educated co-eds:

"Do you think you will stick at college for four years," continued Charles.

"I hope so," I ventured, "Dad wants me to if possible. I suppose I could stop next year and go to Normal, but I should like to go on!"

"Lots of nice girls at Normal, pretty ones, too," said he watching the effect of his words. "Girls shouldn't go to college. It is like cats doing dogs' tricks!"

"What an idea!" I gasped choking over the insult added to half a walnut in the cake frosting. "You certainly are old fashioned. Aren't girls human beings the same as boys? And when did cats belong to the dog family."[6]

Nan continued the repartee by chiding Charles who, as a mere part-time student, seemed to be overly concerned about "what happens on the hill"— obviously not his true milieu. Neither Charles nor Nan is shown in an especially attractive light in this exchange, but Nan must have felt it was illustrative of a certain frame of mind.

FACULTY AND FRIENDS

Frank, a distant cousin of the chauvinist Charles, was a conventional literate chap. Thankfully Frank did not share Charles's annoying conviction of male superiority. Nan and Frank had a more traditional boy-girl relationship. Family ties aside, Charles and Frank definitely were not friends. This complicated the young men's mutual acquaintance with Nan. Nonetheless, Nan was much more at ease with Frank, who was one year her academic senior, and the two frequently arranged that their paths up the hill in the morning intersected. They skipped classes to enjoy "walks and talks" about the hill and the city: "Just at the foot of the hill grew an old gnarled white hawthorn which seemed to have been there for a long time, but never grew very fast. In spring it was covered with the whitest blossoms and for some reason I always see it when I recall these care free days with Frank!"[1] In spite of hating the colour red and risking the discomfiture of some of Fredericton's citizens who disassociated themselves from military personnel, Frank joined the officers' militia. Nan put aside her suspicion of soldiers and strolled the streets of Fredericton with her young man. Frank, however, soon moved on to medical school. The grassy slopes, evening receptions and pleasant walks of college days became sweet memories and the basis for nostalgic reflection.

Before Frank of the pleasant walks and before the cheeky Charles, there was Stephen, of whom we know nothing at all. All three young men exist in Nan's memoir without a surname. Notwithstanding several familial clues, it is impossible to attach an identity or a future to these young men. Again, why was Nan reluctant to identify places, institutions and names other than those of direct family members? It is a question I repeatedly asked myself as I perused

Nan's papers. Might there exist a possibility that even forty years later, one of these young men (or their children and grandchildren!) might be revealed and embarrassed by an innocent romantic liaison from Nan's youth? Or did the reluctance lay simply with Nan herself? It is tempting to detect a certain coyness in Nan's later storytelling. By omitting selected names and places, she creates a hint of mystery about herself for future readers or biographers to ponder. As a mature writer, Nan had developed a keen interest in psychology, and her reticence might be attributed to a psychological theory she studied along the way. Were some of her "remembered" experiences somewhat exaggerated or less than factual? Possibly she felt the experiences themselves were more important than the characters? Did she wish to create a morality play, illustrating the universality of human experiences and behaviour? Will we ever uncover her motives?

Like campuses everywhere, the University of New Brunswick had a reputation for pranks and hijinks. Nan observed rather than actively participating in a particularly memorable Hallowe'en venture. "Tommy's" old carriage was kept in a shed at the top of the hill, and "the pranksters decided that it might be a good idea to take it down the hill and leave it there.... Several of them took hold of the shafts and very quietly ran it down the hill for fear of disturbing Tommy in his apartment [in the Arts Building]. When they reached the bottom, a voice from within the carriage called: 'That's right, gentlemen, now take me up again!'"[2] Tommy was Dr. Thomas Harrison, professor of English language and literature and chancellor of the university, and who fortunately fell into the "beloved professor" category.

UNB held a rather unique graduation ceremony, dubbed Encaenia (a derivative from the Greek word meaning festival of founders). It was first celebrated in 1830 and the ceremony evolved over the years, with a raucous cannon salutation to the graduates highlighting Encaenia from 1876 until 1936. In 1896, however, the year of Nan Ross's graduation, the Encaenia cannon did not function properly and the gallant young men of the class decided to salute the graduates by firing a cannon from the Fredericton military barracks. The women graduates were called in as accomplices to the misdeed, as it was "... explained that if each boy were escorted by one of the women, they were sure the police would not molest them."[3] Nan figured this recognition of the feminine element of the class was the young women's just reward for enduring the friendly superiority of their male counterparts for the past four years. A militant attitude on the part of the young women was not required in this instance—simple dignity and intelligence sufficed.

This was the social and natural setting of UNB in the mid-1890s. Nan's part in some of these events make an interesting aside, but she entered UNB a serious-minded, disciplined student. She was eager to plunge into any and all courses offered. Her natural inclination and only previous experience was in the field of literature, in which she had an admittedly good grounding, thanks to her Woodstock high school teacher. Nan, always the voracious reader, was ready to move beyond the sentimental novels she had devoured and to approach the classics of western philosophy, language and literature.

The university was very much alive with academic vigour and a small, but significant, number of notables were found on both the faculty and the graduate rosters. Prominent among the graduates prior to the 1890s were Sir George Parkin, educator and principal of Fredericton Collegiate School; Hon. William Pugsley, lawyer and briefly premier of New Brunswick; Sir George Foster, professor of classics at UNB, Member of Parliament and Senator; Charles G.D. Roberts, noted poet (and his three brothers); Roberts's cousin and fellow poet, Bliss Carman; as well as a conspicuous number of judges, university presidents and chancellors, newspaper editors, doctors, lawyers and military men. Nan's respect for the faculty pre-dated her graduation from UNB and grew more fervent with passing years. In 1926, she affirmed, "Under the instruction of some of the finest minds that ever directed education in the province, ... it is not surprising that there should have graduated men who have made their names known in the land."[4]

Few in number, but mighty in knowledge and style, the faculty of the 1890s was comprised of some imposing figures. UNB had financial difficulties and its reputation was challenged by a growing number of newer colleges and universities. Dr. Thomas Harrison became president in 1885 and continued to teach English literature and mental and moral philosophy. Even as chancellor in the mid-1890s, he taught mathematics to Nan and her freshmen contemporaries. According to Nan he managed to entertain the students enough so they could absorb at least as much of his subject as was required. Harrison was more remembered for his presence: "He was a large man and it must have taken many yards of silk to make him a gown. But to see him sail into class, twirling his spectacles in one hand, silken draperies billowing about his feet was to feel that any price was cheap that could so successfully outline his personality."[5]

The venerable Dr. Loring Woart Bailey came from Harvard in 1861 to preside in the science lecture hall. Dr. Bailey had studied the "new" sciences under Louis Agassiz, a founder of the National Academy of Sciences in America and Harvard's Asa Gray, the theorist of Christian Darwinism. Initially, most theologians believed Darwinism and Christianity were incompatible. The phenomenon of Christian Darwinism was employed to argue that orthodox Christians need not reject Darwinism, because such Christians would have the theological resources to adjust their natural theology to Darwinism. Darwin, however, rejected this notion.

First-hand contact with the great minds of the day as revealed by Dr. Bailey was a marvel for the freshman students of UNB: "It was an advantage that the [university's] economies of those days decreed that the science professor should compass the whole range of scientific thought in his teaching. This worked to the advantage of the student, for it became necessary to give him not a smattering as might have been the case in later years, but a bird's eye view of all science."[6]

Bailey was said to have felt intellectually isolated at the Fredericton campus. There was no one to share his inquiries into microscopic natural life. He was given the tag "Skim Bailey," because his many duties apparently left him little time to do other than "skim" student papers and exams. He was secretly serenaded by students with his own musical ditty: "Oh, we'll hang Skim Bailey to a sour apple tree." Nan declared "Skim" the most beloved professor of her student days and it was easy to send her memory back to observe him peek from behind his study blind as the student voices were raised in his honour.

Dr. Harrison, a graduate of Trinity College in Dublin, had a preference for Trinity-educated graduates or faculty. He enticed two gentlemen from Trinity whose names stand out beyond all others in the annals of the University of New Brunswick in the 1890s. They brought a wee bit of academic glamour and mystery and above all, prestige (although it came in later years), to the English and languages departments. Both became political leaders in twentieth-century Ireland.

The first of the two Trinity graduates Harrison brought to UNB was William Frederick Stockley. Stockley was appointed chairman of English and French languages and literature in November 1885. He was twenty-six years old when he arrived in Fredericton, and his discourses on Elizabethan drama and customs enthralled the students in the Old Arts Building lecture hall. His popularity was assured by his striking, comforting resemblance to the familiar image of Shakespeare himself: "There was something mystic about Dr. Stockley's class room as though a presence or a genius had brushed us. He always left the classroom with a hurried step, his college cap ready to be lifted the moment he passed, his gown floating along the aisle as if he hurried to some far distant duty."[7]

When Nan Ross encountered Stockley's literary magic, he had just returned to UNB after a one-year leave of absence. In September 1890, Stockley had gone back to Ireland, leaving behind in Fredericton the rumour that his proposal to a young Fredericton woman had been rejected. He returned to UNB, married, and continued his teaching career at Fredericton until 1902, when he took his talents and experience to St. Mary's College in Halifax. By 1905, he was back in Ireland and immersed in the social and political changes of his homeland. When the first Dail Eirann (lower parliamentary house of the Irish Free State) was formed in January 1922, Dr. William Stockley was the representative for Trinity College, Dublin.

It is, however, the aura around Willie Stockley's good friend and replacement professor of modern languages that has remained the most compelling and vivid of the Trinity College men at UNB. In 1890, Dr. Douglas Hyde, with his recently acquired Doctor of Philosophy in literature, needed some convincing to take over academic duties vacated by his friend Willie, and become one of only eight faculty members at a university in the Canadian wilderness. Stockley reasoned that the thirty-one-year-old Hyde needed a time away from Ireland. A UNB professorship would enhance his résumé upon his return to Ireland. The academic magnets of Boston and New York, cities where many young Irish Nationalists resided, were not far away and Willie must have revealed that the romantic prospects in Fredericton were quite favourable.

Douglas Hyde, Irish nationalist, founder of the Gaelic League and professor at UNB, 1890–91. Photo courtesy of Project Gutenberg Canada, 19028.

This proved sufficient for Hyde. In September 1890, the new professor arrived in Fredericton and bunked in to the Officer's Barracks (and mess hall) on Queen Street. Fortunately Hyde kept a diary during his UNB years, and he corresponded regularly and openly with his sister in Ireland. The neophyte professor lectured enthusiastically on French, German and English literature. His lectures branched off into discussions of socialism, proportional representation, J.S. Mill's theories about politics and liberty and related topics. According to Hyde's candid diaries, some of the UNB lady students "knew nothing," although some were "very pretty indeed." It was a shame the inquisitive Miss Ross missed the brief Douglas Hyde era at UNB.

Hyde also revelled in and romanticized his participation in Canadian winter culture. Snowshoeing, ice-skating, sleigh-riding, camping and hunting with Native people supplemented his interest in dancing, drinking and partying in general. He found Fredericton women pleasantly unreserved. However, a concern for the political fate of Charles Parnell, the Irish nationalist and Home Rule leader, and the desire to re-unite with his family and homeland combined to allow Hyde to bid a reasoned farewell to New Brunswick in June of 1891.

When Nan Ross entered UNB in the fall of 1892 and Hyde's friend Willie Stockley had returned from his sabbatical, Hyde's presence, or as Nan noted, "his genial shadow" was still deeply felt. The fall 1892 *University Monthly* published a sentimental (could it be ironic?) Hyde poem, "To Canada":

> ... I pine for her mighty embraces
> In the home of the moose and the seal,
> And I pine for her beautiful places
> And sad is the feeling I feel
> When snowflakes remind me of her.

Great things were in store for both educators. Hyde was a founder of the Gaelic League in 1893 and the first president of Ireland under the constitution of 1937. Stockley was a member of the Dail Eireann of 1922.

Nan's Faculty of Arts curriculum focused on the classics, but there were other fashionable and radical notions in the air. Prior to Nan's enrollment, Hyde had lectured on socialism, possibly as related to the Marxist aspirations within the labour sector of the Young Ireland movement. The works of Karl Marx were cited but Tolstoy was not taken seriously and nihilism was reckoned as subject matter for novels and dark adventures. In general, these "idealistic cults" were not considered with much authority. Even in 1939 Nan contended, "Not many college graduates... are capable of good judgment, because they need to apply their knowledge to practical life before they can actually discriminate."[8]

Ann Harvie Ross was extremely proud of her graduation in spring 1896. She would treasure forever the campus, the experience and "... those nights the stars seemed to pour into the blue vault as if shaken from some horn of plenty into human ken. While soft breezes laden with elusive scents known only to Nature's pharmacists played among the burgeoning willows. A million sensations tripped lightly through our being every day.... And now it was over."[9]

The University of New Brunswick remained nameless throughout "Passing Through," yet Nan's loyalty to the institution lasted all her life. She applied for and was admitted as an alumna immediately upon graduation. Although there was no formal alumni organization in 1896, Nan was one of the first group of five women to be admitted to that congregation. She attended Alumnae (female graduates) meetings in 1926 and 1927 and over the years wrote several enthusiastic articles about her alma mater. Friendships and contacts from UNB and Fredericton carried her through the troubles and joys of the coming years.

Annie Harvie Ross (Nan), a Canadian university graduate studying in the United States, in 1897. Photo courtesy of the University of New Brunswick Archives, MG L7 Series 3, File 1, #2.

AN AMERICAN NURSE

The violets had barely wilted on the pastured hill of the university before Nan found herself at home with her family in Woodstock. Four years of studies and examinations had left her mentally exhausted. The university graduate was a curiosity to her own family, to relatives (those brash young Doaktown uncles) and to the folk of Woodstock. In terms of the real world, Nan likened her newly educated self to a hothouse plant suddenly and ruthlessly deposited in a hotel lobby for all the world to see. The world, in its many masks, would pass through the hotel lobby.

Nan was not deluded by the merits of her university degree, but she was quite uncertain how to apply the knowledge and maturity she had acquired. In retrospect, Nan equated the insecurity of her future with the economic depression that afflicted the Canadian and local economy in 1896. It was also a period of very low population growth in the Maritime provinces. While the population in the rest of Canada had grown by 14 per cent in the years 1881–1901, the Maritimes population had increased by a paltry 1.5 per cent. Although somewhat fascinated by the world of business (taken in a very broad sense), Nan concluded that her options, and the only practical options for all educated women, were teaching or nursing. With foresight, if not conviction, she had secured through the Normal School in Fredericton during her final year at the university, a New Brunswick grammar school teaching licence. Hence she was, in theory, somewhat prepared to earn her own living.

The editor of Woodstock's newspaper (probably the *Carleton Sentinel*) offered Annie (reverting to her familiar Woodstock name) a position as social column reporter. Obviously she was literate and familiar with the community, however, Miss Ross did not view commenting on the society of Woodstock a useful or stimulating occupation. From a distance of forty years she observed, "Had I accepted his offer... I might have arrived at my writing goal sooner and by a less arduous route."[1] Fear of making a wrong initial choice also led her to turn down the only teaching position that came her way: she did not consider Grand Falls, 125 kilometres up the Saint John River from Woodstock, to offer future prospects. The limited career dilemma was therefore finally resolved by a pragmatic decision to pursue a vocation in nursing. Admittedly, Ann was in a hurry to get on with her career-finding task. Nursing seemed to satisfy an undefined sense of mission and social welfare acquired through study and a youth spent questioning societal wrongs.

Applications to a wide range of teaching hospitals resulted in only one acceptance and in fall 1896, Annie set off for Boston to enroll at a small teaching hospital in nearby Somerville, Massachusetts. This hospital (typically name-less in her autobiography) offered a small allowance to student nurses, thus relieving her of further financial dependence on her parents. The general hospital Annie attended may have been the medical facility of the Massachusetts General Hospital that treated physical ailments. However, Massachusetts General Hospital records do not confirm her attendance. A psychiatric division of this hospital, formerly named the McLean Asylum for the Insane, was renamed McLean Hospital in 1895, in order to reflect a more inclusive range of treatment. Located in a separate, tranquil setting, it became and remains, a world leader in the treatment of mental illness and the training of mental health care providers. The facility's reputation and concern for mental illness would have made a lasting impression on a "probationer" nursing student from Woodstock, Canada. It would be satisfying to affirm that Annie's entry into the medical and caring professions was through the McLean Hospital.

Nan's initial homesickness in the United States was eased by the companionship of other young Canadian women also enrolled at the nursing school, as well as by the physically strenuous work required of the students. In spite of the popularized ministries of Florence Nightingale and Clara Barton, nursing was not yet considered a profession. Training was demanding and at times demeaning. For six months one was a Probationer. The education received while in residence at a training hospital was considered as compensation for the practical nursing labour and service provided to the institution during the course of training. Candidates had to be at least twenty-one years of age, "strong and healthy" and with perfect hearing and sight. Butler Hospital for the Insane in Providence, Rhode Island, mirrored the McLean Hospital's connection with the Massachusetts General Hospital and announced in its annual report for

1897 the philosophy of integrating physical and mental disorder studies: "There is no reason why the nurses should not become thoroughly efficient in the care of nervous and mental diseases, and also competent to undertake any ordinary case in general nursing, and to be much more valuable in hospital work."[2]

At Nan's hospital, as in so many training hospitals of the time, the success of the program depended in a large measure on the management style and personality of the matron. Because of her educational background and presumed better judgment, Nan gained the confidence of the matron, who entrusted her with a variety of responsible and daunting tasks. Without companions, she was sent to inner Boston wholesale houses to purchase homeopathic and allopathic (traditional) drugs. Annie was also alone at her first obstetrical case at a home in the east side of Boston—potentially a traumatic experience for all concerned! Nonetheless, a "schism" between the matron and the senior nursing class ensued, resulting in the matron's resignation and, after only six months, the withdrawal from the hospital and the training school of Nan and several other lower-ranking colleagues.

In an abrupt change of direction and through the influence of this matron, Nan secured a job in the city as a travelling "salesman" for a grocery specialty house. Although a novice in this non-traditional position, she was quickly transferred to Providence, Rhode Island, and was once again left to her own devices. Her employer arranged boarding facilities with a respectable Providence family. The business world was indeed insightful and instructive, but "in those days women had to watch their steps, being weak things prone to destruction according to popular opinion."[3] On much later reflection, Nan would state unequivocally, "As far as men with whom I did business were concerned they were much less apt to get 'fresh' as we said in those days, than the doctors, some of whom considered nurses fair game and were not above defying the regulations for the occasional evening off no matter how disastrous it might prove to the nurse."[4]

Here was an opening for Nan, writer and social activist, to expand on the theme of exploitation of female medical practitioners. But… she didn't pursue the matter at this point in her memoir, or to the best of my knowledge, on any other occasion.

Business was not the world for Nan. Within a year, with a little money in her purse and the ingrained motto to get on with the task and finish the matter at hand, Nan "risked" returning to nurse's training. She wisely chose Philadelphia as the city in which to resume her medical training. Philadelphia had long been recognized as a leader in American medicine and in the training of nurses and doctors.

The state of Pennsylvania had a tradition of accepting women into various levels of the medical profession. The Woman's Medical College of Pennsylvania, designed specifically to offer medical doctor training for women, was established in 1850. By 1897, at least three Philadelphia academic and institutional hospitals had highly regarded nurses' training schools. Each training school boasted having graduates of the British Florence Nightingale School of Nursing on staff as teachers, practitioners or administrators. According to much later biographical sketches, the Philadelphia Polyclinic (later a part of the University of Pennsylvania) is identified as the institution at which Miss Ann Harvie Ross recommended her nursing studies.

In the fall of 1897 (or 1898), with renewed vigour and commitment, Nan embarked on "… three strenuous years, years, in which I often wished myself elsewhere."[5] As in the early years of her childhood, Nan recalled most vividly the impressions and anecdotes gathered during her first year of work and study at the Polyclinic. True to the images preserved in photographs and texts, nurses (particularly matrons) were upright, efficient, extremely tidy and very starchy. Discipline and maturity were assets of the highest order.

Typhoid fever was rampant in the growing, steaming cities of the Atlantic seaboard. Water reservoirs were unreliable and it was not until 1912, with the completion of Philadelphia's water filtration system, that the danger of typhoid fever developing into an epidemic was eliminated. In 1898, patients from the Spanish-American War with desperate injuries as well as typhoid contracted at medi-camps at Chickamauga, Georgia, filled the wards. Typhoid victims were treated with doses of whisky alternated with strychnine, or were subjected to submersion in tubs of shockingly cold water to reduce temperature. This treatment, which amounted to torture, was abandoned in favour of cooling sponge baths after a resident doctor experienced a mild attack of the disease—and the treatment. Nan's first experience with sudden death occurred in the deep hours of an early morning. She carried a lamp as orderlies moved the body of the deceased past the dissection laboratory and across the darkened hospital yard to the morgue. Was she frightened? "Certainly terrified, but when a thing had to be done, it had to be done through with even if one felt every nerve about to go rigid."[6] Nan's personal motto had been applied.

It seemed inevitable that Nan's health would suffer under the unsavoury working and living conditions experienced by the student nurses. Nan blamed her anemic condition on overwork, heat prostration and an unhealthy, very selective, diet. The stifling atmosphere of the operating theatre sterilizing room was unbearable and Nan became seriously ill. A brief recuperation at the seaside was prescribed. A doctor at the seaside resort community where she convalesced

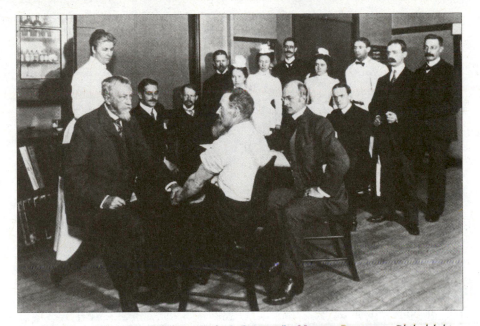

Dr. Silas Weir Mitchell at his clinic in the Infirmary for Nervous Diseases in Philadelphia 1902. Annie was an earnest graduate of this prestigious Philadelphia Polyclinic in 1901. Photo courtesy of the National Library of Medicine, B 08 398.

advised her against continuing the nursing program, but in her true "things-must-be-done-at-any-cost" attitude she was back at the hospital within a week.

Nan frequently exhibited feistiness in dealings with other students, staff and gentlemen who showed an interest in her. In one instance, very near to completion of her junior year, Nan was "crimed"—disciplined for a perceived misdemeanor—that involved the attentions of a doctor who spent too much time lingering about her post in the sterilizing room. Punishment for the infraction entailed going for a certain period of time without the distinctive double-frilled cap that a practising nurse wore perched high upon her coif-fured head. "Criming" also involved the more serious consequence of being disqualified from receiving the gold medal for the year. Nan bore this stigma with a bemused and virtuous presence only briefly, before the matron reversed the sentence, on the basis that the whole matter had simply drawn too much attention to the young woman in question.

Annie dealt with the matter of friendships with gentlemen rather obliquely in her memoir. The reader is therefore delighted to learn of the re-entry of Frank (of the pleasant walks at UNB). Frank visited "Nan," as he had known her at UNB, in Boston during her first nursing school venture, in the fall of 1896. He was on his way to medical school in Philadelphia. Again in the spring of 1897, when she was in her grocery sales career, he paid an impromptu visit to Providence, Rhode Island. It was "… a glorious morning so we wandered off and spent the afternoon in the Park talking of the million and one things which interest youth, with no thought of food or anything but the time limit set by his train [and] a beautiful park the Roger Williams…."[7] There is a hint of melancholy as the sentence trails off and a new chapter commences. Did Frank's presence at medical school in Philadelphia (most likely at the University of Pennsylvania) have any bearing on Nan's decision made in the very near future to resume her nursing education in that city? No matter, for they rarely saw each other and the notion to follow Frank would be much too difficult to admit. Dr. Frank eventually became a distinguished specialist in a town in the Midwest: "So much for the romances of college life and their permanency in this work-a-day world."[8]

As with graduation from UNB in 1896, graduation from Philadelphia Polyclinic in 1901 was anti-climactic. In a determined effort to escape the confines of a large hospital, Nan took a position as a private duty nurse. At the Philadelphia Polyclinic, Nan had come into contact with the work of Dr. S. Weir Mitchell and the Department of Neurology. Mitchell's contribution to the study of nervous and mental diseases was monumental. As a neurosurgeon he identified and pioneered the treatment of nerve injury pain. It was through doctors in this department that Nan received her first private practice assignments and developed her ongoing interest in the physiology of mental diseases. For six months Nan enjoyed the variety and civility of caring for individuals who were generally appreciative of her ability. From a historical perspective, her most interesting case involved the care of the ailing chatelaine of the Lippincott family, of publishing house fame.

The spacious Lippincott mansion on Philadelphia's Walnut Street was a social and business setting in an era of elegance and wealth. Like many grand homes in the vicinity, the residence was soon replaced by high brick office buildings and pavement. Dr. S. Weir Mitchell was a prolific writer of medical texts, Lippincott's specialty, as well as dramatic and action novels. Lippincott & Co. published several of his works and it is easy to speculate that he played a role in bringing a Polyclinic nursing graduate to the attention of the Lippincott family. And for Annie, it was rather pleasant for a change to care for a charming elderly woman in comfortable and gracious surroundings. She was now firmly set as an independent thinker and yet she still had serious misgivings about the direction her career should take.

MATRON OF WOODSTOCK'S HOSPITAL

Nan's departure in 1902 from Philadelphia and her hasty return to New Brunswick was certainly abrupt. The only explanation Nan offered for her action was given with considerable embarrassment. She "simply did not get enough to eat" at the hospital where she was presently employed! Corned beef and cabbage as sustenance before going on private night duty was not tolerable. One might question whether this was her only motive. It seems safe to say that Nan was also lured back to Woodstock—"to the town where my parents lived"—by her family ties.

The town primarily responsible for her education and upbringing lacked any form of hospital care. The community was justifiably concerned. A public meeting was held in March 1902 and Ann Ross, one of Woodstock's eminent daughters with recent nursing experience in Pennsylvania, was consulted. A prominent local businessman, a lawyer, mayor and benefactor in the person of Lewis P. Fisher, aided by the provincial government, the Carleton County Council, the Municipality of Woodstock and a host of local citizens (who voted $50 to become members of the hospital organization) collaborated to establish the Carleton County Hospital. Nan's parents, Christine and Robert Ross, were still living in the town and could have been counted on to urge their capable daughter to return to Woodstock and accept the position of Matron at the new hospital. A young Woodstock doctor also offered his encouragement.

And so it was that Nan returned to Woodstock, accompanied by another Pennsylvania nurse, both agreeing to work for living expenses only. The hospital association leased the stately but simple Miles Moore family home for two hundred dollars a year and made it over into a ten-bed hospital. It was a

Main Street, Woodstock, New Brunswick, c. 1900. Home of the Robert F. Ross family from 1885 until 2010. Photo courtesy of the Provincial Archives of New Brunswick, Isaac Erb fonds, P11-84.

"cottage hospital," without benefit of a resident doctor. The hospital boasted an operating room inconveniently located on the second floor as well as a family-style kitchen and laundry. Citizens of Woodstock, who would pay $1.69 per day should they be admitted to its care, were very possessive of their new facility. Following its opening on August 18, 1902, some felt comfortable and confident enough to inspect the hospital uninvited and to remark openly on its administration and ministry. After one year, Nan felt she had done quite enough for the old hometown. The salary was non-existent and as she later observed, "… fifteen years after, no one remembered that I had started this work… [although] there is always the satisfaction of knowing that at the request of the young doctor, who is no longer on duty, I was there at the beginning."[1] Nan was correct in expressing her disappointment at receiving no recognition for her role as founding Matron of the Carleton County Hospital. Regrettably, a brief typewritten history of Woodstock, written in 1974, records the first Matron as one Addie M. Ross.

So, back it was to Philadelphia and resumption of private duty work. During 1903–4, Nan cared for ten patients, mostly in the gritty, less desirable parts of the city where her only recorded recollection is a lengthy tale of saving the life of an errant mouse that lived in a patient's bathtub. Before long the "pull of institutional work" convinced Nan to accept a position as head nurse at a newly established private room department of an (unnamed) hospital in the city's Germantown neighbourhood. Another challenge faced the now twenty-nine-year-old administrative practitioner. The new unit was still in the planning state when both Nan and her assistant became seriously ill. A severe attack of bronchitis sent Nan to Atlantic City for a brief respite, but this did not prevent this health condition from reoccurring—nor from her tackling the new job. The hospital's own start-up difficulties included a telephone service with no central system, a second-floor operating theatre with a sloping floor, and living quarters for the head nurse featuring a network of noisy overhead sewer pipes that emitted unpleasant whiffs of odoriferous gases. Regardless of working and living conditions, Nan was extremely mindful of the qualifications and prestige of some of the nation's greatest medical men who served in Philadelphia-area hospitals, including the Germantown hospital. Drs. William W. Keen, Musser, Hobart Hare, Owen Jones Wistar, along with the previously noted S. Weir Mitchell, all made outstanding contributions to the study and treatment of diseases. They wrote highly regarded textbooks, garnered honorary degrees and had clinics and awards named in recognition of their work. These medical luminaries shared an interest in writing literary and adventure novels. Nan felt it an honour to work with these gentlemen. And yet in the simple matter

Bridge across the Saint John River looking toward Woodstock, New Brunswick. Photo courtesy of the Provincial Archives of New Brunswick: Canoeing on the River, P530-13.

Carleton County Hospital was opened August 1902 in the Miles Moore home in Woodstock, New Brunswick. Annie Ross was the first matron of the ten-bed hospital. Photo courtesy of the Provincial Archives of New Brunswick, Carleton County Historical Society Collection, P205-11.

of charting patients' conditions, Nan never overestimated her superiors and "… made haste… to adopt the simplest methods when working with great men."[2]

Nan's bronchitis persisted. A well-known chest specialist recommended the logical solution—a complete change of air. The Canadian prairie boasted vast regions of fresh air. Nan admitted she had "lost her nerve" for surgical cases. The New Brunswick grammar school teaching certificate cached away since 1896 could now prove useful. It seemed providential. All these factors pointed Nan towards the West and an easily procured interim teaching assignment near Regina, commencing September 1905.

"WESTWARD HO!"

Westward Ho! proclaimed the heading to chapter eight of "Passing Through." The theme of Charles Kingsley's 1855 adventure novel of the same title, although set in Elizabethan times, had frequently been applied by contemporary admirers to the energetic and heroic nineteenth-century drive westward across the North American continent. Images of wagon trains, rugged men and wary immigrants with dreams of freedom and free land came to mind. In August 1905, the North-West Territories and Assiniboia were poised to assume status as Saskatchewan and Alberta in the Dominion of Canada.

Annie Ross fairly leapt on the westbound Canadian Pacific Railway (CPR) train. The nurse and aspirant teacher was amazingly energized by the prospect of her own Westward Ho venture. The province of Saskatchewan was also in a celebratory mood as the September 1st Inauguration Day for the province's first premier, Walter Scott, drew near. The City of Regina had been declared the new provincial capital on May 23. Annie's five-day rail journey ended at an unmarked station near that city. There she was greeted by a family with whom she would live for the next five months. Nan marvelled at the genuine hospitality, hard work and conviviality of this family of six children, parents and farm hands: "Anything more completely the opposite of the life I had been leading would be hard to find. After the years of brick walls that were the houses of Philadelphia, it was a soothing experience to see all this restful coloring and the wide horizon of the plains."[1] It appeared she had made a wise choice.

A small collection of farm children daily faced their new serious-minded schoolmarm from Philadelphia. Of course there was no problem with discipline when the teacher's philosophy was summed up: "... After all children are not hard to manage, if you make your yes, yes and your no, no!"[2] Ann (or Nan or Annie, or by whichever name she introduced herself in each new setting) did harbour some doubts about her teaching ability and these were confirmed by the first visiting inspector. Nonetheless, her newly optimistic attitude that it was much better to deal with "healthy organisms" (schoolchildren) than sickly ones persisted and "… eventually I did learn the trade putting into it the stick-to-it-iveness of all my past."[3]

Ann experienced a delightful sense of fun and belonging with this rural family. Her brother James paid a brief visit and was also caught up in the cheerful surroundings. Although the new teacher tried hard to keep her medical experience a secret, for fear she would find herself acting as midwife and duty nurse on unplanned occasions, one of her fondest memories was a nursing story. An Ontario visitor to the family barn had passed too closely to a high-strung mare. The horse promptly munched off the gentleman's moustache, taking a portion of the man's flesh as well. Ann was called into service to stitch the wound with the only surgical materials at hand—cambric needle, silk thread and plain carbolic. It is unfortunate that Ann's tenure at the "near-Regina" school lasted only until Christmas 1905. The family had been good to her and her time with them was probably the happiest of her teaching career in Saskatchewan.

Optimism then carried Miss Ross further west. Settlements in the new province were springing up primarily west of the Dominion Surveyor's delineated 3rd Meridian. The 3rd Meridian runs north–south through central Saskatchewan at 106 degrees longitude. Buying and selling of homesteads in the area west of the Meridian was brisk. The settlement of Mortlach, about 100 kilometres west of Regina, was planning to hire its very first schoolteacher. Mortlach had started life in 1904 as a flag stop on a branch line three kilometres south of the CPR main line. English, Gaelic, French and Scottish interpretations are offered as sources for the name of the settlement, although the village site was homesteaded in 1902 by Khamis Michael, an immigrant from Iraq or Turkey (sources vary). The total population in 1906 was 127, of whom only four were women. But there was a post office, coal and lumber suppliers, hotel, general stores, implement and harness dealer and grain elevator. A brand-new school constructed at a cost of $1,095 awaited the new teacher. Seventeen pupils were enrolled. By the end of term there were forty pupils seated in crowded rows before Miss Annie Ross.

The first three-member school board, with D.W. Hossie, the Massey-Harris harness and implement provider, as chairman, administered a budget that did not extend to school supplies and texts. The new Saskatchewan Department of Education offered matching-grant incentives if money was raised locally.

Mortlach Saskatchewan Public School under construction (top centre-left) in 1905, await-ing its first teacher, Miss Annie Ross. Photo courtesy of Mortlach Museum, Saskatchewan.

The community, therefore, rallied to raise funds in the popular ranching and rural manner. A box social was organized and a hundred dollars was raised for books. Miss Ross was fascinated by this custom and quickly realized that the event was actually a popularity contest, in the guise of a fundraiser, to identify the most attractive young woman in the district. The contents of the decora-tively adorned boxes of baked items were secondary. Annie's box went for a very respectable five dollars; and yes, there were a very considerable number of bachelors about Mortlach but "… generally the bachelors were useful without expecting too much."[4] They quietly and anonymously chopped wood for the teacher's stove, but Annie was swift to ward off any possibility of becoming a rancher's wife.

Another affair of a much less pleasant nature surfaced. Along with the grow-ing number of settlers and labourers came the concern for police protection and a Royal North West Mounted Police officer was assigned to the Mortlach area in 1905. Annie had expressed the seemingly naïve (possibly flippant) view that if people conducted themselves in a proper manner, police protection would not be necessary. The resident officer unwisely responded, within hearing range of the community, "that I [Annie] was a person who needed a good deal of police supervision or words to that effect."[5] Such a remark was open to wild interpreta-tion and the resulting furor eventually landed at the teacher's doorstep. Before long, the local folk (particularly "the bachelors") came to the realization that the teacher in need of police supervision hailed from a different community and that Miss Ross's behaviour was not open to question or comment. Nonetheless, Annie was deeply affected by the scandal and credited her saved reputation to the intervention of that "gallant knight," the "Turk" who was so influential in the Mortlach area: "In his broken way he [Khamish Michael] explained… that he had known there must be some mistake and had gone personally to the town where the story was supposed to have originated and found that it was a case of mistaken identity."[6] Miss Ross personally rebuked the officer whose remarks had precipitated the scandal and rebuffed the adage subscribed to by the ladies of the community: "Where there is smoke there is fire."

While this scenario was being played out in the community, Annie was cheerfully enjoying her classroom work. One diligent fifteen-year-old eighth grader would be remembered with great satisfaction and fondness. David Neil Hossie, son of the school board chairman, went on to be a member of the first graduating class of the University of Saskatchewan, graduating with honours in Latin and English in 1912. He was the province's first Rhodes Scholar to attend New College, Oxford. Young Hossie was called to the English bar, served with the Royal Field Artillery in World War I and was awarded the Distinguished Service Award and a decoration from the Serbian government. He returned to Vancouver where he became a respected, formidable figure in the legal community and a Queen's Counsel. His eighth-grade teacher outlived him by twelve years, but continued to take pride in his accomplishments until the day she died.

In her memoir, Annie never mentions Mortlach by name or the names of people of the area (with the exception of the notable Hossie family and "the Turk"). It was through hints in much later correspondence concerning David Hossie and his future fame that led back to Mortlach. With the location identified, research through census records and local history and helpful historians was much easier.

Annie's contract at Mortlach ended with the new year, so she took the opportunity to return to New Brunswick for a lengthy visit with her family. In doing so, she missed the most extreme winter recorded in the southern regions of the prairie. Cattle perished by the thousands, as the townsfolk and farmers struggled to endure the mighty freeze. There was an abundance of teaching positions in this impossible land. True to her stick-to-it-iveness doctrine, Annie returned to Saskatchewan in the spring of 1907 and accepted a position at Rosthern, north of Saskatoon.

Rosthern was a stable farming community with settlers from Germany, eastern Canada, Galicia and Great Britain. But it was the immigration of the Doukhobors from various regions of southwestern Russia in 1899 that strongly influenced the character of the larger prairie community. Doukhobors rapidly became an ever-present subject of curiosity and speculation. One of the three defined Doukhobor Colonies in the Canadian West, the Prince Albert Colony (or Duck Lake or Saskatchewan Colony) on the banks of the North Saskatchewan River, was adjacent to Rosthern. The Prince Albert Doukhobors were pacifist agriculturalists who strove to replicate the communal life that had ultimately forced them to leave their homeland. With help from Lev Tolstoy, Quakers and sympathetic foreign state ministers, they found refuge in the vast prairie of North America. Even in their Russian homeland, the sect was characterized as a "peculiar people" and this description followed them to their new home. A popular book, published in 1904 and the work of a disillusioned Doukhobor supporter, bore the title *A Peculiar People*.

Annie's encounters with the Doukhobors of the Prince Albert Colony were minimal, because the Doukhobor children attended a Quaker-run school near the colony's Petrovka settlement and had little association with local children. In response to the Sons of Freedom Doukhobor sect's custom of marching great distances in the nude to protest government regulation and as an expression of their rejection of material goods, other settlers reacted with disgust or stunned amusement. Annie's opinion of the behaviour of the "peculiar" neighbours was no different from that of most other Canadians. Such antics were pointless and ... somehow un-Canadian. However, because of her first-hand (though brief) association with them, Annie acquired an enduring fascination for these people. Her questioning of Doukhobor philosophy, nineteenth-century nihilism and the evolution of twentieth-century communism led her in later years to write articles, letters and a book-length manuscript on the subject of the Doukhobors.

As a teacher with a keen sense of history, Annie also acknowledged the proximity of the Native and Métis cultures and the stories of Louis Riel, Batoche and Duck Lake. Years removed from Rosthern, she recalled teaching a little boy by the name of Ernest McNabb, son of a future Saskatchewan Lieutenant-Governor. In 1940, McNabb Jr. commanded Canada's first fighter squadron, won the Distinguished Flying Cross, the Czech War Cross and was awarded the Order of the British Empire. One does not like to question the accuracy of Annie's memories but alas, Ernest was born in 1906! Possibly an older brother was in Miss Ross's elementary school class at Rosthern in 1907.

Annie wound up the school year at Rosthern in June 1907, then headed for the city. Saskatoon had two schools and was greatly in need of a third. Miss Ross was assigned the seventh grade in a two-storey red brick school that later served as a fire hall. Like the bustling city rapidly coming together on the high banks of the South Saskatchewan River, Victoria School was exploding with sixty students (mostly boys) aged nine to sixteen packed into one grade seven classroom. Annie's reputation for discipline was severely challenged, but she believed she held her own against this horde. When she managed to have one particularly rebellious and duplicitous sixteen-year-old expelled, the teen's father demanded his reinstatement. But Annie "rose in wrath" and refused to have the fellow in her class. Such was her ire that it was recalled with passion in her memoir: "Terribly handicapped by a lack of proper home control, they [rebellious students] go through life thinking the world owes them the same favors that have been conferred upon them by two indulgent or too careless parents. But why teachers should be so tortured by such problems … is beyond me…."[7]

One thing not lacking in the great Canadian West was a choice of bachelors. Even Annie herself wondered why she had failed to meet a man in whom she could be truly interested when there were so many available. Men friends were becoming less and less a part in her life. The bachelors of Mortlach offered a life of hard work and little culture. On one occasion Annie had gone to Prince Albert to spend the day with an amusing Mr. "T." They strolled in a park-like setting, in a scene reminiscent of the charming day in Boston's Roger Williams Park with UNB flame Frank: "It was such an afternoon as one might look for romance or foolish fondling, but alas, the mosquitoes were so thick that a smudge was necessary to even sit a while in the shade."[8] In Saskatoon, she

On the left, overcrowded and understaffed Nutana/Victoria Elementary School, Saskatoon, where Annie Ross taught 1907–8. The building later became a fire hall. Photo LH 1085 courtesy of the Saskatoon Public Library, Local History Room.

encountered childhood playmate, "Pum," from New Brunswick. He lived in the western city, along with his mother, and was now an established newspaper-man: "… Here were all the hall marks [sic] for an exciting love affair based on our childhood…. But it just couldn't materialize under [his] mother's watchful eye."[9] What a disappointment! Once again circumstances, as much as prefer-ence, had dashed a promising relationship. In spite of this biographer's cre-ative dissection of early Canadian newspaper directories, "Pum" of Saskatoon remains a mystery man.

Annie left Saskatchewan in the fall of 1908 with few regrets. She had loved the prairie scene with its vastness, vegetation, changing colours and especially the power of the river. But again something was calling her further west.

"INLAND PARADISE"

One might say that destiny led Annie to the small, rugged town beside a cool dark lake in the western mountains. Or maybe it was rumour, or hearsay, or ties of friendship. Miss Ross was not the first New Brunswicker or native of Fredericton, Woodstock or any of the settlements along the Saint John River who found their way to Nelson, British Columbia. A veritable network of New Brunswickers connected the lives and aspirations of many of the nearly 7,000 inhabitants of Nelson and the mining and exploration sites in the mountains surrounding the west arm of Kootenay Lake. Family associations and familiar names appeared with regularity at gatherings and in many walks of daily life. Annie's choice of Nelson as her next world to experience was made all the more exciting knowing others had remained and prospered in this young city in the splendid wilderness of interior British Columbia.

Although characterized as a "booming mining town," with timbers and waterfalls crashing in the distance and a swirling population of husky and hungry prospectors, Nelson's seekers and settlers had quickly erected and established most of the amenities expected in a growing Canadian Edwardian-era community. By 1908, the municipality, incorporated in 1897, boasted a majestic, granite post office, an equally impressive courthouse, a daily newspaper (at times more than one newspaper), stolid cathedral-like churches, a gaol, a wood-frame city hall, a Canadian Pacific Railway station, several banks, a swiftly growing number of grand homes of unique, late Victorian architectural styles—and, best of all, an entire city block devoted to a collection of buildings known as Central School. Plans, construction and finances were under way for the replacement of the original 1892 rambling wooden structure. The new deep-red brick, Queen

A Kootenay Lake sternwheeler or paddlewheeler, the common and popular method of transportation along Kootenay Lake to the City of Nelson until the mid-twentieth century. Photo courtesy of British Columbia Archives collections, F-02455.

Anne-style school with twelve classrooms would be thoroughly modern and leave little to be desired in design and equipment.

With an opera house, a modest public library, a city-owned and -operated electric light and power plant at Upper Bonnington Falls fifteen kilometres west on the Kootenay River, a streetcar system (inoperative, however, in 1908 due to financial and technical troubles) and a flourishing number of businesses, saloons and hotels, Nelson was in all appearances to newcomers a centre of stability, commerce, culture and community. Actually finding one's way to this charming little city located at the outlet arm of the elongated stretch of Kootenay Lake had then, as now, a measure of difficulty beyond simply following a rail or a trail west. There was the necessity of selecting an appropriate pass in the Rocky Mountain barrier between British Columbia and Alberta. (Alberta was part of the North-West Territories until 1905.) West of the Rockies, the routes followed circuitous waterways of lakes and rivers.

In 1908, most travellers, as well as goods coming from eastern Canada and labelled "destination Nelson," disembarked from the main line CPR train at Revelstoke, British Columbia, then transferred to a rail line running south along the Columbia River to Arrowhead at the head of Upper Arrow Lake. Here another transfer was made to one of three sternwheelers, the *Kootenay, Minto* or *Rossland,* for the long day-trip south on Upper and Lower Arrow Lakes to Robson. From Robson, near the junction of the Columbia and Kootenay Rivers, it was a short forty-kilometre train ride east again, courtesy of the Columbia

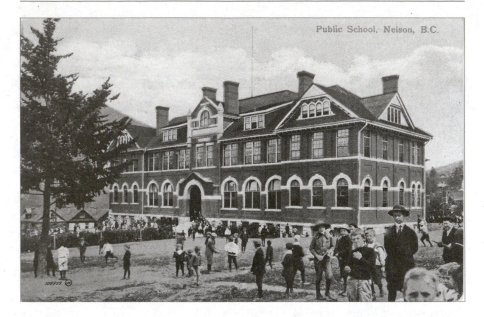

Nelson's large and modern Central School where Miss Annie Ross ruled the sixth division from 1908 to 1910. Photo courtesy of Touchstones Nelson: Museum of Art and History, #0596 acc. 7812.

Twenty-eight students pose for a class photo in Nelson's Central School, 1909. Photo courtesy of British Columbia Archives collections, B-01419.

& Kootenay Railway & Navigation Company. The rail line ran parallel to the Kootenay River in the river's final downhill charge to the Columbia. Around a sweeping bend of the Kootenay River, the traveller caught sight of the City of Nelson inching its way up the backdrop mountain.

There were other routes: the more southerly route through the Crowsnest Pass, then onto the sternwheeler (the "Crow Boat") up Kootenay Lake and down its west arm to Nelson; or via the Nelson and Fort Sheppard Railway from Spokane, Washington, detraining at Nelson's Mountain Station above the city. Expectations were always high when approaching Nelson, and one was generally thankful to have finally arrived. Consequently, the newcomer often felt she might as well settle, as the coming and going was rather complicated— even in fair weather.

Annie Ross was in a very positive frame of mind when she arrived in Nelson in August 1908. The past was left in New Brunswick, Pennsylvania and Saskatchewan. The future was in the Kootenay. It had been a very simple matter to secure a teaching position at Nelson's Central School. Dr. E.C. Arthur, a Nelsonite of considerable distinction and influence, was also the secretary of the school board. With good humour, Annie recognized the challenges ahead and observed that even Dr. Arthur "… was a notoriously bad writer and his letter seemed to read, 'Antics will begin on September first'."[1] Antics were part of the daily dealings of an elementary school teacher. She would cope.

Rather than return to family and New Brunswick for the summer recess, as had been her custom, Annie prefaced her move to Nelson with a trip to California. From Vancouver (or possibly Seattle), she boarded a ship for San Francisco where a nursing friend lived. The city was still recovering from the devastating 1906 earthquake, but the old mission culture was fascinating and the return ocean voyage provided an opportunity for Annie to try her sea legs. Even seasickness was casually brushed off! The main line of the CPR carried her up through the Fraser River canyon. From Kamloops, she took a side trip via a branch line into the Okanagan Valley for a brief view of the lovely fruit-growing valley and to visit "T.," the gentleman last met in the mosquito-ridden park near Prince Albert. Apparently "T." had married and settled in the valley; but we do not know whether or not Mr. "T." found true love and happiness in that sunny clime.

Upon arrival at Nelson's CPR waterfront station via the Arrow Lakes and Kootenay River route, Annie probably checked in at one of Nelson's hotels that offered suitable accommodation and boarding. The Strathcona Hotel, operated by the Phair family from Fredericton or the more formal Hume Hotel, established (but recently sold) by former Fredericton and upper Saint John River folk, would have offered a welcome haven. However, a most significant event is told in Annie's words: "It was here [Nelson] very soon after my arrival that I met the man who was long afterwards to become my husband. We met quite unromantically at the boarding house where we had meals."[2] Margaret Brown, the boarding house proprietor, was a canny, widowed Scotswoman with previous experience at the CPR's Banff Springs Hotel. Her home in the Scottish Highlands had been in the Balmoral countryside and King Edward VII was a sometime-visitor to the family farm. Mrs. Brown's boarding house at number 507 on aptly named Carbonate Street (one block above Silica Street) was the venue for wit and stories.

In August 1908, William Garland Foster also arrived to take up a position in Nelson. He too had moved slowly and deliberately across the country to meet his destiny in the dining room of Mrs. Brown's boarding house. Garland Foster (as he was known) was born near Ottawa in Carleton County, Ontario, in 1879, making him four years Annie's junior. He attended Ottawa Collegiate, and commenced a journalistic career as a reporter for the *Ottawa Free Press*. He then moved westward, first to the *Winnipeg Telegram,* then to Portage la Prairie as editor of the *Evening Review,* followed by stints as the news editor of the *Victoria Colonist* and the *Victoria Times.* He then backtracked to Nelson where he was editor and manager of the *Nelson Daily News.* Garland Foster appeared a thoroughly likeable young man who set out to increase readership of the *Nelson Daily News* and generally raise the profile and quality of the paper. He became a household name in his chosen city, a member of the gentlemen's Nelson Club, the Press Club and a councillor for the Board of Trade. Both William and Annie were at the time of their meeting preoccupied with the careers and prospects that had brought them to Nelson.

Miss Annie Ross took over management of the "antics" of the sixth division class at Central School on August 24, 1908. Eleven teachers (all women), 534 pupils and the affable principal, Mr. Albert Sullivan, were scattered about the property occupied by Central School. Five classes filled the main building, three were located in an older building removed to the corner of the school block, two divisions were exiled to the fraternity hall, one was located in the equally cramped high school four blocks uphill, and another was to be found in a church basement.

Dr. Arthur and his four fellow city school trustees were immensely proud of their school. They and their predecessors had lobbied for several years before the necessary funds were secured from the electorate to construct a much larger and well-deserved structure. As Dr. Arthur had bluntly reported in 1905, "there is no other city in British Columbia that has such a wretched public school building as Nelson."[3]

The Public Schools Annual Reports included in the leather-bound British Columbia Sessional Papers record an accurate and statistically detailed description of every school and schoolhouse in the province. These formal facts belie the clatter, chatter and rattle of doors and windows that accompanied the construction of the new Central School in the fall of 1908: "A new brick building with granite facings was started with the hope of being finished by the new year. But we taught under difficulties that term, the chipping of granite playing a tattoo for the absorbing of knowledge."[4]

William Garland Foster, editor of the Nelson Daily News *1908–1915. Photo courtesy of Touchstones Nelson: Museum of Art and History, #0106.*

Nelson came under the classification of "Graded City School of the Second Class" and, as such, the city provided a portion of the schools' budget over and above the per capita grant provided by the provincial government. Cost per pupil to the government was approximately fifteen dollars and even teachers with university degrees and appropriate certificates and experience like Miss Ross received a basic seventy dollars per month. Mr. J.D. Gillis in his report for Inspectorate #3 Nelson for 1908 deplored that "the supply of good teachers must always fall short of the demand as long as the salaries offered them continue to be smaller than those paid in callings that require less preparation, are less exacting and less destructive of nervous energy."[5]

In spite of all the difficulties, Annie felt Central School staff under "Sully's" leadership constituted a happy family. By 1910, Mr. Sullivan had risen to the position of district inspector and graciously acknowledged that his staff at Central School was just about the best in the province! The provincial government had recently initiated a free textbook program under the supervision of former Nelson teacher, Mr. Wilson. This was definitely an advantage to both teachers

William Garland Foster, twenty-nine-year-old newspaper editor, in 1908. Photo courtesy of Sheila and Phil Mayville.

and pupils and the 1908–9 term looked like a good year all round.

Socially, culturally and even athletically, there was much to occupy one's time in Nelson. Teachers, professionals, politicians and former New Brunswickers became Annie's circle of friends and associates. She had hardly unpacked before Mrs. Wilhelmina Pearcy, one of Nelson's three high school teachers, and Mrs. Fraser brought Miss Ross, a graduate of the University of New Brunswick, to a regular monthly meeting of the University Club of Nelson. The University Club of Nelson was organized in December 1903 by an earnest group of gentlemen who shared an intellectual inquiry into the social and educational issues of the day as well as a pride in their diverse alma maters. The Club's constitution stated: "All graduates and undergraduates of Universities of recognized standing shall be eligible for membership." A clause in the original draft constitution that had declared, "Its purpose shall be discussion of matters affecting or interesting the members as University *men* [emphasis added]…" was amended to read "Its purpose shall be discussion of matters affecting or interesting *its members.*" These two clauses made it quite clear that membership in the University Club of Nelson was open to all university graduates, including women.

From the outset, the University Club of Nelson embraced the establishment of a University of British Columbia as its primary goal. And indeed, the small, geographically remote organization emerged as an unlikely but effective and recognized force in the establishment of the University of British Columbia at Point Grey in Vancouver. Given her experience in the forefront of co-education at the University of New Brunswick, it is not difficult to understand why Annie was attracted to this cause. At the 1908 annual general meeting, which was only the second meeting she attended, Annie was elected the first woman secretary-treasurer and Mrs. Pearcy was elected president. Monthly meetings featured a local or visiting guest speaker. The text or a summary of the educational opinion-paper presented was recorded with due solemnity in the *Nelson Daily*

The Ottawa family of William Garland Foster in 1895. Sixteen-year-old William is back row left. His parents are Ann and Benjamin and his siblings Mary Ann (Molly), Stephen, Ann Jane (Jennie), Lola and Matilda (Tilly). Photo courtesy of Sheila and Phil Mayville.

News. For the next year and a half, Annie's familiar scrawl (no more legible than the penmanship of fellow member, the good Dr. Arthur) recorded the minutes and discussions in the blue buckram minute book.

As secretary, Miss Ross recorded the delivery of a timely paper, "The Woman Problem of the 20th Century" by University Club member—Miss Annie H. Ross. The *Nelson Daily News* of April 20, 1909, picked up on the presentation of this "most interesting and cleverly-thought out paper." The presenter had rather critically outlined the suffrage movement and concluded that giving women what they were asking for "… would merely be paving the way for a few ambitious women to overturn conditions as they were." Dr. E.C. Arthur "… spoke in the highest appreciation of Miss Ross' paper and said that personally, he had always been in favour of giving women the franchise." As newspapers do, the headline to the article in question was somewhat inflammatory: "OPPOSES THE SUFFRAGE." Was this *Nelson Daily News* article a subject of discussion around the dining table at the boarding house frequented by the editor and the protagonist?

The suffrage issue, of course, did not fade away. Annie retained her coolness on the subject for several years to come. However, Annie Verth Jones, MD, a University Club member who enjoyed a working friendship with Annie Ross, was prominent in the votes-for-women world. While some prominent women of Nelson demurred on the subject of suffrage, Dr. Jones and Isabel Arthur, MD, wife of Dr. E.C. Arthur, could always be counted on to endorse the logic of the movement at any opportunity. Annie would come to rue the day she expressed her dissatisfaction with the principle of universal suffrage!

Not given to attending feminine church-related functions or undertaking rigorous mountain pursuits, Annie was more comfortable observing the beauty and history of the natural scene about her. She developed a keen interest in the Kootenay's rather recent past, all the while appreciating the civic advancements made by the young city in its management of power and water utilities. Nelson was indeed an up-and-coming community. In a manner similar to the University Club of Nelson's enthusiasm for the establishment of post-secondary education in the province, the Nelson teachers' association was proud to host the twelfth annual British Columbia teachers' convention held March 29–31, 1910. Business meetings, civic receptions, workshops, public forums, demonstrations, model lessons and photographic sessions—the Nelson organizing committee had planned a thorough and engrossing series of events. Over two hundred teachers from the very smallest, soon-to-be forgotten, one-room schools like Renata on Arrow Lake, Cascade, Meadow Spur and Cambourne to the important and self-important professors, inspectors and superintendents were energized by the speeches and activities. Annie and a coterie of Nelson teachers attended and acted as hostesses at the various functions. It was an opportunity to meet, mingle and show off the majestic new Central School: "The handsome front windows of the

Minute Book of the University Club of Nelson, March 12, 1910. Recording Secretary A.H. Ross. Image courtesy of Touchstones Nelson: Museum of Art and History.

Nelson school, with their attractive display of flowering plants, are the envy of the teachers who have a less broad outlook from their school rooms."[6]

Long anticipated by the Nelson University Club, a University Site Commission was mandated by the provincial government in April 1910 to hear submissions on the location of the provincial university. Site Commission members travelled to fourteen communities, including Nelson, where hearings were held June 17 at the new Rattenbury-designed Nelson Court House. Although Nelson Mayor Harold Selous urged the selection of his city as the perfect, unique site for the university, the University Club of Nelson had officially resolved to promote the selection of the largest centre of population, Vancouver, and a campus at Point Grey, as the most appropriate site. The hearing constituted the type of impressive civic occasion Annie Ross would have enjoyed.

However, Annie was contemplating a move. Admittedly there had been a great many staffing changes and "readjustments" at Central School in the past year. But the West was still to be explored. A puzzling allusion in her memoir to "my fiancé" seems to run counter to Annie's decision to accept a position at a primary school in Golden on the CPR main line. Robert Landells, the attractive then-young teacher at Annie's Woodstock, New Brunswick, school c. 1890 was now the principal at Golden, and he had been among the delegates to the 1910 teachers' convention in Nelson. Possibly Mr. Landells was influential in spiriting a fellow New Brunswicker with admirable teaching skills to join his staff in an even more rugged mountain community.

A melancholy reverie written in 1939 provides no explanation: "So for three [two] years I enjoyed the charm of this inland paradise. A love affair, a good position, ideal climate and fascinating scenery—what more could one wish with a background of friends? But the more we have the less we appreciate it. In after years one gets to know that the ups and downs of love and its vagaries are largely imaginary."[7]

MRS. GARLAND FOSTER

*G*olden—the name alone raised expectations and excitement. When Annie arrived in the late, golden summer of 1910, at "… that delightful Alpine village caught between the Rockies and the Selkirks…", she indeed believed it would be "… a stimulating place in which to live."[1] The community of Golden was then hardly more than the western base camp for the maintenance of the CPR line through Rogers Pass and the Rocky Mountains. Its fame as a centre for climbing and winter adventures was not foreseen until three Swiss guides arrived in 1912 and brought their expertise and artistry to scaling mountain peaks. In the robust little town, there was a small school (classed "Rural") and three teachers for three divisions with a total of eighty-nine students.

Miss Ross seemed quite content with her thirty-four students and her sixty-five dollar per month salary. She retained her admiration for former New Brunswick Principal Landells and found his sobriety and genteel appreciation of good music engaging. Robert Landells had proven to be an unlikely, modest hero in the community when he located and assisted in the rescue of two young men who were inadvertently swept away in their boat by the raging flood of the Columbia River. He was one of those dedicated, respected, bachelor teachers fondly recalled by the students as well as the townsfolk where he taught for nineteen years.

Annie's Golden year was simply an interlude. Christmas saw her back in Nelson for two weeks, staying with her friends (and Garland Foster's), Myra and Frank C. Green. To Annie's interest and delight, Garland Foster was a guest at the Christmas dinner table of these former New Brunswickers at their home on Kootenay Street overlooking Cottonwood Creek. Late in the summer she resumed her annual cross-country visit to family in New Brunswick. Upon returning to Nelson in the fall of 1911, Annie found herself without a teaching position. Either Central School had its full complement of teachers, or Annie found she preferred the small rural schools. As "… teaching had become for me neither a vocation nor an avocation, but an adventure…"[2], she accepted the only position available in the very large British Columbia Inspectorate [District] #7—a one-room school at Cascade.

Like Golden, Cascade was a self-descriptive name for yet another short-lived boomtown in the Kootenay Boundary country of British Columbia. Cascade sprang up in 1896 on a benchland below a powerful cascade on the boiling Kettle River. Here the Kettle River turned south towards the American border. The settlement, which anticipated construction of a CPR branch line (Columbia and Western Railway) between Castlegar (the Robson junction with the Arrow Lake steamers) and Midway, was only twenty kilometres east of the Boundary community of Grand Forks. Immediately below the Kettle River gorge, an English syndicate had constructed an impressive powerhouse that would provide electricity to the West Kootenay Power and Light Company grid. Cascade was briefly the epitome of a Boundary boomtown—wagon trains,

One-room school at Cascade, British Columbia, near Christina Lake, where Annie Ross taught 1911–12. Photo, taken 1910, courtesy of British Columbia Archives collections, B-09172.

The staff of the Nelson Daily News, *May 5, 1912. Editor W.G.Foster seated prominently at centre, Gretchen Phair Gibson in white blouse, S. Archie R. MacDonald (present but unidentified), husband of Elizabeth "Nain" Roberts of Fredericton. Photo courtesy of Touchstones Nelson: Museum of Art and History, #2010.03.01.*

construction camps, saloons, hotels, provisions depot—and typically, it was devastated by fire. The cataclysm took place just a few weeks prior to the arrival of the first railroad locomotive in 1899. Another fire in 1901 and the conclusion of railway construction tolled the death knell of the community. Although a presentable school had been constructed during the boom of 1899, when Miss Ross arrived from Nelson in 1911, she found she had been preceded by a parade of teachers who had presided at regular intervals at the one-room Cascade school. As in most rural schools in the district, attendance was erratic, trustees unreliable and teachers frequently indifferent to the callings of their profession. Needless to say, things at the rustic little school were in a rather sorry state.

However, on the surface, Annie appeared to enjoy the children and the natural setting of the townsite. Her salary was a generous eighty-five dollars per month. No doubt a portion of it was spent on rail tickets to Nelson. One curious remark applied to her situation at Cascade is open to interpretation: "Ants and their habits took the place of any community interest I might have had. After all animals and insects are not so different from human beings in many ways."[3] Was she simply lonely for more civilized companionship and a more sociable community? Or had she become a little jaded about the people in her life in general?

Wherever her wanderings may have taken her, Annie had not burned any bridges. September 1912 saw her back in Nelson as the principal of Hume

School. Hume School, named in recognition of a local pioneer family from New Brunswick, was situated in the residential community of Fairview, adjoining Nelson. Bogustown, the original name for this area just east of the city's centre, was as old as Nelson itself. The rural-style, frame two-room school constructed in 1899 had originally had fifty-nine students, but had since grown to four rooms, housing four divisions, four teachers and 170 students when Annie assumed her principalship. Until the community was incorporated into Nelson in 1922, the school was known variably as the Hume or the Fairview School. Annie was gratified that her teaching experience was finally recognized. It was at Hume that Miss Ross gained the reputation for strictness, fairness and determination that was to characterize her public and private life for many years to come: "I toiled over a pleasantly stimulating adventure, whose ups and downs were welcome if the results were commensurate with the effort."[4]

Life centred on school, community events and friends. Nelson was moving ahead. In October 1912, the Governor General and his wife—the Duke and Duchess of Connaught—arrived by lake steamer, and Thomas Wilby, driving a Reo Special touring car, passed through Nelson on the first ever cross-Canada motoring trip. Wilby's venture was called the "All Red Route." A Curtiss airplane had recently circled the mountainside town; the arsonist responsible for a series of disturbing fires (including destruction of the town's large smelter) was captured and charged; and household science was added to the school curriculum. Nelson was the place to be. Annie's home was a suite in a Josephine Street house two blocks above Baker Street, Nelson's main commercial (alternately muddy and dusty) thoroughfare.

The *Nelson Daily News* figured prominently in Annie's social life. Her old friend William Garland Foster, editor and general manager, had several New Brunswickers on staff. Gretchen Phair (later Mrs. Gibson) of Fredericton, secretary at the newspaper, became Annie's lifelong friend. The (Sir) Charles G.D. Roberts family of growing literary fame was represented at the newspaper by news reporter Lloyd Roberts, second son of Charles and Mary Roberts. In 1912, Charles G.D.'s favoured sister (Lloyd's aunt) Jane Elizabeth, called "Nain," also moved to Nelson, because her husband, Samuel Archibald Roberts MacDonald, had been hired as advertising manager for the paper. Elderly Emma Roberts, Charles and Nain's mother and Annie Ross's sewing class teacher back in the Fredericton mill village, was part of the Fredericton-to-Nelson exodus. It is safe to assume Annie resumed her acquaintance with the Roberts clan. (Nain had also attended the University of New Brunswick in the early 1890s.) But the Roberts family did not have happy recollections of Nelson. Lloyd, who earned a literary fame of his own, was particularly fond of his generous and

imaginative Aunt Nain, and devoted a whole chapter of his early family mem-
oir to her. Nain's marriage to S.A.R. MacDonald was extremely unhappy. Of
her time in Nelson, Lloyd wrote, "She became little better than an exile in
the heart of the Kootenays."[5] In 1914, S.A.R and Nain and their three sons left
Nelson for Winnipeg. The move to Winnipeg proved equally unfortunate and
unhappy for Nain.

Nelson grew and prospered in the years prior to the Great War. A cable
ferry crossed the West Arm of Kootenay Lake near Nelson's attractive Lakeside
Park. There was a towering brick fire hall and the city's streetcar system had
been settled on a firm financial base. The majestic triple-decked SS *Nasookin*
was built and launched at the lakeside quay. A Chakho-Mika Carnival in July
1914 was a fun-filled open-air festival for the whole family.

Annie and several teachers from the Nelson district were returning home
from summer school in Victoria when the chilling pronouncement of war
in Europe struck the headlines. Nelson's reaction to the outbreak of war was
swift and sure. Reservists, a goodly number of remittance men, and those
with strong British ties enlisted, and on August 28, 1914, the first contingent
of Nelson men left for military training in Victoria. William Garland Foster,
along with nearly half the male staff of the *Nelson Daily News,* was among the
early recruits. Garland Foster joined the 30th Overseas Battalion and in May
1915 took up a commission with the first battalion recruited from the interior
of British Columbia—the 54th Kootenay Battalion, Canadian Expeditionary
Force. Annie was shocked at his decision to enlist. Although "friends" all these
years, there was no understanding between them and "too late I realized that I
had not the right to say yes or no."[6]

Due to prior experience in Ottawa as the Governor General's foot guard,
Garland Foster was recruited as an officer. While others moved on to the
Canadian forces training camp at Vernon, British Columbia, Garland Foster
remained in Esquimalt near Victoria for officers' training. Christmas 1914, with
a stalemate already apparent in the trenches of Europe, found him gratefully
back in Nelson. And then the unexpected happened: "Then he arrived suddenly
one day after Christmas holidays and announced that we were going to be mar-
ried. Just like that!"[7] Annie knew this was an ultimatum. With world conditions
such as they were—and Annie approaching forty years of age—waiting was not
an option!

Only the briefest formal account of the Foster-Ross nuptials was recorded.
The *Nelson Daily News* reported the editor's marriage on January 16, 1915, in
twelve strict lines in the following Monday's paper. There was no descrip-
tion of a tall, dark-complexioned bride of stately, mature bearing joining in

marriage with a mustached, trimly pressed lieutenant in the Canadian Armed Forces. Preparations for the wedding were swiftly made. No time for gown, parties and trimmings. Quite likely the entire proceeding was a well-kept, but briefly held secret. Family, teachers, newspaper people, and New Brunswickers were not informed. The couple simply arrived on Saturday, January 16, in the parlour of Dr. Gilbert and Mrs. Lillian Hartin, 806 Vernon Street, Nelson, British Columbia. Rev. Dr. George C. Pidgeon of Vancouver officiated as the "Lieutenant in the Canadian Forces is quietly married to former New Brunswick girl."[8]

It was remarked that Lieutenant Foster would resume his military duties and Mrs. Foster would continue to reside in Nelson. The wedding took place in the evening and the couple left immediately after the ceremony on the steamer that would carry them to the railroad the following day. Annie stayed with her husband on the westbound train until it reached the stop where she could safely disembark and catch an eastbound train, re-trace her route and be at school on Monday morning!

There was some consternation in Nelson circles around the secrecy of the Foster-Ross nuptials. School trustees chastised Mrs. Foster and then declared a holiday in her honour. Five days after the wedding, the groom received a

417 Carbonate Street, Nelson, where William Garland Foster lived while editor of the Nelson Daily News. *Photo by Ron Welwood, 2010.*

William Garland Foster, Officer in the 54th Kootenay Battalion, 1915. Photo courtesy of Touchstones Nelson: Museum of Art and History, #85.278.50.

congratulatory telegram from Canadian news publishing "greats" E.H. Macklin, chief business manager of the *Winnipeg Free Press,* and J.F.B. Livesay, general manager of Canadian Press (and father of future stellar poet Dorothy Livesay). On behalf of the representatives of the Western Associated Press organization, they sent wishes for a long, happy and prosperous life. Like many wartime weddings, there was little time for frippery, festivities or family.

Life settled into a wait and pray, work and worry cycle. Final farewells to the 54th Kootenay Battalion, which had been officially formed May 1, 1915, under the command of Lieutenant-Colonel Mahlon Davis, were held in Nelson in early June. But first there was a formality faced by the wives of all military men. Annie was required to sign a release giving permission for her husband

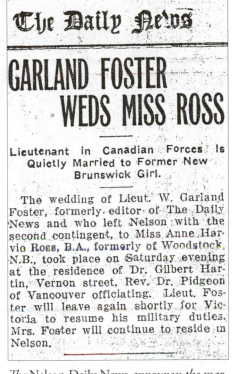

The Daily News

GARLAND FOSTER WEDS MISS ROSS

Lieutenant in Canadian Forces Is Quietly Married to Former New Brunswick Girl.

The wedding of Lieut. W. Garland Foster, formerly editor of The Daily News and who left Nelson with the second contingent, to Miss Anne Harvie Ross, B.A., formerly of Woodstock, N.B., took place on Saturday evening at the residence of Dr. Gilbert Hartin, Vernon street, Rev. Dr. Pidgeon of Vancouver officiating. Lieut. Foster will leave again shortly for Victoria to resume his military duties. Mrs. Foster will continue to reside in Nelson.

The Nelson Daily News *announces the marriage of its former editor William Garland Foster to Miss Annie Ross, January 16, 1915. Image courtesy of the* Nelson Daily News, *January 18, 1915, p. 7.*

to undertake military service. This was viewed much like signing a death warrant. It brought home the finality and upheaval created by the Great War in which the country was now truly embroiled.

The demonstration of patriotism and pride in sons and fathers of the West Kootenay who signed on for service was as enthusiastic and colourful as anywhere in the country. The men and officers of the 54th, whose names were all published in the *Nelson Daily News* on June 3, 1915, were celebrated with a picnic at Procter up the west arm of Kootenay Lake, concerts and dinners. The largest crowd ever in the history of Nelson witnessed the departure of the 54th on June 11. The Battalion, preceded by Boy Scouts, banners, bugles and pipers, swung down Baker Street to the CPR station. Two trains of recruits from the East Kootenay appeared on cue and hitched up with the twelve railcars noisily filling with the soldiers of the 54th. The men were transported to a life "under canvas" at Camp Vernon where they would undergo a regime of physical and logistical training. For Annie, the Nelson revelry was just "too much." Her years of nursing in the United States in the aftermath of the Spanish-American War had given Annie a perspective on suffering few Canadians understood or imagined. She eschewed the show of patriotism and concentrated on plans for the future.

Since it appeared that her husband would be confined to the Vernon military camp for several months, Annie decided she would not return to school in September 1915 but would instead find a place to live near the army base. Prior to their marriage, Annie had purchased a small house at 1122 Stanley Street in Nelson. The house would be rented and Annie would move to Vernon. The new Mrs. Foster bid her own farewells and also entrained to the North Okanagan community. Although close to her husband's "work," there was nothing more tedious than whiling away the time with similarly unoccupied wives: "A chance I had to substitute for one of the teachers in the town seemed to offer some amusement, but my husband never liked the idea of married women working so I gave that up."[9] This was not an encouraging attitude for an independent

"The Boys of the Nelson Daily News*" serving with the 54th Battalion at training camp in Vernon, 1915. Garland Foster seated left. Photo courtesy of Touchstones Nelson: Museum of Art and History, #84.14.12.*

Troop ship Saxonia, *which transported the men of the 54th Battalion CEF to Britain in 1915. Image courtesy of the Great War Primary Documents Archive. "The Maritime War – 1st Canadian Troop Convoy." (www.gwpda.org)*

woman who would continue to make her own way and her own decisions in the weeks, months and years to come.

With winter coming on, even the dry belt of the Upper Okanagan was damp and chilly. The men welcomed the news that on November 15, 1915, they would depart for Halifax. The 54th Battalion was now under the command of Nelson-area resident Lieutenant-Colonel A.G. Kemball, C.B., while Garland Foster was promoted to captain and quartermaster. Annie got a jump-start on the troop train and travelled on ahead to Ottawa. There she met Garland Foster's parents and enjoyed a brief surreal lunch and a couple of hours together at the Foster family home. Long anticipated final farewells were endured and the train carrying the 54th rolled on to Halifax. The Cunard liner *Saxonia*, requisitioned as a troop carrier, sailed November 21 and docked at Plymouth eight days later. Here the troops disembarked and trudged on to Bramshott in eastern Hampshire. Bramshott was a vast troop city under construction and was destined to be a final home to thousands of Commonwealth soldiers.

As for Annie: "He crossed... I went home [to Woodstock, New Brunswick]."[10]

WAR ALARUMS

For all its peculiarities and idiosyncrasies, Annie's 1939 memoir "Passing Through" provided a pathway through her early years. By the time the memoir reached 1915, forty years of reflection, minor adventures and asides had been told. As her life unfolded, it became more obvious that the absence of specific names, places and dates was purposeful. Her style of storytelling had been firmly established, but as her life story and attentions moved overseas and she was freed from associations with Canada, Annie seemed more open to noting names and places. Her perceived need for anonymity was gone and the guessing game she earlier played with an unknown or potential audience became irrelevant. Discoveries, personalities and memories were far too powerful to be ignored. She would have to be more open with herself and her world. It was her duty to identify and laud the extraordinary acts of ordinary people in these troubled times. History and context assumed greater importance and "Passing Through" becomes more illuminating.

From October 1915 until March 1916, Annie paced the floor of her parents' home in Woodstock. In Annie's estimation, the female community's preoccupation with local womanly war efforts such as knitting and making up soldiers' kits were trivial. Such activities were helpful but of little consequence. In February 1916, Annie received word that William, still lingering at the Canadian training camp at Bramshott, was hospitalized with pleurisy. That was Annie's final call to action. Against her family's wishes, Annie secured a cabin on the Allen liner *Corinthian* sailing in March from Saint John. She joined the overseas exodus and sailed for Britain and the world of the European conflict. Annie was extremely alert to the horrific challenges and sorrows ahead, but simply could not remain uninvolved. She tucked a flimsy paper Shorthand Writer's Note Book into her luggage. One hundred pages cost one penny. Annie is not known to have kept many other written records of her life, but like so many other men and women of the Great War, she felt compelled to record through correspondence and journal at least some of the events happening around her.

On the back cover of this little note-book, Annie scrawled, at least thirty years later, the words, "contains notes of … lighter moments in England." This type of gentle comment was quite typical of other even more dedicated wartime diarists. First-hand accounts of casualties and suffering were often sparingly recorded. For example, the editor of the letters and diary of Clare Gass, a nurse in the Canadian Army Medical Corps, observed that weeping was not allowed and events rather than emotions were easier to enscribe: "The closer she [Clare Gass] is to the front, the less she recounts."[1]

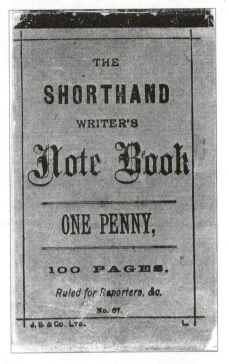

The cover of Annie Foster's penny War Diary, recording the "lighter moments" of 1915–1916. Image courtesy of White Rock Museum and Archives, 1995-17 File 1 Diary.

While Annie's wartime journal remained primarily an account of extracurricular, "lighter" comings and goings, it was a marvellous discovery for a biographer and offered a great insight into her cares and personality. Long after the Great War, Annie kept her war memory book close at hand. She did not offer it to the University of New Brunswick Archives along with her other writings, photos and papers. Instead, the notebook ultimately found a home in the White Rock Museum and Archives, in the community that Annie called home for the last forty years of her life.

Thankfully, Annie's first Atlantic crossing passed without incident. Memory of the sinking of the *Lusitania* by a German submarine off the coast of Ireland on May 7, 1915, weighed heavily on the passengers. As the *Corinthian* steamed through the Danger Zone, many remained dressed and alert all night, life preservers close at hand, while the captain and crew kept up morale with conversations and entertainments.

Annie made the first entry in her notebook on April 8, 1916. Other than mentioning that her husband was able to take time from the Bramshott Common military camp and meet her at the train station in London, there is no reference to the dreadful battles raging across the English Channel. For the present, William and Annie could be tourists in London and enjoy their short time together. London was strangely and delightfully familiar. The landmarks, historic sites, buildings, shops and streets were all part of Annie's education and upbringing. She found little to recommend at the Windsor Hotel in Westminster. There was no central heating, and warmth was found only in the bathroom with its network of pipes and spigots. Annie's complaints about the quality of English cuisine were familiar (then as now) to the consumers of English meals. Waiters in the upscale dining room spoke English only in the morning when the menu was also in English and, shockingly, porridge was served only under protest. French was the language of communication at the evening meal. Even more distressing to Annie was the sight of women in the hotel lounge smoking "… in a dreadfully masculine way. The old dowager rested her cigarette on her chin and spread her ample bulk over the largest chair. Another dame of reverend age sucked on hers till her cheeks fell in. No wonder Englishmen marry actresses."[2] The colonial Mrs. Foster was so impertinent as to inform a taxi driver whose rate she deplored that she and her husband did not intend to buy the vehicle, merely drive in it: "Apparently the longest way round is the surest way home."[3]

Their first order of business was to find suitable accommodation for Annie as near to Bramshott as possible. Annie began an exasperating search for a temporary home from a tiny suite in the Royal Anchor Hotel in the nearby village of Liphook. The Anchor boasted that Queen Victoria had on occasion slept in the bedroom adjacent but this fame was of little interest to the very practical Mrs. Garland Foster. In an ironic reversal of expectations, the lady from the land of frozen rivers, mountains and prairie found the heating arrangements in English residences primitive and "chilliness personified." A handful of coals only accentuated the cold and dampness. Fortunately, Annie had the good grace to recognize, through some bitter tears, that although "… about this time I was ready to take the next boat back… [I] must have tried my husband's patience sorely."[4]

In time, she located rooms for one pound per week in a vine-covered cottage in the pleasant village of Shottermill, formerly a centre for broom-making and other rural arts. Mrs. Emsley, wife of the military camp's senior chaplain and who had also crossed on the *Corinthian,* lived nearby. The two ladies entertained themselves by visiting the Peasant Art Industries community at

Margaret Macdonald (second from right), Matron-in-Chief of Canadian Nursing Services [Canadian Medical Corps], at her office in the Strand, London. Photo courtesy of Canada Department of National Defence/Library and Archives Canada, PA-005229.

Haslemere and the Hutcheson Museum. Peasant Art Industries, a creation of Ethel and Geoffrey Blount, was a well-known artistic community integrating work, leisure and the country life industries movement and was of particular interest to the two ladies. Toys, weaving and wood decoration first admired at Peasant Art Industries occupied Annie's imagination for years. She became a personal friend of the Blounts and, curiously, an ardent admirer of their toy-making abilities. Also within brisk, healthful walking distance were Tennyson's home, the Kiffold Yew Tree (England's oldest tree) and the haunts of novelist George Eliot.

Annie often took walks in the countryside with Mrs. Emsley or William on his brief leaves. But such charming incidents were not part of the present reality and Annie was altogether too observant of the people and properties about her. On June 8, 1916, she had a serious conversation with her journal regarding two topics of deepening concern to her: the welfare of children and nutrition. As a teacher and a nurse she found the number of neglected children playing in the streets highly disturbing. Through a questionable line of thought, she linked her stern observations with women's suffrage: "Have decided that the vote is the last thing the women in England need—I never saw such god-forsaken children. Why should a race of females who cannot properly bring up their own offspring be trusted with the national responsibility? It would solve a lot of problems both in the care of children and national problems to make cooks of the whole lot of them—rich and poor."[5] The dreariness of English cookery has always been the object of complaints from foreigners and Annie fell right in step with this tradition: "Imagine any self respecting housekeeper using margarine for shortening."[6] She elaborated: "The results [of poor nutrition]—pale, jaded, old wise-looking infants, lame halt hunchbacks, stooped—and a occasional one that thrives in spite of things."[7] Such rants were not entirely uncharacteristic. As Annie became more politicized and gained confidence in her own opinions and experience she acquired a reputation for outspokenness and obstinacy. This was merely an indication of encounters ahead.

Even before she left Canada, Annie had called upon her latent nurses' training and offered her services to the British Red Cross. Just as she had signed William's permission for military service, William permitted his wife to take up hospital work—as long as it did not involve scrubbing floors and labouring chores such as those undertaken by the wartime British Voluntary Aid Detachment personnel. Three months had passed since Mrs. Foster had arrived in England. She had taken the necessary inoculations. Her nerves were wearing thin and she had not heard from the British Red Cross. Following another tirade in her journal (on June 27) in which she again labelled English women failures as mothers and cooks, Annie, accompanied by Mrs. Emsley, took an assault on London. It was now July 4 and she was determined to set things in motion on the nursing front. Nurse Foster presented herself at the office of Miss Margaret Macdonald, Matron-in-Chief of Canadian Nursing Services (Canadian Army Medical Corps), in the impressive Cecil Chambers Building in the Strand.

Macdonald was a formidable woman in her own right. She and Annie shared many characteristics and life experiences. A native of Pictou County, Nova Scotia, Margaret Macdonald had trained at the New York City Hospital, and then taken up private-duty nursing in the city. She epitomized the new professional nurse—disciplined, courageous, knowledgeable and caring. Her biographer describes how Major Macdonald "… blossomed into a materfamilias when she was in charge of Canada's military nurses in the First World War."[8] It fell to Macdonald to reject Annie's application to serve with the Canadian Nursing Services on the basis of Annie's ineligibility to enter the Canadian military. Nurse Foster was a British subject, in good health and her training was more than acceptable. However, Annie was over thirty-eight years old and married. Macdonald advised Annie to try the Canadian Red Cross services, if she was not taken on by the British Red Cross.

Mrs. Emsley in tow, Annie hastened to 83 Pall Mall, headquarters of the British Red Cross and St. John's Ambulance. Here she learned "… that some misunderstanding had prevented me being called and they supposed I was already on duty!"[9] On the spot she was offered her choice of two immediate positions. Did she prefer a military hospital in distant Lancashire or one at Isleworth in Greater London between Richmond and Hounslow? It was not difficult to select Isleworth for its proximity to the Bramshott military camp. Insurance, banking, purchase of British Red Cross uniforms at Selfridge's Department Store—all was accomplished by early afternoon, leaving time (and five pages of description in her notebook) to visit, enjoy and enthuse about toy exhibitions and their curators in central London. Annie had developed an all-consuming interest in museum-piece toys of all types and styles, representative of all decades and materials. Some toys were distinguished for their historical personal attachment, others for their artistic qualities or commercial value. True to her admiration of Mr. and Mrs. Blount "… the absolutely unique exhibit was that of the Peasants' Arts Society, which was beautiful enough for a picture."[10]

William and the 54th Battalion, having endured one of the most wretchedly wet winters in Britain's history, were still lingering at Bramshott. Annie was now to be truly involved in the war effort before her husband had even set his boots on the continent. William and his wife had a quick farewell and, on July 7, Sister Foster began her war service nursing career at Percy House Military Hospital, Isleworth.

SISTER IN SERVICE

*P*rior to the Great War, Percy House, erected in 1883, had been a conventional workhouse school, but like many of England's private and institutional buildings, it was hastily converted into a military convalescent hospital. Wards and support buildings were spread about a cloister and courtyard area. This arrangement necessitated much hustling in and out and up and down. When Annie Foster arrived, there were only four nursing sisters caring for 300 patients. Sister Foster was put in charge of 100 beds. As she had anticipated, the work was never-ending. Preparation of the wounded for examination by the chief medical doctor seemed to occupy a great deal of time and required infinite patience. One particularly crusty old army surgeon was of the opinion that many men were malingerers prone to "swing the lead." Annie did not share this assessment and had the deepest respect for the wounded men, many of them mere youths.

Neither a true military nor civic hospital, Percy House was classified as an Auxiliary Home Hospital, staffed by the British Red Cross or the Order of St. John. The professional medical staff was assisted in every way imaginable by 300 members of Britain's Voluntary Aid Detachments (VAD). VADs were "… untrained volunteers, recruited by the Red Cross and given a few weeks' rudimentary first aid training by the St. John Ambulance…."[1] Those at Percy House (almost exclusively women) were frequently residents of note from the surrounding villages. Some of them, Annie observed, became quite skilled in nursing duties and they generally "worked for joy." As time and the war dragged on, the services of the VADs became invaluable in Britain and at the front. Their role was critical and praiseworthy but at times contentious.

The Matron-in-Chief of the Canadian Army Medical Corps, the stalwart Margaret Macdonald, exemplified this professional wariness of untrained caregivers. She did not countenance the VAD presence in Canadian military hospitals: "As someone forging a place for professional nurses in the military and thus part of a broader contemporary movement for the professionalization of nurses, Macdonald did not want any watering down of the CAMC nursing ranks."[2] This was a subject on which Annie and Matron-in-Chief Macdonald disagreed, but it did not prevent Annie from exerting political and personal influence in a related matter.

Two Canadian nurses (one a Miss Cook, daughter of a minister from Kaslo, near Nelson) were nursing at Percy House when Annie began her service there. Both nurses were anxious to be sent to the continent with Miss Macdonald's Canadian Nursing Service but had been overlooked for the transfer. On her first day off, Annie, with Miss Cook in tow, travelled up to London to pay a call on the affable Sir Richard McBride, former premier of British Columbia and now, at the denouement of his career, Agent General for British Columbia in London. The nurses, Annie explained, "... were able to get attached to their own [CAMC] unit after I went up with one of them to discuss the matter with the British Columbia Agent General. At that time he insisted that I should tell my husband that I must get into our own [CAMC] service. But my husband objected to any wire pulling in such a matter and anyway the British [Red Cross] service offered a better chance for leave when he got leave."[3] A later offer from CAMC did not guarantee that she would *not* be sent to Salanika. Annie, having no wish to emulate Florence Nightingale's career in Turkey, did not pursue her inquiry. Sister Foster put aside any interest she may have had in being closer to the front and stayed on at Percy House, where between October 4, 1915, and December 31, 1919, nearly 5,000 men were treated.

William and Annie, expecting the 54th Battalion to depart for the continent at any time, met at Bramshott Camp or in London as often as their days or hours off permitted. Parting became more difficult each time. When Annie arrived at the camp on the evening of August 13, the troop train had pulled out a few hours earlier: "As I had now said good-bye five times not expecting to see him again, you would also think I might have been used to it. But this time was worse than ever and I went back to the hospital feeling that this was just one of those things that come one after another and make life almost unbearable!"[4]

William, having assumed the position of Adjunct, was the professional journalist in the family. He wrote surprisingly uncensored reports back to Nelson that were published in the *Nelson Daily News*. In the August 25, 1916, edition, a letter dated July 29 described the local battalion as "... well over strength, as

Nurses and orderlies at Percy House Military Hospital (a former workhouse), Isleworth, Middlesex, in 1916. Nurse/Sister Annie Foster at centre of the group. Photo courtesy of Peter G. Higginbotham.

a result of the drafting in of men from other battalions… [though] the bulk of our men, however, are those with whom we left Vernon last November."[5] Knowing the readership was anxious for any morsel of news, he went on to note the welfare of other Kootenay men. An adjacent article told of the work of Annie, Nurse Cook and a nurse who was the sister-in-law of former Nelson mayor, Harold Selous. Late in July, William was of the notion that " … his wife will in all likelihood be sent to France in the Red Cross service."[6]

August 13, 1916, was a sort of D-Day for William's 54th Kootenay Battalion. The Kootenay men, under their own Lieutenant-Colonel Kemball, left for the battlefields of France and Flanders. They joined the Princess Pats (Princess Patricia's Canadian Light Infantry) and were introduced to the gruesome mud and debris of the front line. On September 15, they saw action for the first time. Throughout October and November, along with the British, they were engaged in the third stage of the First Battle of the Somme, where tanks were used for the first time in the conflict. November 13, 1916, was " … the most grueling and exhausting in the experience of the Battalion. [On the 18th] … our Battalion gained high praise for the manner in which they kept direction when advancing under very trying circumstances…."[7] Casualties were significant. As in many true wartime stories of love and separation, it would be a long time before Annie and William would meet again in London or Bramshott.

And so Annie's war work continued at Percy House Hospital. Fortunately, Percy House was situated in a privileged and historic part of Britain. London was easily accessible by train; Hampton Court Palace and Richmond and Kew Gardens were not far away; former homes of past-centuries' celebrities Nell Gwyn, Alexander Pope and David Garrick were nearby; and the church of Isleworth itself merited four pages in her journal entry of September 15, 1916. An entry in this notebook dated August 16 explained Annie's frequent ventures to toy exhibitions, museums and craft and antiques shops. She had been commissioned by Canada's Minister of Trade and Commerce, Sir George Eulas Foster (no relation), to "report on the London toy trade." George Foster was a little-known, but highly experienced, Canadian career politician. He served in the cabinet of seven prime ministers and was a delegate to the Paris Peace Conference of 1918–1919. To Annie, he was also a native of Carleton County, New Brunswick, a fellow graduate of the University of New Brunswick, and the Conservative Member of Parliament for King and York Counties, New Brunswick, from 1882 to 1900. Quite how or why Sir George was interested in toys at this critical time in history is hard to imagine, but he did select a dedicated and thorough contractor.

War was coming closer every day. The first German Zeppelin shot down in England dropped out of the sky within flaming sight of Percy House. Annie turned her attention more fully to her young patients' medical and mental conditions. She saw humour in their schoolboy antics and their discomfort in accepting the good cheer and noble intentions of the visiting ladies of the auxiliary: "I got to understand the qualities that endear Tommy Atkins to the world."[8] Finding the right balance between medical care, tolerance and understanding was a constant quest. Annie took particular interest in the manifestation and effect of skull injuries. She would draw on her experience with these impairments for many years.

Christmas presented a particular challenge. Staff, patients and, no doubt, the good ladies of the town, decorated the wards. There were yellow paper chains, green wreaths, red ribbon festoons, and Allied flags and a frieze of Christmas bells above the fireplace. Many men, although discharged from the military, were unable to go home to their families. The unmanly art of needlework had been pressed upon them in their convalescence and a competitive spirit resulted when a public exhibition of crafts at the hospital awarded prize ribbons.

Annie's earlier observations on the quality of English food were more than confirmed by her hospital and wartime experience. The men were always hungry. Bean and pea meal was substituted for flour, butter was unheard of, and sugar was doled out by the fraction of a teaspoon. Practical measures were applied even to outdated and awkward nurses' uniforms. The St. John's Ambulance care-giver's "… tiny black velvet bonnet perched on the top of the head with strings tied under the chin"[9] was quite absurd. The "New Woman" was emerging in subtle ways, and Annie rather ruefully admitted that she came to dress like the local people, even on those days when she was not in uniform.

It was Annie's intention to record "the lighter moments in England" in her little notebook, and on the whole she was faithful to that assignment. It is only through careful analysis of her difficult scrawl that hints of pain and sadness are found. The "Toy Report" was her primary time-off occupation and her research was often combined with whirlwind sightseeing in London. On November 6, Annie and her new friend, Miss Phelan, ticked off (and described accurately and enthusiastically) an incredible list of must-sees: St. James Cathedral, Lambeth Palace, Westminster Abbey (conspicuously sand-bagged), St. Paul's Cathedral, St. Martin's-in-the Field, the National Gallery, and, of necessity, the Canadian military Pay Office and the British Columbia Agent General's office, where they read newspapers from home. They were amused to learn that, in the opinion of the verger of St. Martin's, a window had been bombed by suffragettes due to encouragement from Germany. "Mental indigestion" was how Annie described the day.

Another passion or diversion was an interest in English etchings, prints, frames, and ceramics of all designs and composition. Annie wrote knowingly of "pinchbeck," "mezzotints" and "stipples," but would only rationalize the purchase of an art piece or artifact when she was certain she was getting the better end of the sale. Several times she returned to an elderly framer in nearby Chiswick to have treasures appraised or attended to. These artworks would become mementos of her time in England and sources of inspiration for further study and appreciation. As her residency in England lengthened, she grew bolder in making small bargain purchases. One day in mid-November 1916, Annie and Nurse Maude visited Mr. and Mrs. William Giles, who lived and worked in their own charming studio. Mr. Giles had invented a specialized printing press and a frame-making device. He was to become the president of the Society of Gravers and Printers in Colour and the publisher of *Original Color-print Magazine*. Annie was greatly taken with Giles' prints and creations, and confessed, "One [image] with the sheep in the foreground I must have when I can commit an extravagance with impunity."[10] If indeed, Annie had acquired a Giles woodcut or print, which it appears she did not, she would have left something of considerable value to her estate!

There were times when Sister Foster permitted herself to speak out on war issues other than medical care and food. In her psychological assessment of the wounded men, she sensed a growing tension attributable to "carelessness of consequences" in the higher command. She became more fully aware that the consequences of war would continue long after the conflict had ceased and most of the physical wounds had healed.

War talk often seemed to lead to discourse on women's suffrage. Annie wisely softened her position on votes for women and now accepted that suffrage would, in fact, follow the conclusion of hostilities. Women had more than shown their courage and shouldered enormous responsibility at home and abroad in the past two years. Women had earned the vote. Among other momentous changes, suffrage would lead to a demand by women for a voice in international politics. Given the vehemence with which a particular clever female acquaintance spoke regarding the non-involvement of America in the war, Annie observed that the future "will be quite exciting at times!" America was more and more in the news and in daily conversation. On December 18, 1916, President Woodrow Wilson issued an American Peace Note, followed in January by a "Peace Without Victory" speech to Congress. Wilson planned that he alone would mediate the end of the war. Hope did not last for long, since on January 31, 1917, Germany announced the resumption of unrestricted submarine warfare. A general war weariness pervaded Great Britain, its institutions, its people and, in particular, the military forces.

Some critical entries in Annie's notebook were definitely not about the lighter moments of life. No sooner had William left for the continent in August 1916 than Annie found she tired very easily and experienced frightening hemorrhaging from her lungs. This was a reminder of similar chest complaints she had experienced during her early nursing days in Philadelphia over sixteen years earlier. Dr. Lowry, a non-military specialist, could find no cause. When this "throat and lung" trouble recurred in October, Lowry enunciated "Stomach" and wrote a long prescription. However, Annie noted, "I knew a lung hemorrhage when I saw it, so added my own treatment by taking father's old remedy, beech wood cresote [sic] for luck."[11] This disturbing condition came at a very stressful and busy time for a full-time supervisory and working nurse, but the work had to go on.

Just before Christmas, Annie proclaimed in her journal that she would be quitting at Percy House at the new year. The 54th Kootenay Battalion had spent Christmas on the line and the day "... was somewhat memorable ... as towards midnight the Bosche [enemy] put down a very heavy strafe on our front and support trenches because of our having fired on him when he attempted to fraternize earlier in the day."[12] William would be getting leave early in 1917, his first since August, and she wished to be free to meet him. By the end of January, William's leave had not come about, but Annie was nevertheless on her way to her old rooms at Shottermill for a necessary period of rest and recuperation. She felt she had been at Percy House a very long time: "The night of my departure the men celebrated, whether their freedom, their joy at my going, or regret, I was never sure, but the harmless demonstration took the form of a pillow fight...."[13]

February 1917, then March, and William's leave was again cancelled. The 54th was suffering major losses, including the loss of its Commanding Officer Colonel. They were experimenting (not always successfully) with the deployment of gas canisters against the enemy. It was time for Annie to get back to work. In mid-March, she took up her next British Red Cross assignment at Maxstoke Castle, Warwickshire, which stood on a two-hectare estate just a few kilometres east of Birmingham. Owned since 1599 by the Dilke family and dating from 1346, Maxstoke was every inch and every stone a castle. The visitor approached via an avenue of trees and a grassy carpet of daffodils, snowdrops and violets (reminiscent of Fredericton), crossed a water-filled moat, and entered the medieval courtyard through ancient wooden doors. Although it was a convalescent Auxiliary Home Hospital like Percy House, only thirty soldiers were cared for in the castle's spacious banquet hall. The occasional soldier, already in a fragile mental state, was spooked by the tales of resident ghosts and secret Jacobean chambers. As the nurses made their nightly rounds, there was every likelihood they would be mistaken for a ghostly apparition. Annie was to write a charming, light-hearted article on the history of Maxstoke for the *Vancouver Province* eighteen years later and both "Passing Through" and her wartime journal offer pleasant descriptions of the estate.

Although nothing untoward took place at Maxstoke, Annie felt isolated and "fed up" after three weeks, and was up to London for a new assignment by mid-May. Her spare time in Warwickshire had been spent devouring art history books and biographies of artists. Could it be she missed the shops, galleries and toy exhibitions of Greater London? What a change was in store! Her next assignment, Brunner Mond Hospital (BMH) in Middlewich, Cheshire (between Chester and Manchester), was farther from London than Maxstoke. Middlewich was a grimy industrial city and Brunner Mond a huge munitions factory. Brunner Mond Company had recently become infamous for an atrocious disaster that occurred January 19, 1917, at its gigantic operation in Silvertown, in the East End of London: "Working flat out to meet a chronic shortage of shells for the war effort, the Brunner Mond works exploded, killing 73 people and laying waste a huge expanse of Silvertown."[14] This was the biggest explosion seen in London before or since.

The company hospital was looking for a nursing sister who was a strict, yet kindly, disciplinarian. Annie wondered what she had done to fit that criterion. Convalescent soldiers at BMH were reputed to jump the fence of the institution and, upon descending, were greeted by young damsels of the town. When a local police sergeant confronted Sister Foster with this complaint, she responded in defence of the soldiers by inquiring about the girls who were leading the young men astray. In fact, Annie blamed neither the girls nor the chaps, for it was a dismal life they led: "The sidewalks of the town were corrugated iron so that workmen wore clogs to work."[15] The stench and heaviness in the summer air was particularly stressful on the men who had been gassed. On this matter, Annie, with her own handicap of weak lungs, was particularly sympathetic.

Finally William's long-awaited ten-day leave—his first since leaving Britain on August 13 the year before—was granted. Annie fled to London on June 5, where conflicting train and hotel arrangements added an element of panic to their reunion. Twenty-two years later, Annie remembered the leave:

> These leave days were queer—a sort of living "twixt heaven and hell," as it were. I shall never forget the day I took leave of him after his holiday—actually the last time I saw him. I was to stay a day longer in London in order to see him off to his train. At that last minute he thought he had lost his pass and tickets—a sort of psychological retreat no doubt. A hurried search revealed them safe in his baggage. One saw him get into his train, with a sort of suspended animation feeling. Death awaiting him in time, leaving life behind was no doubt my husband's feeling. He got in his car, spoke to another officer who sat opposite. The bell warned. I saw the other officer turn his head away as if he had had too much. I knew the moment had come. Leaving life, happiness and all that home had meant to us behind. I walked as one slowly congealing to the taxi stand.[16]

The depth of the emotion shown in this parting is particularly poignant and reminds the readers of scenes immortalized later in films depicting wartime separations.

With her added anxiety about events in France, Annie found the rounds at Brunner Mond more and more difficult to endure. She was aware that there was a growing wish on the part of Canadian and British authorities to facilitate the return of the wives of Canadian servicemen to Canada, even though some wives, such as herself, had contributed significantly to the war effort. It was the summer of 1917; surely hostilities would be over within a few months? Annie resolved to take advantage of this opportunity and secured passage from Liverpool for August 14. She hastily left Britain after taking a few days off for illness but "... finally I did get away to London, where the usual difficulties over passports added to farewells were not likely to improve my *condition*" [italics added].[17]

HOMECOMING

*T*he clattering, stuffy and crowded train journey to Liverpool was equally trying. Annie's companions on the train and ship journey were members of the family of the late Sir Richard McBride who were bringing Sir Richard's ashes home to Canada for burial in British Columbia. Only when she had settled into her cabin aboard the White Star liner *Megantic* did Annie experience some "surcease." The ship, carrying three hundred invalided officers back to Canada, had already survived an attack by the German submarine *UB-43* on February 25. Such was the nature of trans-Atlantic travel in 1917.

Annie had far greater concerns, for she recognized her *condition* as pregnancy. She was exhausted, weakened by the persistent difficulty with her lungs and poor nutrition—and she was forty-two years old. The ship's doctor was widely acknowledged as "… so drunk by eight o'clock in the morning that he did not know his own name."[1] When it became evident that Annie was suffering a miscarriage, she insisted on being put in the care of a military doctor on board, since the "drunken beast" of a ship's doctor "… would hardly be the best person to trust in the case of complications arising from an interrupted pregnancy."[2] Annie felt somewhat more secure under the care of Dr. Major Hogan, who was on leave from the battlefields of France in the same vicinity where William was presently serving. Hogan had previously practised at the highly respected Dalhousie Medical School. How Annie must have longed for the care and sympathies of her fellow nursing sisters. Although only two-and-a-half months into her pregnancy, Annie later confided to friends that she had lost twins during that horrible Atlantic crossing.[3]

It was a long and sad voyage—made even longer as the ship dropped in first to Halifax, then to Quebec City, and finally, Montreal. Here, Annie boarded a train to Ottawa to spend a week with William's family, whom she hardly knew at all. A week later, she was able to return home to Woodstock and the comfort and love of her aging parents.

Annie's recovery from her seventeen months in Britain was slow and mentally painful. In the security of her childhood home, she spent many waking hours contemplating the principles of the Society for Psychical Research she had tentatively joined while overseas. Founded in 1882 at Cambridge, the Society studied allegedly paranormal phenomena in a neutral, scientific manner. Somewhat akin to the spiritualism she had witnessed as a child, the Society offered an insight into these times of sudden death when "… the veil between life and death must have worn thin."[4]

Sunshine came back into Aunt Annie's (or Aunt Nan's) life when she went to Maine to visit her sister Margaret, now Mrs. Percy Homer. Margaret was the mother of two delightful little girls, Christine, aged four, and Margaret, aged two. Nan (as she would again be known to many close friends and family) would devote four full pages of "Passing Through" to recalling the games, toys, teddy bears, imaginary playmates and stories she shared with these little girls. Just as her mother had taken her to the family pond at Manners Sutton, Nan took her nieces on nature walks and introduced them to bugs, beetles, blossoms and berries. Back in Woodstock, Nan and Margaret's brother, James, his wife, Clara, and an exceptionally beautiful baby boy provided further reason to smile and hope again.

These diversions, however, were short-lived and Nan's mind frequently returned to what she called her "war worries." These forebodings were now matched by what was to become an added global scourge during the later days of the war—influenza. Both her parents, Christine and Robert, suffered a (thankfully) mild attack of this disease. A full year after Nan's return from Britain, the war clouds hung over Europe as dark and heavy as ever. On an evening early in October 1918, the Ross family read press reports of terrible Canadian casualties in an action near Sancourt in the vicinity of Cambrai where the 54th Battalion had been engaged for some time: "Although my husband was not mentioned, there was mention of two adjutants being wounded."[5] It was several days before confirmation was received that William was indeed a casualty. He had sustained critical lung and shrapnel injuries. Nan immediately made plans, including certification of her own health and the state of her "lung lesions," to attend to her husband's care. However, the intensity of the war coupled with severance of communication lines and now the adversities accompanying the influenza

Trench near Sancourt, France, where William G. Foster was wounded September 30, 1918.
Photo courtesy of the University of New Brunswick Archives, MG L7, Series 3, File 1, #14.

epidemic made such travel plans quite impossible. Nan sensed and feared the worst: "For two weeks I hung betwixt hope and fear…. It must have been a terrible task for my brother to bring the final telegram."[6] Nan believed her Celtic Scots insight had taken over her subconscious and accounted for recent curious dreams: "My mother often knew when we were in danger without any visible means of doing so. I recall vividly the day before my husband's death, which allowing for the difference of time was six p.m. October 14, 1918. For hours a strange restlessness pursued me, a desire to do something."[7]

There was a wretched irony in that William's death on October 14 (which, like any other wife and mother, Nan had feared and anticipated for three years) had come so close to the end of hostilities on November 11, 1918. Paralyzed with shock and sorrow, Nan found some healing refuge in sleep and reverie. A particularly poignant letter dated October 15, 1918, arrived from a British nurse who attended Captain Foster in his final hours. She wrote gently of how the medical staff had tried so hard to save Captain Foster who had been a perfect "brick." Quite hastily, while battles still blared on the horizon, Captain Foster was laid to rest with a small number of other Canadian men in the British Cemetery on Bucquoy Road near the town of Ficheux. Nan Foster was never to visit the little cemetery where her husband was buried. However, a thoughtful infantryman delivered to Nan a grainy brown photo of the trench at Bourlon Wood where William was injured. The small photo, a shocking anomaly in a folder of formal, pleasant Ross family portraits, resides in the Annie Harvie Ross Foster fonds at the University of New Brunswick Archives.

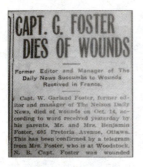

The Nelson Daily News *reports the October 14 death of its former editor Captain William Garland Foster. Image courtesy of the* Nelson Daily News, *October 19, 1918.*

CAPT. G. FOSTER DIES OF WOUNDS

Former Editor and Manager of The Daily News Succumbs to Wounds Received in France.

Capt. W. Garland Foster, former editor and manager of The Nelson Daily News, died of wounds on Oct. 14, according to word received yesterday by his parents, Mr. and Mrs. Benjamin Foster, 593 Pretoria Avenue, Ottawa. This has been confirmed by a telegram from Mrs. Foster, who is at Woodstock, N. B. Capt. Foster was wounded

The many tributes and condolences Nan received all spoke of her husband's dedication to his men and his duties and of his remarkable efficiency, tempered with good cheer and affability. She was particularly taken with the letters and a battalion Christmas card sent by William's military batman, Mr. Hatch. She took these condolences and tributes to heart and carried on.

The flu was attacking with militaristic vehemence. The local Woodstock clergyman was an early victim; the town's kindly old doctor (the type of legendary frontier medical man) succumbed to overwork; and Nan's toddler-nephew came close to death. The community called on Nan, with her nurse's training and experience, for help. This she willingly offered. After several months back at her nursing profession, and just as she was defining plans for her own future, Nan, the caregiver, herself contracted the flu. Upon her partial recovery, the doctor surprisingly recommended that she move on as soon as possible, as the change could be nothing but beneficial. On July 17, 1919, the Foster family learned that William had been posthumously awarded the Military Cross "… for conspicuous gallantry and devotion to duty at Cambria on September 27, 1918."[8] This was a further source of pride and encouragement to the widow.

Annie Foster had resolved to begin where she left off. She would return to Nelson, the small city where she had met William, where she still owned a home and where she had friends. Although 5,000 miles further from the front than New Brunswick, Nelson, the home of the 54th Battalion, had suffered heavy losses. Over 800 men and officers from the 54th alone would never return to the Kootenay area. By the time Nan was fit to travel, the Nelson School District was able to offer the returning teacher a position at a one-room rural school in Balfour, commencing January 1919. As she rode the familiar CPR line across the country for which her husband had fought and died, Nan felt somewhat restored and ready to face life anew and alone.

Balfour was a very small service and fruit ranching community, as well as a steamer transfer point, located on a sunny benchland at the outlet of Kootenay Lake into the Kootenay River. Reputedly Balfour took its name about 1889 from Lord Arthur James Balfour, future Prime Minister of Britain (1902–5), but at the time of Annie's arrival an Arthur Balfour was an up-and-coming chief secretary for Scotland. This Balfour family had significant mining interests in the area.

Thirty kilometres by paddlewheeler would take Annie down the west arm of Kootenay Lake to her old home in Nelson on the weekends. Balfour seemed like a good re-introduction to the world of children, education and well-being. Mrs. Garland Foster (the variation on her name she would henceforth use professionally) was paid a generous $1,020 per year to teach twenty-five pupils at the Balfour Rural School. She was the most highly qualified teacher in the school's nine-year history. A reputation for discipline, recognized and encouraged by Mrs. Foster herself, had preceded her to Balfour: "Rigorous scholarship filled the [1919] term conducted by Mrs. Garland Foster, B.A.…"[9]

One observant little girl, Isabel McKay, was qualified to comment on Mrs. Foster more personally, because the teacher lived with the child's family and had become a friend of her mother's. Mrs. Garland Foster "had great goals," according to Isabel, but the little girl also vividly recalled the heart-wrenching story of the teacher's miscarriage of babies during a stormy Atlantic crossing. Mollie, a niece of Annie's Nelson friend, Myra Green, spoke well of the teacher Mrs. Foster even fifty-four years later. Although as a teacher Mrs. Foster was prone to dispense advice quite generously, she would also find several other community venues for her opinion in the very near future. The post-war days posed many serious issues unimaginable even twenty years earlier. It is not surprising, but also not without irony, that because of her outspoken manner, Mrs. Garland Foster was noted among the suffragettes of the community.

Balfour had become well known throughout the province following the construction in 1911 of the rather grand CPR hotel, Balfour Hotel (also known as the Kootenay Lake Hotel), on the plateau above the ship wharf. A backdrop of mountains, glistening fast-moving water dominated by dark evergreens, with patches of orchard emerging on the mountainside, was just what the adventure tourist of the day was seeking. A circle tour by rail and paddlewheeler from the Rockies through the Columbia and Kootenay River systems featured a stopover at the Tudor and chateau-style Balfour Hotel. The "tennis set" and pseudo-élite of Nelson were also attracted to the resort-like setting. By 1916, however, the brief glory days of the Balfour Hotel were over. The province's Prohibition Act of 1917 also discouraged frivolity and the pursuit of leisure. A more practical purpose was found for the attractive building, and in 1917 it was re-opened by the federal Military Hospitals Commission as the Balfour Sanatorium. Over a hundred veterans afflicted with lung disorders underwent treatment with good doses of fresh mountain air and sunshine, while also enjoying the billiard tables and tennis courts of the former hotel.

By coincidence Annie was also to benefit from the proximity of the sanatorium. When she experienced difficulty in climbing the steep bank from the boat landing to the townsite, she consulted the sanatorium doctors about her own lung condition. X-rays verified that she had in fact suffered from tuberculosis. Thereupon, following the advice of a former military medical colleague, Mrs. Garland Foster, as a Great War widow and veteran herself, applied to the army for health service benefits. She had no difficulty in securing the benefits, " … perhaps because nursing sisters being so few comparatively [to the number of veterans] and having so much gratitude hurled at them, were more easily put through [the] department. Perhaps, I should be thankful, although a 50% TB disability is not a thing to be thankful about."[10]

Annie was now a civilian and would look at life in a more reconstructionist manner. In July she left Balfour after a satisfactory school term, but she would continue to seek a new direction for her life.

In utter contrast to any other experience in her adult life, Annie took a notion to "get back to the land"—a land upon which she had never toiled. She later rationalized that this primitive instinct was influenced by the re-establishment of land grants offered to returning soldiers. In her case, however, she was primarily still in search of peace and healing.

Prior to the Great War and his marriage, William had purchased three hundred acres of undeveloped land in the Pend d'Oreille country south of Nelson, very close to the American border. Annie was determined to try living on this large parcel of mountain forest. The Pend d'Oreille (spelling varies) River flows into the Columbia south of the City of Trail, and would one day be controlled by several hydroelectric dams on both sides of the border, but in 1919 the area was very thinly populated by a hardy, disparate collection of would-be prospectors, former prospectors, fruit and cattle ranchers and their struggling families.

One bold move or "mad fancy" was followed by another. On August 14, 1919, the *Nelson Daily News* passed on the following local gossip: "Mrs. Garland Foster has purchased the Symonds Ranch [at Nine Mile Creek on the Pend d'Oreille] which adjoins her property. She will take up ranching and is expected to arrive ... about the 20th of the month."[11] This information surely astounded those in Nelson who remembered the energetic, somewhat stiff but formidable schoolteacher and now activist Great War widow. Mindless of the opinions of others, by September Annie was the resident owner of 1.25 square kilometres of timbered mountainside on the extremely rugged landscape high above the powerful Pend d'Oreille River. Nine Mile Creek School had opened in January 1916, and every year since a new teacher had tried her luck with the eight to eleven pupils who found their way to the one-room schoolhouse. Initially, the school was supported by local district funds but by June 1919 only seven students attended and no funds were forthcoming from the school district. Although the Public School Report for 1920 notes a teacher, eleven students, and a local contribution of forty-five dollars, the Nine Mile School was officially closed in June 1919.

The closure of a rural school was unacceptable to the area's most recently arrived resident and large property-owner. Indeed, the *Nelson Daily News* kept its eye on Mrs. A.H. Foster, noting on September 2 that she had arrived at her Pend d'Oreille "estate," and the following day had "... taken charge of the Nine Mile School, which opened on Tuesday with a good attendance."[12] The school's abandonment by the authorities had presented Annie with the opportunity to fulfill another step in her pursuit of the rural, pioneer life. She described the situation: "There was a school in the neighbourhood, which I could have, in fact it rather sought me...."[13] In a quiet natural setting, she would teach children an appreciation for botany and nature studies such as she had learned from her own parents in rural New Brunswick. She would promote and experience healthy outdoor living, in stark contrast to the lives of families in the dark industrial towns of Britain of so recent memory. In order to bring the number of pupils up to minimal enrolment figures, as Nine Mile Creek's next teacher, Annie brought two children (from unnamed families) into the former Symonds home with her.

Discouragements soon followed. Bears roamed the paths and yards. One child became very ill and before winter set in Annie realized the venture was untenable and she retreated to Nelson: "This was the first time I had failed to go through with an undertaking."[14] The entire Pend d'Oreille episode merits barely half a typewritten page in her memoir.

What was Annie thinking? Why did she choose to live at the Symonds Ranch? The Pend d'Oreille backcountry is remote and marginally accessible to this day. None of the government or archival documents entirely explained Annie's actions, so on a late spring day in 2006, I visited the Pend d'Oreille country myself to try to understand Annie's Pend d'Oreille quest. An hour's drive from Nelson was a high, forested benchland accessible by a deeply rutted dirt road above the Pend d'Oreille River. This was the Nine Mile Creek area. Several mown fields revealed the outlines of long-abandoned buildings, among them some that accurately matched Annie's descriptions of the Foster and adjoining Symonds properties. On a bright spring afternoon, it was pleasant to envision a tall, silvering-haired woman in a long dark skirt collecting about her a dozen children from nearby rural properties. It was idyllic in setting and sensibility. But come winter? Even rural New Brunswick forty years earlier could not have presented more daunting conditions. Is it any wonder this Utopian venture lasted a brief three or four months? It is not surprising to note that never again did Annie Garland Foster stray far from pavement, plumbing and pillows.

Nonetheless, the good matron's next major undertaking back in the civilized City of Nelson was even more astonishing.

CIVILIAN LIFE

*A*nnie often managed to have two or three careers and causes on the go simultaneously. Her conversation was current, varied, and, as noted, opinionated. Teaching and living in Balfour or the Pend d'Oreille community had been experiences in isolation; nonetheless, these experiences served as a natural progression into community life. Mrs. Garland Foster would now assume a public profile within and on behalf of the Great War Veterans Association (GWVA).

The GWVA was established in Canada in April 1917 in response to the federal government's meagre pensions, rehabilitative, medical and practical services, and general lack of planning for the returned men and their families. The veterans and, especially, the families of those who did not return, needed a strong, knowledgeable, and dedicated voice to present their needs to an uncaring government. Upon the safe return of the men, the government mistakenly assumed life would simply return to its pre-war routine.

Annie had too much practical experience to accept this "back-to-normal" concept. In fact, she was disturbed by the attitude of some vets who, after a brief adjustment, settled back into their easy ways and seemed comfortably unconcerned about the plight of their comrades. She wrote: "Although I had gone reluctantly to the war, this after the war way of looking at the other fellow's troubles seemed so selfish.... The struggle for existence in civil life seemed to destroy that comradeship which was so striking when they first came back."[1] As a veteran of the war herself, Annie qualified to join the Nelson Branch of the GWVA. The Ladies Auxiliary was not for her. The predominantly male organization welcomed her energy and her knowledge of and insight into federal political motives and ensuing legislation and regulations. Annie was so seriously

Formal portrait, taken in 1919, of Mrs. Annie Garland Foster, former teacher, Great War veteran, advocate for veterans and their families, candidate for City of Nelson Councillor. Photo courtesy of the City of Nelson.

committed to the men's recovery and re-establishment that she was eager to translate her concern into social and political action.

Very, very few women had walked this political path before her, but she was willing to lead the way in British Columbia when the road was finally open. Step by step between 1916 and 1919 women were gaining the right to vote in provincial, federal and local civic elections. The first women to be granted the vote in the federal system were those who were members of the military in their own right (predominantly nurses) or those who had close male relatives in the armed forces. In August 1917, Roberta MacAdams, an Albertan nurse with the Canadian Army Medical Corps serving in England, contested a provincial legislature seat under the Alberta Military Representation Act. This act had created two seats in the legislature for the sole purpose of providing representation to soldiers serving overseas. Nurse MacAdams, known to her contemporaries as "Sister" (the familiar designation of a professional nurse at the time), ran under the clever slogan "Give one vote to the man of your choice and the other to the sister" and became the second woman elected to a legislature in the British Empire. Although experiencing very great personal hardships at this time, Annie must have taken note of the CAMC nurse's accomplishment and been greatly heartened by MacAdams' victory.

January 1920, with the Pend d'Oreille experience well behind her, was the appropriate time for Annie to raise two banners—one for the veterans and, finally, one for women's full participation in the electoral and political process. Fortunately, Annie (and her fellow Nelsonites) failed to recall her fairly prim assessment, delivered ten years earlier, opposing women who sought the vote. Every undertaking from January 1920 onwards would bear witness to her quest for justice, health and the well-being of those who served their country in time of conflict as well as for women and children. The new Mrs. Garland Foster was not so much an advocate of women's voting rights as an advocate dedicated to righting any injustice or neglect that afflicted women and their children.

Although GWVA purposes were widely known and seemed irrefutable, the organization's primary goal of promoting preferential employment for returned soldiers and its generally conservative perspective sometimes resulted in clashes with trades and labour councils and with the Industrial Workers of the World. Nonetheless, it was quite common for branches of the GWVA to endorse, and even select, candidates to run for local political office. The Nelson branch, which had a membership of four hundred in 1920, was not particularly vocal and its activities were not recorded in the group's British Columbia veterans' weekly newspaper.

In a provincial government by-election of January 24, 1918, Walter Drinnan, British Columbia GWVA secretary-treasurer and a candidate selected in a Vancouver riding at an open convention of veterans' organizations, faced off against Mary Ellen Smith. Mrs. Smith defeated Drinnan in the first provincial election in which there was a woman candidate, the first in which a woman was elected, and the first in which women voted. Such conflicting allegiances and alliances challenged the priorities of the recently enfranchised and growing GWVA electorate.

There would be no such dilemma in Nelson. At an exciting public meeting of returned men and sympathetic citizens held in the GWVA rooms on the evening of Saturday, January 10, 1920, Mrs. Garland Foster announced her candidacy for an aldermanic seat in the City of Nelson. She aimed to represent Nelson's West Ward on the city council. Earlier in the week, with only days to spare before Election Day on January 15, Mrs. Garland Foster had been invited by the Nelson GWVA to stand for city council. The former teacher and veteran would represent both "constituencies" … so to speak. A nominating committee sought other veterans to step forward as candidates but none were so inclined. The meeting unanimously endorsed Mrs. Foster's candidacy and quickly named a large committee to register nomination papers and campaign on her behalf. Eleven men and five women electors signed her nomination papers, when only three signatures were required. It was made clear that "Mrs. Foster will stand for election as an independent, unassociated with any ticket except the veterans' ticket."[2]

In her nomination acceptance speech, Annie G. Foster indicated that the vital plank (in the minds of the vets) in her campaign would be implementation of a municipal housing scheme for returned men and their families. On other matters, she held that:

- the "majority should rule" on the Prohibition matter;
- she endorsed the concurrent referendum bylaw establishing a municipal library;
- there is no need for an increase in taxes;
- educational assistance to the children of war widows should be forthcoming; and
- the candidate advises a vigorous industrial policy.

Annie also advocated the development of cottage industries such as weaving and the production of natural products like flax—a personal interest acquired through association with Doukhobors and the crafts movement in England. There was little time for door-knocking and speech-making. Only three of eight aldermanic candidates showed up at a candidates' public meeting at the Nelson Opera House on the eve of the election. Annie was in good form that evening, calling on her hospital experience to illustrate her knowledge of certain city functions, such as plumbing. With three out of four candidates to be elected in each of the city's two wards and the solid backing of the GWVA, Annie's success on January 15 was not surprising. She was the choice of 217 voters, second only to Mr. John Bell with 288. "City Has First Lady Alderman" pronounced the newspaper on the following day. The editorial page, while noting that the new council was composed of well-qualified and well-represented *men*, was mostly gentlemanly and gallant in its praise of Mrs. Foster: "Possessed of a brilliant intellect, a broad and comprehensive grasp of public affairs, unusual ability to express in clear concise English the views which she holds and of more than average business capacity, Mrs. Foster is bound to prove a valuable member of the new city council. She can be depended upon to give the citizens of Nelson broad-minded, intelligent and efficient service...."[3]

Annie's head was not turned by the generous words of the *Nelson Daily News;* after all, her late husband had been managing editor until 1915. In reality, women in public office presented such a novelty that most frequently they were not taken seriously. Even Alexander D. McRae, millionaire Vancouver landowner and future leader of the Provincial Party of British Columbia, was rather flippant in his personally scribed congratulatory note: "Hail to Nelson's first alderwoman! Congratulations lady. I shall expect to see Nelson swept and garnished on my next visit."[4]

Municipal council terms were one year in length. There was no time for learning curves or periods of adjustment. City hall would be Annie's second home (for a year at least) and business commenced immediately. Nelson's city hall was a decorated and well-proportioned two-storied wooden frame structure

Nelson City Hall and former Court House at the foot of Ward Street as it appeared in 1920, when Mrs. Garland Foster served on Nelson's City Council. Photo courtesy of Touchstones Nelson: Museum of Art and History #823.

overlooking Kootenay Lake at the foot of Ward Street. In 1909, this crowded, busy building (formerly the area's courthouse and provincial government building) had been jockeyed from its original position near the intersection of Ward Street and the boulevard of Vernon Street to a less impressive site half a block down Ward. Architect Francis Rattenbury's commanding granite courthouse replaced this old wooden structure at the civic crossroads.

Returning Mayor J.A. "Long Jim" McDonald presided at the first meeting of the 1920 council on Monday, January 19. A sizable delegation of women observed the proceedings. Following reports from department administrators, McDonald announced appointments to the city's standing committees. Mrs. Foster would chair the Street Railway Committee, represent the city on the Kootenay Lake General Hospital Board, and sit on the Court of Revision and the Parks, Cemetery and Health committee. Her first official act was one of lasting significance. She seconded the motion to adopt and implement the bylaw passed by referendum January 15 that created the Nelson Municipal Library in accordance with the province's newly enacted Public Library Act. Miss (later Dr.) Helen Gordon Stewart had primed her friend Mrs. Foster on the benefits of supporting the creation of public libraries in rural and smaller municipalities.

Helen Stewart was just beginning a long career as the first chair of the Public Library Commission of British Columbia. She travelled the province dispensing cartons of books, organizational wisdom, and encouragement to dozens of book-thirsty communities. Nan ("Nan" again to her very close friends) and Helen made a fine pair of crusaders.

The business of City Council, which met every second Monday, moved along at a steady pace and council matters were assiduously reported in the local press. The novice alderman might well have registered a certain satisfaction following the February meetings. Library board appointments were made, and, along with City Medical Officer Dr. Isabel Arthur, Alderman Foster was authorized to investigate a site for an isolation hospital in the event of an epidemic. However, the thorny matter of a ticket-pricing scheme for the city's financially strained streetcar system was addressed but not resolved.

Nelson had boasted an internal rail system since December 1899 when the privately owned Nelson Electric Tramway Company opened a line through the commercial centre of the city to the adjoining lakeside residential area. From the outset, the streetcar system was plagued with electrical supply and maintenance problems, culminating in chronic debt and take-over by the city in 1914. Debt and difficulties accumulated and the city administration was constantly on the lookout for cost-saving schemes. The expense-saving probability of engaging streetcars driven by one man and phasing out the current two-man cars was also debated in February. The Street Railway Committee's recommendation not to convert existing two-man cars, but to consider acquiring a one-man car when new rolling stock was required, was adopted.

A delegation from the GWVA, in accordance with the aims and issues of the organization, objected strongly to the recent "… appointment as foreman of the city's electrical department of a man who is not a citizen of Nelson over the head of a man who has served the city for over six years in this department and was overseas for four years."[5] The position had also not been advertised in the press. The GWVA spokespersons no doubt took heart from the presence and implied support of their own vice-president in her aldermanic chair. During discussion of the city's portion of the school's budget, Alderman Foster strongly warned against reducing teachers' salaries. The new alderman was doing her job and her agenda was on track.

This was a further source of pride and encouragement to the widow.

NELSON CIVIC AFFAIRS

Mrs. Garland Foster, as she was regularly referred to by the press, was now a curious and interesting local political figure. The *Nelson Daily News* would avidly follow her career. Her participation in city business was recorded in council minutes and her every word, tone and manner discussed over tea-cups and tin coffee mugs. Although her electoral achievement was certainly a significant accomplishment, Annie devoted only one full page in her memoir to her term as alderman of the City of Nelson. In 1939, when it was time to revisit 1920 and Nelson City Council for her memoir, somehow the year and the place may have seemed too remote or the issues too irritating. Interestingly, the most honest insight into Annie's personal assessment of her political career is found in an unlikely and unassuming place.

On an unknown rainy West Coast afternoon, Annie had pasted newspaper articles (frequently undated and unsourced) related to her various careers and interests into a cheap school scribbler. On the back cover of this notebook, in an inky, barely legible scrawl, she left several sketchy clues to the highlights or the most memorable moments of her political career. The first impression of these jottings is that it is a shopping list, summaries, or merely random notes. On closer examination, and given knowledge of the personalities and fractious issues at the time, these hasty scribbles become rare glimpses into Annie's true feelings. The notes reveal a humour and an irony not often evident in the public record left by Alderman Mrs. Garland Foster. Here were the key phrases and images surfacing from her memory bank possibly thirty years after her time as a civic official. These were not words she would have dreamt to be of interest to a future biographer yet each jotting is potentially a story in itself.

Alexander Duncan McRae, future leader of the BC Provincial Party, MP and Senator, congratulates Annie Foster on her civic victory. Image courtesy of White Rock Museum and Archives, 1995-17 File 2.

Mrs. B. repeatedly requested alterations to the level of the street near her home.

Mrs. S. had serious issues with the city water supply. Alderman Perrier's remark that the loss [vandalism] of the horses' tails on the Lakeside Park's merry-go-round might be rectified by a "re-tail" licence bylaw to pay for the "re-tailing" of the horses was duly recorded. And then there was the matter of the street railway employees' holiday time and the Tag Day spectacle. In barely legible writing at the bottom of the back cover of the scribbler, Annie had summarized her estimation of her civic political career: "City Father vs. City Mother." But it was one quote by Silver King Mike, "Vote for that woman. Men no good—Woman no worse," that led the biographer on a fascinating side journey to find Silver King Mike.[1]

Annie got by financially on her pensions and alderman's stipend and devoted herself full-time to her civic duties and related causes. Every month brought new issues, but several matters hung on the agenda much longer and seemed unsolvable. March 1920 was a particularly significant month for Alderman Foster. She successfully pressed for the enforcement of an existing strict, but ignored, bylaw governing the production and sale of milk produced by dairies within the city. She mused publicly whether there might be other questionable bylaws "hidden away." In keeping with her election platform, Annie then led council to take steps in promoting the provincial government's housing scheme

SILVER KING MIKE

Silver King Mike (Harris Ginsberg) was a singular Jewish merchant with an intriguing past in New York and the mining camps of Colorado. His biography is not told in a paragraph, but in 1897 at the age of fifty, he became janitor at the Silver King Mine on the mountain high above the collection of buildings called Nelson. By 1900, he had set up a second-hand furniture store in Nelson and "... became that colourful pioneer curio who seems to germinate in a new country, the butt of much amusement yet, in Mike's case, an accepted and even beloved figure, well known on the streets of the town."[2] Mike's quip about voting for a woman was seconded in the scribbler and in Annie's hand by an overheard but encouraging comment, "The best man on the Council this year is a woman." These positive remarks were countered by the remark "Italians—do not vote for Ma Donna."

for returned men. The city must urge the provincial government to amend the scheme to provide loans for the purchase of existing homes, rather than only for the construction of new homes. Such a scheme would prove more practical and more inviting. At this appropriate juncture, Alderman Foster took a two-week leave from council work and boarded the CPR for Montreal and the Fourth Annual Dominion Convention of the Great War Veterans Association. As Vice-President of the Nelson branch, Annie was the first woman delegate to the veterans' national convention. On March 23, the City of Montreal hosted a banquet for the 400–500 delegates at the elegant Windsor Hotel. While *Saturday Night* published her photo with a suitable complimentary caption,[3] the *Nelson Daily News* fairly burst with pride in printing the byline in from Montreal. The paper reported:

> The Chairman announced, "The lady comrade has the floor." Never before had a comrade of the feminine persuasion stood up to address a convention of GWVA until Mrs. William Garland Foster of Nelson arose, immediately the hub-bub of irregular debate and impromptu caucusing ceased and the house became as still as a listening post. Mrs. Foster came to the front... and spoke on equalizing pensions, the cloud of black lisse draperies framing her head and shoulders, adding its silent eloquent appeal.[4]

The Montreal reporter neglected to describe the speaker as rather tall, digni-fied, and with silver-streaked ebony hair, but his sympathies lay with those of the war widow and nursing sister who was continuing to serve her comrades and their families. It was particularly poignant when Nan revealed how "… we officers' widows have asked permission to go without our pension, so that the widows of private soldiers might have more…."[5] In describing this wonderful evening, Nan liked to inject a lighter tone by noting that in the mode of fair-ness, the waiter "proffered" her a cigar following the banquet.

There was much serious work to be done at the general sessions, and the delegates from the West Kootenay (Annie was joined by Mr. Owen of Trail) did not shy away from discussing, debating and recording the proceedings. Later Nan would present thorough reports to both the Nelson and Trail GWVA gath-erings. The GWVA was extremely conscious of its immense political and social lobbying power. Over three thousand resolutions were submitted to the con-vention. Of these, a dozen or so found their way into federal government policy and legislation. A resolution, similar to the matter very recently before Nelson City Council, that recommended the extension of loans to returned men for

Nelson's impressive late-Victorian main thoroughfare, Baker Street, in 1908. Photo courtesy of Touchstones Nelson: Museum of Art and History, #66.2.50 neg. 806.

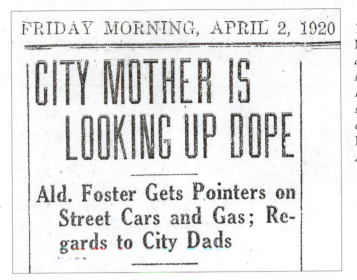

FRIDAY MORNING, APRIL 2, 1920

CITY MOTHER IS LOOKING UP DOPE

Ald. Foster Gets Pointers on Street Cars and Gas; Regards to City Dads

The Nelson Daily News *takes an attention-grabbing swipe at Alderman Foster's money-saving efforts. Image courtesy of the* Nelson Daily News, *April 2, 1920, p. 2.*

the purchase of existing homes, gained national support. Rate increments and single payment gratuities to pensioners, those with permanent disabilities, and the dependents of fallen men were demanded. The 1920 convention resulted in a federal Returned Soldiers' Insurance Act, designed for those who could not, due to their wartime physical condition, qualify for life insurance. Value of the policy was eventually maximized at five thousand dollars. Considerable press within and without the organization was generated by the open door membership policy. Opinions varied. Should membership in the GWVA be extended to those who had served on the home front and to those who had served in previous wars and combats? This policy, which offered the additional benefit of increased GWVA membership, was eventually adopted. Old wounds concerning Quebec's less-than-enthusiastic participation at the outset of the European conflict were salved by the eloquent speech of a Quebec delegate and the honest cordiality of the Montreal hosts.

Governments at all levels, particularly the Liberal-Conservative government of Prime Minister Robert Borden, had been negligent in their duty to the men who had served their country and continued to suffer in so many ways. GWVA would hold their government responsible. This battle for justice was not over.

Never one to lose an opportunity to further the welfare of her city or exercise her civic concerns, Alderman Foster stopped off in Ottawa where she consulted the Ottawa Car Company on the advisability of purchasing one-man streetcars for the City of Nelson. As evidenced at February city council meetings, the matter was a prominent current issue in Nelson. Instinct told

J.A. McDonald, Mayor of the City of Nelson during Annie's tenure on City Council. McDonald and Foster did not always agree on matters of civic affairs. Photo courtesy of the City of Nelson.

Annie that Nelson's steep grades and winter conditions required maximum safety features, including two men in each car. The Ottawa Car Company confirmed this. The company also advised a trial purchase of a single one-man car before converting all of Nelson's rolling stock. The *Nelson Daily News* headline of April 2, "City Mother is Looking Up Dope," was a backhanded compliment to her commitment to duty.

In Mrs. Foster's absence, Mayor McDonald and the remaining aldermen had reversed their opinion on the one-man car option in an effort to find a partial cure for the city-owned streetcar system's financial malaise. Annie, however, came forth with an interesting revenue proposal involving mere pennies, no fare increase and no layoff of personnel. Her scheme was labelled the "Psychological car ticket" venture. People needed to be induced to ride the streetcar. Riders must be offered a bargain. The existing five-cent fare would remain, but books of twenty-five tickets would sell for one dollar—a savings of one cent per ride. An exchange of strong words ensued at the April 12 council meeting, with Alderman McHardy being particularly intransigent. But Alderman Foster, as chair of the Street Railway Committee, was adamant. Psychology won the day and the new rate structure was adopted. Nelsonites showed their gratitude and used the streetcar. Over the next several months, improvements (lighting, re-wiring of the bandstand and changing rooms alterations) were undertaken at the streetcar's Lakeside Park terminus. All this contributed to the popularity—and increased revenue—of the streetcar.

The suddenly sound financial position for the operation of the streetcar was not lost on the members of the crew. In September, the men petitioned the Street Railway Committee for an increase in salary. This startling request re-opened the four-cent versus five-cent ticket debate. Nan appealed to council: "The traffic was the largest in the line's history. Under the best of circumstances, she said, the street railway would probably never earn more than operating expenses as long as it had a short line."[6] Meanwhile, the newspaper helpfully observed that "Receipts … for 1920 are consistently out running the estimates figured at the first of the year, according to a financial statement prepared for the City Council."[7] The streetcars' role in this balance sheet could not be refuted and it was agreed the four-cent trial system would be continued for three more months.

Meanwhile, when Alderman Foster was attending GWVA business in Montreal in March, her city's council had decided to engage a Vancouver engineer to assess and offer improvements on the state of Nelson's streets. This measure was yet another instance of contradiction between city procedure and the GWVA policy (and Annie's election platform) that returned men must be given precedence in consideration for employment when any level of government position or contract was involved. The Vancouver engineer in question had not served in the war. With the support of Alderman Patenaude, the matter was held over for consideration.

If "psychology" had been council's watchword in April, it was replaced by "philanthropy" and "philosophy" in May and for several months thereafter. Dispersal of the city's tax revenue was a common ethical and practical problem. The YMCA appealed for relief from city rates (water, light, scavenging) on the indisputable basis of the good work and facilities it provided to the community. Mrs. Foster held the position that the YMCA, along with other worthy institutions, were not civic institutions and tax relief considerations could not be justified. When the Board of Trade requested an additional $1,000 grant in recognition of the publicity it afforded Nelson by its many activities, she quipped audibly enough for the reporter to hear, that she wished she had applied for $1,000, as her trip to Montreal had given the city some fair publicity as well!

It was during these discussions that Nan gave notice that she would be presenting a bylaw to regulate the popular fundraising activity of soliciting funds in public places. The Tag Day debate was under way. The *Nelson Daily News* reporter chuckled to himself when he observed that Alderman Foster's draft tagging bylaw created quite a "breeze" at the May 12 (and several subsequent) council meetings. Here was a story worth following!

Local charities and worthy-cause protagonists were accustomed to soliciting raffle tickets, donations and "tags" on the streets and in certain welfare-conscious shops of Nelson. In return for a donation or purchase, the donor was given a tag to show his or her benevolence. It appeared this unlicensed and unregulated solicitation was becoming all too common and potentially harmful to those businesses operating under city trade licences. A bylaw would require "taggers" to purchase a trade licence or secure permission from the city council to make sales on the street. Annie Foster's Bylaw 320 would sanction public solicitation (and hence lusty competition) on only four days per year specifically designated as Tag Days. The regulation would apply in the central commercial area of the city. The clincher was the final clause of the draft bylaw which advocated a fine up to fifty dollars for an infraction and up to a month's incarceration for failure to pay said fine.

Mayor McDonald and the church-and-charity ladies of Nelson took umbrage at the insinuation that funds thus raised through teas and entertainments were not entirely well spent. (Annie's scrapbook jottings cryptically noted this "spectacle of ladies opposed.") Five council members put their heads down and preferred to ignore the Tag Day ruffle. There was no seconder for the bylaw and hence other forms of business licensing to generate funds were pursued. At the instigation of the Prohibition Party and via the Police Commission, inquiries were also made into the sale and possible licensing of "near-beer" (under two and one-half proof) in local establishments. This was an opportunity for Annie to question instances where "near-beer" was served by women in the hotels and bars of the city. Mrs. Foster inadvertently cited such a person by name. This transgression was reported in the press, much to the consternation of hotel proprietor Madame Monteleone.[8] By the end of June, the Trades Licence Bylaw had been agreed upon. Business licence rates were raised and extended to include those in the professions, business, investments and banking and others hitherto unlicensed. Even astrologers, seers and clairvoyants were compelled to pay fifty dollars every six months according to Bylaw 321. Under Annie's direction, the city's Parks, Cemetery and Health Committee dealt with maintenance (including the carousel horse-tail vandalism incident), vagrancy and entertainments in city parks.

A respite from the Tag Day debacle came in the form of the Fourth Annual Convention of the British Columbia branch of the GWVA, held in Fernie June 3–5. Annie, of course, was the Nelson delegate and she reported at length for the *Nelson Daily News*. The provincial organization endorsed the resolutions of the Montreal National Convention. Pensions, allowances, first claim on employment opportunities, life insurance, training programs for the able and the disabled—all in keeping with promises the soldiers had been given upon enlistment—were endorsed. A disquieting and seemingly irrelevant resolution urging governments to prohibit or restrict immigration or purchase or lease of lands by "Orientals" was also sanctioned. Uncharacteristically, Alderman Foster offered no comment on this latter issue.

By July, Mrs. Foster was president of the Nelson GWVA. In her dual civic and veteran capacity she was called upon to welcome the commissioner of the Salvation Army, Major Gillespie, to Nelson. Formalities such as this and judging embroidery at agricultural fairs and acting as hostess to visiting dignitaries' wives were not particularly enjoyable, but they were part of her role and Mrs. Garland Foster could be relied upon to fulfill her civic duties. She would want it to be recorded here that on October 16, 1920, William Lyon Mackenzie King, Liberal leader of the Opposition of the government of Canada, was honoured at a businessman's luncheon at the Hume Hotel in Nelson. Eighty residents enjoyed a meal and the comradeship of Mr. King and his party. Mrs. Annie Garland Foster was not among the dignitaries invited. The lady alderman was not a business figure, nor was she a member of the Liberal Party, but she was most certainly, given her elected position, a Nelson dignitary. Her distinction as a woman in the forefront of the community quite rightly entitled her to an invitation. Nan was no doubt accustomed to such slights of reason and protocol.

As noted, in May the YMCA's application for tax relief had resulted in considerable moral evaluation by the council. A similar set of dire financial circumstances faced St. Joseph's Roman Catholic Convent School. In June, Aldermen Perrier and Patenaude alerted council to the possibility that St. Joseph's could well close. Many of the two hundred children enrolled there would then suddenly be deposited at the doors of the city's public schools, if some sort of rates or taxation rebate was not forthcoming. This would pose an unheard-of expense to the Nelson School Board. As in the YMCA case, Alderman Foster offered sympathy, but stood on her principle of non-intervention with churches and charities.

A similar matter regarding taxation of church property had quite recently come before the Supreme Court of British Columbia in Victoria. A judgment allowed that church properties could be subject to taxation. Not long after the St. Joseph's School matter arose, however, the British Columbia Appeal Court reversed this Supreme Court decision. On appeal by the Bishop of Victoria, the case *Bishop of Vancouver Island v. City of Victoria* ruled that St. Andrew's Cathedral in Victoria was exempt from taxation and the City of Victoria was restrained from selling the church land as a counterclaim for unpaid taxes. This principle of freedom from taxation for buildings used for public worship could potentially be applied to the Nelson dilemma. However, September 27 a motion came before Nelson City Council for the city to offer financial assistance to the City of Victoria for a further appeal of this decision. The case would now go to a Judicial Committee of the Privy Council in London. Alderman Patenaude registered the only dissenting vote in Nelson's support of the City of Victoria's case. Until the Judicial Committee of the Privy Council rendered its advice, the British Columbia Court of Appeal decision stood and church properties could not be taxed. The Judicial Committee ultimately affirmed the Court of Appeal decision and there the matter rested.[9]

Although against some measures of relief from taxation, Alderman Foster was genuinely behind City Medical Officer Dr. Isabel Arthur's recommendations for provision of treatment to those citizens with advanced tuberculosis (TB). Presently TB sufferers were not welcome at district hospitals, and although it was hinted that Balfour Sanatorium was to be closed, the two experienced medical women advocated maintenance of a special cottage at the Balfour site for city patients. Health and welfare were matters in which Annie's competence and abilities were respected and acknowledged. This personal credibility was not extended to other arenas.

In addition to obvious scenic, transportation, mineral and forest assets, the young City of Nelson was blessed with an abundance of waterfalls, rapids and reliable sources of hydroelectric power. From 1897, when John Houston, Nelson's first mayor, developed a power-house on Cottonwood Creek Falls within the city's limits, the city had invested early and wisely in the ownership and production of hydroelectric power. Power was a magnet for industrial expansion as well as a comfort for citizens. The Nelson Board of Trade, an influential and at times aggressive force in the promotion of industry and business, advertised the availability of inexpensive power. Throughout 1920, Mr. J.H. Haslam of Regina, Saskatchewan, was in constant correspondence and communication with the Board of Trade and the City of Nelson. He endeavoured to negotiate an agreement to purchase Nelson's surplus power to supply a pulp and paper mill he envisioned in the area. City council was not accustomed to conceding electrical rate decreases to private corporations and Alderman Garland Foster was particularly alert to Nelson's ability to sustain demands on electricity production. In October, Haslam bid to purchase all the city's excess power, while Annie urged the city to thoroughly study a recent Board of Trade report on the pulp and paper industry. Like the merry-go-round in Lakeside Park, the pulp-paper-power issue went round and round and little light was generated in the process.

Concurrently, Alderman Patenaude was pressing for another action involving use of Nelson's legendary surplus power. Although "… it would be inadvisable to tie the city up with long-term contracts [such as the Haslam deal], rates should be arranged that would have the effect of encouraging the use of current in every possible way."[10] A lower rate would be established for higher consumption. Hence Nelsonites were urged to consume more power and thus produce more revenue! Annie questioned the advisability of extending use of appliances when the city was simultaneously considering an outside offer for surplus power. Such discussions led her to note with frustration that "… the report was going around that she was opposing [the] pulp proposition without

To the Electors of Nelson

⁋ After repeated requests of a large number of citizens I have agreed to be a candidate for mayor. Owing to the short time elapsing before the election I shall not be able to see all my supporters, but shall count on them working for me and voting for me just the same. Realizing that Nelson is at the parting of the ways, I am prepared to assist in laying the foundation for future progress; and I am also prepared to devote my entire time to the task. A programme will be announced later to include the war memorial, schools, public utilities, sports, publicity, roads and public meetings.

ANNIE H. FOSTER.
Phone 468L. **(Mrs. W. Garland Foster)**

Annie Foster's notice in Nelson's mayoralty campaign January 1922. Image courtesy of the Nelson Daily News, *January 9, 1922.*

good reason and… she would like to give the public her reasons for opposing it."[11] Getting the attention of the council and sympathetic reporting from the press led to several prickly exchanges with fellow council members. Annie alluded to her personal misgivings about the investor from Regina. Nonetheless, on November 27 Haslam received a contract proposal, open until July 1921, by which the promoter would agree to purchase from the City of Nelson not less than 4,000 horsepower per year for twenty years. The location of Haslam's pulp and paper industry was not stated. Allegedly, the gentleman was satisfied with these terms, but the matter never proceeded to a voter's money bylaw and Nelson was not subjected to the prosperity and aroma of a pulp and paper mill.

City power rates were not adjusted as long as Mrs. Garland Foster sat at the council table.

A less contentious, but more lasting and historic feat for the council of the day was the process and politics leading to the amalgamation of the city with the suburban area of Fairview, the site of Hume School where Annie Ross had been principal prior to the Great War. Alderman Garland Foster was the prime proponent of this expansion. She understood the strict amalgamation process, the financial benefits to the city and the practical civilizing benefits to the Fairview residents and their school. Greater numbers equalled greater clout in both the civic and provincial rings. Upon registering her motion of amalgamation, the newspaper headlined: "Alderman Foster Will Mother the First By-law."[12] The subsequent referendum to admit Fairview into the city took place January 13, 1921, in conjunction with the annual civic election. The "yes" vote was a lasting tribute to Nelson's first woman elected official.

During the final months of her one-year term, Annie occasionally steered clear of some controversies. A provincial referendum on Prohibition held October 20 relaxed the law and allowed government control over liquor sales, rather than outright Prohibition. Annie did not participate in the public debate. She also avoided involvement or comment on the December 1 provincial election that resulted in a Liberal government, although she had reason and opportunity to know all the issues and candidates very well.

By early December, there were rumblings of dissatisfaction with city government. At a public meeting (held in the city council chamber!), a contrived plan to select a slate of candidates for the January 13, 1921, election was set forth. Alderman Foster attended the meeting and when invited to speak, laconically said "… she much enjoyed hearing the news expressed as to the defects of the present Council year and only wished that more citizens had exercised the privileged of being present at the Council sessions and lending support."[13] Annie might well have felt quite vindicated by the press summation of the year's accomplishments: "Whether under the stimulus of Mrs. W. Garland Foster's four cent fare or from the improvements at Lakeside Park… or from the 'natural causes,' traffic on the City's tramway system registered a remarkable growth this season over last year's record traffic."[14] However, it became very obvious early on that Annie Garland Foster was not to be favoured with inclusion on the civic slate of nominees. Surprisingly, it was not until early January that she formally announced through the press that she would not be running in the 1921 election: "When I recently discovered that there was a small group of citizens bitterly opposed to a woman as chief executive, I gave the matter no further consideration. I have never been a suffragette, and it is not my intention at this late date to disturb the perennial equanimity of Nelson by introducing such ancient prejudices."[15]

Annie's interpretation of suffrage was rather pragmatic. She recognized and espoused the human rights issues implied by votes for women, but found the militancy associated with the movement distasteful and disquieting. It was not uncommon for community-minded women (and men) of the time to encounter this conundrum. She dealt with the situation in her own rational way.

Nineteen years later, Nan reflected that by using devious, feminine ways she had achieved significant results in her brief tenure on Nelson's city council:

> … I saved the city many thousands of dollars and prevented having their excess electric power tied up for nearly a hundred years. At the time I was considered a spoilsport by my colleagues. The real reward… came when transportation journals in New York commented favorably on the fact that I had made the street railway pay by making it cheaper to ride than to walk…. I did manage to make it popular with the result that that year it showed a profit in spite of the low fares.[16]

Politics was probably not the ideal venue for Nan's social action. Ironically however, politics was one of the few paths to influence and power that was opening up to women in the mid-1920s. Nan, Annie, Alderman and Mrs. Garland Foster had been courageous enough to publicly shed (even partially) the "blue-stocking" image and take on a role as social activist. Corporate, bureaucratic or professional power for women was rare indeed. Success in these arenas required pre-ordained influence, much higher education and frequently an elevated social status. There would always be another road, another approach, and Annie Garland Foster would stay the course.

CHAMPION OF VETERANS

One week in January 1921, Annie Garland Foster stepped down from two positions of authority and responsibility. City council matters passed to a team of new "efficient" (all male) administrators. And as president of the Nelson Great War Veterans Association, she turned the gavel over to her long-time supporter, W. Pascoe, who "... verbally expressing the esteem of the membership and appreciation of her devoted work for the association during her term of office..."[1] presented Annie with the past-president's pin. She was taken aback by Pascoe's kind words, but expressed her sincere pleasure at having been of service to the veterans. She had been elected with the solid support of the returned men and stayed true to the principles of the GWVA by continuing to press for employment opportunities within the municipal civil service, relaxing restrictions on the federal government's Land Settlement Scheme, supporting pensions and scholarships for veterans' families, and continually pressing any matters that affected the health and welfare of veterans' wives and children and, in particular, "the boys" at the Balfour Sanatorium.

Allowing herself no time to catch her breath but now unfettered by public strictures, Mrs. Garland Foster was free to choose her own course in the community. It was in September 1920, when representing the city in health and welfare matters, that Annie had led the charge against both the federal and provincial governments' ruthless plan to close the Balfour Sanatorium and relocate the remaining veterans to Tranquille Centre near Kamloops. Centralist policies dictated this fiscally based decision, which was contrary to the wishes of the residents and the patients. The decision to close the sanatorium was taken despite earlier assurances from the Department of Re-Settlement that this would not

Annie Garland Foster poses in the late 1920s for a Vancouver portrait photographer, wearing the traditional white uniform of a graduate nurse. Photo courtesy of the University of New Brunswick Archives, MG L7 Series 3, File 1, #4.

happen. The city posted resolutions of disapproval to Prime Minister Arthur Meighen, British Columbia Premier Oliver and local Member of Parliament R.F. Green. Nonetheless, the sanatorium was closed in November 1920.

Annie had no further desire to sit on the board of Kootenay Lake Hospital. She adopted the Women's Institute and her contacts with the Department of Health and its chief administrator, Provincial Health Officer Dr. Henry Esson Young, as the means by which she would champion health and welfare issues. As early as June 1920, while still on city council, Annie had attended a lecture called "Public Health and Child Welfare" sponsored by the Women's Institute and given by a Victorian Order of Nurses representative. Along with City Health Medical Officer Dr. Isabel Arthur, Annie believed towns of all sizes should be united in their efforts to secure health inspection in schools and through public clinics. An editorial in the *Nelson Daily News* August 20, 1920, described how public health care was designed to work in rural British Columbia, through health centres that were supported by Women's Institutes, the Victorian Order of Nurses, municipal councils, the Red Cross and various women's organizations, all cooperating with the provincial Ministry of Health. Public education, prevention of disease, the care of schoolchildren and aid to prenatal and maternity cases were the new directions in welfare care. Trained public health nurses were absolutely essential to the provision of these services.[2] Mrs. Garland Foster could have written the editorial herself. She would devote 1921 to the pursuit of these goals and the Women's Institute would be the primary vehicle for the crusade.

Women's Institutes originated in Canada in 1897 as a branch of the Farmer's Institutes, but following the end of World War I, the movement broadened its mandate to include all manner of needed reforms, communication between rural women and responsible citizenship in general. It was a rapidly expanding movement promoting the welfare and talents of women and families throughout the country. It was an all-inclusive organization and for Annie, the Nelson Women's Institute (WI) would provide an audience, publicity, moral support and companionship.

At the Kootenay–Boundary conference in Creston in the fall of 1920 there was a lecture on public health nursing as well as a presentation on weaving by none other than Mrs. W. Garland Foster: "Mrs. Foster exhibited some fine specimens of work, some of which were done overseas, and some in the Kootenay. She suggested that a revival of this homely household art, and a return to homespun, would help many to cope with the high cost of living."[3]

The executive committee of the WI started 1921 by formulating (under the direction of Mrs. Foster) a letter to the Nelson School Board regarding the need for a public health nurse. The board was advised "… that the dept. [Board] would give financial assistance in the matter of salary and that the [Women's] Institute would do their part in the same way, leaving the rest with the School Board…."[4] The school board responded "… stating that the Medical Health Officer filled the requirement of a nurse. A dentist would be a greater necessity to the welfare of the children…."[5] Discussion ensued. Mrs. Foster followed the natural course and moved that a committee be appointed to look into the "dental matter." The committee met promptly and Dr. Isabel Arthur went before the school board February 24 and declared the pressing need for a dentist, rather than a nurse. It was perhaps a good

Dr. Henry Esson Young, BC Minister of Education, Provincial Secretary and Annie's mentor in the field of public health. Photo courtesy of British Columbia Archives collections, 02547 HP 007696.

thing that Annie was by this time on the train to Vancouver Island in the interests of the Child Welfare Association of British Columbia and the WI. Any perceived disagreement between Dr. Arthur and Mrs. Garland Foster would have been detrimental to their respective positions.

In the midst of the WI's involvement with the school board, there was a final hospital board meeting for Annie to attend. As if the public health matters were not sufficient to occupy her time, Annie had also undertaken to participate in a public democratic exercise called the "Peoples Forum." Apparently parliamentary rules were "fearlessly" applied at the forums. Former Alderman Foster gave a brief address on citizenship at a February 7 meeting, while at the following meeting, E.P. Dawson spoke on the Constitution of Canada and the British North America Act of 1867, with Mrs. Foster acting as secretary.

It is undeniable that the southern provincial railway system was essential to the functioning of interior British Columbia communities. Annie Garland Foster's comings and goings, causes and concerns, and her community's ability to reach beyond the mountains and valleys of the Kootenay were totally reliant on the network of railroads. The large classic chalet-style CPR station at the foot of Nelson's Baker Street was the focal point for the activities that made Nelson the "Queen City of the Kootenays."[6] It was not until 1916 that a (somewhat) direct "Coast-to-Kootenay" rail connection between Nelson and Vancouver was in place. The Kettle Valley Railway system, the final link across southern British Columbia, moved west from Midway to Penticton, Merritt, the Coquihalla Valley, then to Hope and the main line of the CPR on the Fraser River. Trains arrived at and departed from Nelson daily, heading in both easterly and westerly directions. Thanks to this regular service, Annie was back in Nelson from her trip to Vancouver Island by March 2 in time to preside as chairman at the first meeting of yet another organization: the Graduate Nurses of Nelson.

For a three-month period, from March until mid-June 1921, Nan suddenly disappeared from the Nelson scene. No motions recorded in minute books, no speeches given, no meetings organized. She missed entirely the deliberations surrounding the erection of a memorial to the soldiers from the Great War. Later, references were made to her studies in the child welfare field during a trip east, but she must have been too busy or distracted to report the specifics of her travels and inquiries to the press. Maybe these months (and unrecorded weeks over the next several months) are those to which Annie's friend Gretchen (née Phair) Gibson referred when in 1943 she wrote: "... Mrs. Foster assisted the British Columbia government with its first social welfare plans, going though the country giving addresses on health and welfare subjects to various societies."[7] (A 1964 newspaper biographer borrowed this exact sentence without credit, but changed "country" to "province.") Province or country, at age 46 Nan was poised to make a career move. She was impressed with the career and accomplishments of Dr. Henry Esson Young, Provincial Health Officer. As a Conservative member of the British Columbia legislature, Young had been a popular Minister of Education (1907–1915) and was credited as the "Father" of the University of British Columbia. He had co-authored the British Columbia Royal Commission Report on Returned Soldiers in 1916 and was extremely forward thinking in reorganizing public health services in his province. Annie felt honoured to work on his behalf and "... to sell health to the interior of the province. It was at times a strenuous adventure, in which during a year I covered most of the small towns of the district speaking to women's societies."[8] Dr. Young's purpose was to provide an annual medical examination for every schoolchild and slowly, deliberately establish further public health nursing services as funds and opportunity permitted. All women and families must be taught the fundamentals of hygiene and nutrition: "Every doctor is a public health officer and every public health officer is a doctor."[9] Mrs. Garland Foster was Young's general in the field.

Early in September 1921, the Kootenay–Boundary Women's Institutes held an extremely historic conference in Crawford Bay on the east shore of Kootenay Lake. The agenda covered child welfare, education matters, immigration, home industries, home economics, public health and legislation. At this conference, a raft of serious resolutions were debated. Dr. Isabel Arthur of Nelson championed a resolution requesting the Board of Health set aside funds "… for operative clinics for cases where parents for financial reasons are unable to have defects in their children remedied."[10] Another resolution requested that the Board of Health secure the services of Mrs. Foster as organizer of the child welfare council in the Kootenay, and Mrs. Foster herself bowed to Dr. Arthur's dental campaign and requested dental inspectors in the schools. Resolutions were followed by an address by Mrs. Foster in which she declared that "present mothers… raised a large proportion of sub-standard men."[11] This was rather a shocking, generalized pronouncement that would not be tolerated decades later! Her determination of what was "sub-standard" may have had more to do with childhood hygiene, diet and education, rather than young men's subsequent mental ability, but her point remained that rigorous education in all fields of hygiene, physical education and nutrition by public health nurses was the only means to rectify this condition. Nurse Foster was not averse to speaking her mind in any forum at any time.

The WI's legislation committee reported on the positive social legislation recently adopted by governments: minimum wages for women, broadening of Red Cross and Health Department work, and provision of guardianship and adoption rules. The committee reported that "Mrs. Foster declared domestic servants must be regarded as professional women, having certain wages and certain hours."[12] Annie could well reject the labels suffragette or suffragist, but such an expression of equality and justice as this was surely given the nod of approval by the conference's most illustrious attendee—the most famous of all the suffragettes—Mrs. Emmeline Pankhurst.

Yes, sixty-three-year-old Emmeline Goulden Pankhurst, mother of British feminism, votes for women and two formidable feminist daughters (Christabel and Sylvia), had come to this rural community in the Kootenay as part of a North American speaking tour. The Women's Institute was responsible for this remarkable visitation. Following the WI conference, Mrs. Pankhurst addressed a large afternoon audience at the Eagles Hall in Nelson. To an amazed and attentive crowd, she extolled the work of the WI but spoke primarily, and in detail, of her experiences with a group of British women in Russia in 1917. She had interviewed the occupant of the Czar's Winter Palace in Petrograd

Nelson friends c. 1922. Annie, Jean Douglas, "Pop" Phair, Mabel Affleck and best friend Gretchen Phair Gibson's daughters Jean and Agnes. Photo courtesy of Agnes Gibson Baker and Touchstones Nelson: Museum of Art and History, #62.6.71 (#221).

(St. Petersburg), Alexander Kerensky, but found him an unlikely, weak leader. The Bolsheviks and their principles were an even greater horror, whilst many in Britain were misled in their support of the revolution.[13] All this was very heady material and not exactly the subject matter expected from the founder of the Women's Social and Political Union (WSPU). Nonetheless, Mrs. Garland Foster who had been appointed to formally thank Mrs. Pankhurst for her lecture, must have been profoundly impressed to share the stage with this famous woman. The Nelson woman exemplified the WSPU's motto "Deeds not words."

Four days after the Nelson newspaper reported on Emmeline Pankhurst's visit, the *Calgary Herald* boldly announced on its front page, "Mrs. W. Garland Foster Likely Candidate For The Riding of W. Kootenay."[14] This aspiration for the federal political scene was pure speculation, but the article was rather complimentary and without a hint of irony, it gave Annie Foster her due: "The prospective aspirant for parliamentary honors is… the city's [Nelson's] first lady ex-alderman and ex-president of the local GWVA, and an outstanding figure in the WI and public health work in this [*sic*] province."[15] Definitely a keepsake for the scrapbook!

Early in August 1921, however, Nan had received word that her father, the gentle and caring Robert Fulton Ross, had passed away in Woodstock. Leaving the care of her recently instituted monthly Baby Clinics to other volunteers, and soon after the WI conference, she submitted her resignation from the directorship of the WI and returned home to New Brunswick for a brief respite with her mother, Christine. In 1922 Nan's mother was relocated to her daughter Margaret's home in Maine. Once Nan was back in Nelson (and resumed being Annie), she became immediately engaged in another civic election.

Had she forgotten the unfavourable comments and behaviour she had experienced in the political arena just a year earlier? On January 9, 1922, four days before Nelsonites went to the polls, "Annie H. Foster/Mrs. W. Garland Foster" placed a large ad in the *Nelson Daily News*: "After repeated requests of a large number of citizens I have agreed to be a candidate for mayor…. Realizing that Nelson is at the parting of the ways, I am prepared to assist in laying the foundation for future progress; and I am also prepared to devote my entire time to the task."[16] Her platform included (naturally) a profitable streetcar service, infrastructure maintenance, sports facilities, support for schools and a suggestion that public meetings should be held whatever the mayor's view on a matter in question. A solid slate of businessmen and the incumbent Mayor McHardy soundly defeated Mrs. Garland Foster. She would not run for city council again. She simply returned to her child welfare work and the WI. In February 1922, the WI urged upon "City Council the importance of giving the financial assistance asked for by the Child Welfare Council toward the support of the Public Health nurse for the city in order that the work of providing adequate nursing service for the outlying district may be undertaken without any further delay."[17] The WI backed its petition with a promise of two hundred and fifty dollars towards the salary for a rural district nurse.

Meanwhile, Annie planned to take advantage of a new public health services course offered at the University of British Columbia, but her application was rejected on the basis that she was not a recent enough graduate! She commented: "As I had done a year's war service and had spent another year pioneering in health service for the very government which had inaugurated the health course I began to wonder if old age was catching up with me or what?"[18] Annie chose to ignore the slight and look elsewhere. The American National Public Health Service favoured experience over age and assigned her the task of establishing a health centre in Skowhegan, Maine. This health care centre would be a joint effort of Sorosis (a national professional women's association) and an insurance company. By September 1922, Annie had taken up residency in this familiar part of Maine. Mrs. Foster's bustling efficiency, disregard for red tape and efforts to combine "bedside nursing" with social work were genuinely appreciated by the citizens of Skowhegan. The *Skowhegan Reporter* noted approvingly of several speeches given by District Nurse Mrs. A.H. Foster. The Rotary Club heard her views on "Community Health and Housing." The Women's Club and the Sorosis Club learned of child welfare through "... her article of unusual merit... which she had spent several months compiling."[19] In 1922, the president of the Skowhegan Sorosis Club was twenty-five-year-old Margaret Chase, who in 1930 married Mr. Clyde Smith. Margaret Chase Smith succeeded her husband in the United States Congress and went on to serve in the Senate—the first woman elected to both houses. Quite likely Annie had shared the platform with yet another notable woman of the twentieth century.

Considerations for her own health and loyalty to her comrades called Annie back to Nelson early in 1923. The WI once again occupied a good deal of her energies. GWVA activities were overshadowed by children and health concerns. The Veterans Association was experiencing decreasing membership, and by 1925 amalgamation with other veteran organizations into the Canadian Legion of the British Empire Service League had taken place. Over the next several months of 1923, WI minutes recorded plans for a Child Welfare Conference, establishment of a "women's comfort station" in a central park, securing a stall in the Nelson market, parochial lack of conviction concerning formation of a national federation of WIs, and efforts to assist in the case of a crippled Nelson child. Nearly every issue featured a motion, action or opinion undertaken by Mrs. Foster. In short, welfare and health matters were moving along according to Dr. Young's (and Mrs. Garland Foster's) plans for the province.

In June 1924, British Columbia was gearing up for an especially exciting provincial election. Annie once again fell victim to her principles and the call of the electoral process. Although liberal in the area of social justice, the experienced politician was conservative in taxation, immigration and business matters. Mrs. Foster did not fit in with the backroom dealings of the traditional parties, and so like many soldiers, farmers, labourers and, in particular, disaffected Conservatives, she joined the recently formed Provincial Party of British Columbia. And now she (along with five other British Columbian women) was a Provincial Party candidate! The Provincial Party was led, and virtually bankrolled, by her friend from the Canadian Expeditionary Forces of the Great War (and moral supporter of her aldermanic challenge), General Alexander Duncan McRae. McRae, one of Vancouver's leading industrialists—thanks to his huge canning and lumber trade—campaigned for reasonable, "clean" government and deplored the corruption of his rivals, Liberal Premier John Oliver and Conservative leader William Bowser. General McRae travelled to Nelson and spoke to a large gathering at the Eagles Hall, although the Nelson riding was, ironically, one of only three ridings in the province that did not field a Provincial Party candidate. Mrs. Foster chaired this meeting, as she was, by virtue of her large rural property in the Pend d'Oreille, a candidate for the adjoining Creston riding. The largely rural Creston riding nearly encircled the Nelson riding and many voters wondered why Nelson's own "'mother'" did not run for the riding in which she resided. In truth, her chances of election were greater in the rural areas and as noted in the press, "it might be a surprise… that she owned a much larger acreage in the Creston riding than either of her opponents."[20]

At a meeting in Balfour, Annie's Conservative opponent, the Creston incumbent Fred Lister, proffered that "he liked Mrs. Foster—as a woman, but as a politician she was out of place."[21] On Election Day, Mrs. Foster won the Procter poll (Balfour's nearest neighbour), but the riding went to Mr. Lister. She took a respectable 22.5 per cent of the votes cast for a third-place finish. McRae's Provincial Party, however, shook the province enough to prevent a majority government. The Liberal premier, John Oliver, had been defeated in his own riding and a seat was generously vacated for him in the safe Nelson riding in order that he might gain re-election in an August by-election. The Nelson and Creston ridings had figured prominently in the 1924 election but the name Annie H. Foster would not appear on the ballot again. It would not be until 1952 that a second woman was elected at even the municipal council level in the

Nelson area. Exactly fifty years after her province joined Confederation, Annie Foster had stepped forward for political service with conviction and purpose. For this alone, she has merited honourable mention in British Columbia history.

When Annie went home alone after hours attending clinics, meetings and lectures she brought with her newspapers, current affairs magazines and hefty government reports. She had sold the home on Stanley Street that she and William had so briefly shared in 1915 and lived in the very respectable and convenient Kerr's Apartment Block on Victoria Street, one block uphill from Baker Street. Mrs. Garland Foster, tall, greying, upright in presence and presentation was a well-known figure on the streets and in the shops of Nelson, the town she so valiantly championed. It is difficult to imagine that she had a life beyond the obvious political and social concerns.

She read, she lectured, and from 1922, she had a telephone—but she also wrote. Her reports on conferences and meetings had often appeared in the local press, but the idea of freelance or creative writing for literary or leisurely motives was not generally associated with the deliberately spoken Mrs. Annie Foster. Her typewriter was a favoured companion. It was not common knowledge that Mrs. Foster had in 1921 joined (and was in fact a charter member of) the Canadian Authors Association (CAA). One of her first ventures into the literary world was a book review, not printed but nonetheless awarded first prize in a book review contest sponsored by CAA's *Canadian Bookman* in 1923.[22] By the end of the year, her articles had begun appearing in the *Vancouver Province, Canadian Bookman, Canadian Home Journal, Winnipeg Free Press* and Toronto's *National Life*. Following her failure at politics and modest, but significant, successes with child health and welfare, Annie would assume her third career—research, reporting and writing.

MISSING PAGES

*T*hroughout 1938 and 1939, as Annie typed her way through her life story, recalling and commenting on her experiences, she consistently divided her life into chapters. Although it is difficult at times to accurately pinpoint dates and places, her memoir followed a chronological path and the text was neatly numbered from page 1 to page 248. Abruptly, however, as the chronology approached 1925 and Annie concluded her reflections on the reluctance of new professional social workers to address home nursing chores, the reader realizes that pages 227–232 are missing. Neatly, in Annie's handwriting, at the top of page 226 is a tidy pencilled message "cut 7 [*sic* 6] pages."

Where did these pages go? Are they to be found elsewhere? When were they removed? And most importantly, why were they removed?

Some time between 1939 (when "Passing Through" was completed) and the mid-1940s, when Annie first deposited a selection of her papers and manuscripts at the archives of her alma mater, the University of New Brunswick, she decided the "chapter" dealing with the events of 1925 and 1926 was not to be shared with family, friends or the curious biographer. This was a rather naïve decision on Annie's part, since any capable and sufficiently motivated researcher would have the means and ability to uncover at least the background time and setting for the censored material. Annie's subsequent writings offer only extremely veiled clues to the events and personalities of these missing years. It was word of mouth over teacups and fences and local gossip reaching from 1925 into the early 2000s that provided the clues. Rudimentary oral history!

"The Tale of the Missing Pages" begins in a manner decidedly similar to so many novels, thrillers and documentaries of the day. In May 1915, a young

The white tents of the 54th Kootenay Battalion, Canadian Expeditionary Forces at Camp Vernon, 1915. Both Hanley and Foster trained here before going overseas in November 1915. Photo courtesy of Vernon Museum and Archives. Photo no. 19442.

man—American-born but a resident of Trail, British Columbia, since 1914—volunteered to serve his adopted country in the escalating conflict between Great Britain and Germany. Patrick Hanley, twenty-eight years old and a former Canadian National Railway locomotive fireman, was found medically fit to serve His Majesty in the Canadian Overseas Expeditionary Force with the Trail Company (No. 3 Company) of the 54th Kootenay Battalion. Private Hanley, of moderate height and darkish complexion, signed the Oath of Attestation on June 10, 1915, and along with his Kootenay compatriots entrained for the Vernon Army Camp. No family or flag-waving friends were at the train station to bid him adieu. In fact, Hanley had struck his brother, George W. Hanley of Memphis, Tennessee, off his Attestation Papers as next of kin. Apparently Hanley, orphaned as a child, was estranged from George. On second thought, Patrick Hanley had designated J.A. McKinnon of Trail as his next of kin. Jack McKinnon was a well-known sports enthusiast and Trail civic booster but was neither Hanley's relative nor a close friend.

At Vernon, the Trail contingent formed up with men from Nelson and the East Kootenay. On August 17, Lieutenant-Colonel A. Kemball, commanding officer of the unit, affixed his name to Hanley's papers. Patrick Hanley was a private in the Canadian Expeditionary Force. There were many familiar faces at the all-male tent city, and over the course of the next six months, recruits endured rugged physical training and learned functional mechanical military skills. Raw recruits became the soldiers of the 54th Kootenay Battalion. Captain William Garland Foster, one of the principal officers of the Battalion, served as Quartermaster in charge of accommodations and rations and would have been highly visible to Hanley from his position in the ranks. By August, amidst the shuffling and adjustments in preparation for transfer overseas, Hanley had been promoted to sergeant, then demoted to private in order to remain within the 54th. September saw him lance-corporal, but before long he faced serious disciplinary action for refusing to obey orders. He was threatened with discharge and given a reduced punishment of fourteen days' hard labour. When the call came on November 15, 1915, to escape the mud and tedium of the Vernon Army Camp for the mud and tedium of the equivalent British camp, Hanley shipped off to war as a private.

The majority of the men and officers of the 54th sailed from Halifax on Cunard's *Saxonia*. The contingent landed at Plymouth in December and carried on to the vast troop city of Bramshott. For the first seven months of 1916, the men trained, drilled, slept and ate. For diversity and morale, they underwent the inspection of such notables as future British Prime Minister Lloyd George, His Majesty King George V, and Canada's Minister of Militia and Defence, General Sir Sam Hughes. The Battalion's officers resisted efforts to draft large numbers of men from the 54th into war-weary units that had suffered heavy casualties. Canadian and, in particular, British Columbian soldiers were determined to fight as a unit.

As recorded in chapter sixteen of "Passing Through," on July 29, 1916, Garland Foster penned a long, hearty letter to the anxious folk of the Kootenay that was published August 25 in his *Nelson Daily News*. Foster could not allude to an anticipated date of departure for the Western Front but expressed great confidence in the men and offered encouragement, noting "… ex-Nelsonite, Brig.-Gen. Victor W. Odlum, formerly of the [Nelson] Daily News staff in the days of the late F.J. Deane, is in command of our brigade."[1] Meanwhile, the Canadian public had been struck by the horrific loss of two-thirds of the 1st Battalion of the Newfoundland Regiment at Beaumont-Hamel on July 1. Allied Command's plan to launch simultaneous offensives on the Western, Eastern and Italian fronts in 1916 was well under way and proving extremely costly. By August 13, when the 54th was called to France, Annie Foster had paid her next-to-last visit to her husband at Bramshott and was deeply immersed in her nursing work at Percy House near London.

Annie reports that "in late August 1916, the 'Byng Boys' [under the command of Lieutenant-General Sir Julien Byng, Commander of the Canadian

Corp and future Governor General of Canada] moved from the muddy fields of Flanders to the Somme, where they took over a section of the front line west of the village of Courcelette. They encountered heavy fighting and suffered some 2,600 casualties before the full-scale offensive even got underway."[2] The graphic horrors of the First Battle of the Somme on the western line would soon be a reality. The 54th Battalion, as part of the 11th Brigade of the 4th Division was to face "… an almost unbelievable ordeal of knee-deep mud and violent, tenacious, enemy resistance."[3] William Garland Foster and Patrick Hanley (re-promoted to corporal in April and sergeant on July 1) saw action for the first time in mid-September en route to the Battalion's acknowledged destination—the Somme. Tensions and apprehensions were extremely high. Somewhere "in the field," Hanley was "… reprimanded for neglect of duty while on the line of marches September 30, 1916."[4] Hanley, however, was not to remain in the field or on the line for long. On October 13, as the Battalion was moving into line in front of Courcelette he "… was blown up by a shell and thrown into a trench, in falling he fell on one of his comrade's bayonets which transversed the middle of [left] thigh, entering behind and emerging in front."[5] A second, equally igno-minious injury to the left knee was sustained later that night when the impaled soldier was dropped from a stretcher while being carried off the line. At No. 22 General Hospital in Dannes Camiers (a site on the casualty evacuation chain located along railway lines), Hanley's condition was originally rated as serious. He was thus spared witnessing the further carnage of this First Battle of the Somme, which ultimately resulted in 24,029 Canadian casualties.

Within four days of injury, Hanley was "Struck off the Strength" (SOS) or declared unfit for physical duties, transferred to a Canadian Casualty Assembly Centre and returned safely to the midlands of Britain and the general hospital and later to a convalescent hospital in Nottingham. Following assessment by a medical board at Shoreham, Kent, the invalid was technically "Taken On Strength" but was moved to Woodcote Park Hospital in Epsom Downs, Surrey.

New Year's, 1917, saw Hanley undergoing rehabilitation at the 902-bed Granville Special Canadian Hospital in Ramsgate on the southeast coast. This hospital was an extremely significant unit in the military hospitalization and recovery chain and had recently been designated as "Special" for its treatment of nervous diseases, notably the recently recognized phenomenon of shell shock. Over 9,000 officers and men of the Canadian Expeditionary Forces were even-tually diagnosed as suffering from shell shock and its various, complicated manifestations. Did Hanley have any reason to require the special services of the "nervous" specialists? The record does not say. On February 22, 1917, Hanley limped away from hospital care to take up duties ("on command to") at the

The men of the 54th Battalion march cheerfully and confidently into Vernon Camp in 1915. Photo courtesy of Vernon Museum and Archives. Photo No. 19727.

British Columbia Regimental Depot at Hastings—a facility to assemble men and store and administer equipment and materials.

Again classed SOS, Sergeant Hanley was soon enrolled at the School of Stenography in Seaford for a three-month course, then went on to the Canadian Training School at Bexhill. He seemed to have had difficulty in settling into sedentary clerical tasks. The old knee injury, for which he recorded no improvement, flared up in October and he was back to No. 13 Canadian General Hospital near Hastings for three weeks of treatment. By January 1918, Hanley was a member of the First Canadian Reserve Battalion, but was still pushing a pencil at Seaford or Bexhill. A bout of bronchitis in July necessitated ten days in No. 14 Canadian General Hospital, Eastbourne. Upon his discharge, Hanley's case sheet was boldly stamped "Discharged to Category A." He had been judged fit for general service. By the Armistice in November, however, Hanley was again SOS and, although he had received a commission in the Ministry of Overseas Military Forces of Canada, was transferred to the 8th Reserve Battalion. He remained SOS until he signed discharge papers noting there was no further treatment required. The *Mauritania* and the CPR brought him home to Trail by the end of June 1919.

The war experiences of William and Annie Garland Foster were more deeply tragic and heroic than those of Patrick Hanley and it seems odd to report here on the brief but confusing war record of one Patrick Hanley. The paths of all three, although they originated in the West Kootenay, had seldom, if ever, crossed in the European theatre. Nonetheless, the ties of veterans, fallen comrades and the altered course of human concerns would bring the two survivors of the "War to End All Wars" into contact within a few short months.

While Mrs. A.G. Foster moved from teaching to politics to health and veterans' welfare, Pat Hanley had little to account for himself during the first year or so following his return to Trail. In April 1920, as Nelson's delegate to the Dominion Great War Veterans' Association Conference in Montreal, Mrs. Garland Foster travelled to her neighbour city of Trail to deliver her account of the conference. She was extremely well received by the Trail men. Many were veterans of the 54th Kootenay Battalion and quite likely Pat Hanley was in the throng that heard Nan speak on veterans' and widows' pensions, jobs, medical

"The Aldridge," nurses' residence and medical offices where Mildred Neilson lived and died, Trail, BC, 1925. Photo courtesy of the Trail Historical Society, #0499.

care and the positive influence and power of the GWVA. If present, he would no doubt have recalled the high regard in which the speaker's late husband had been held by the men of the 54th. Although the Trail GWVA was then engaged in a campaign to construct a memorial hall, Hanley was motivated to join the Nelson organization and in August was elected secretary of the Nelson GWVA. Mrs. Garland Foster, now a Nelson Alderman, had assumed the presidency of the GWVA. Pat Hanley and Annie Foster had now been formally introduced.

Following a meeting of the Nelson GWVA on September 1, Secretary Hanley responded instantly and with commitment to a letter received by the organization that deplored the lonely state of existence experienced by the eighty to ninety invalid "boys" at the Balfour Sanatorium. It was unthinkable. The good people of Nelson had forgotten veterans with lung complaints. Annie and Hanley would have been in total agreement that action was required. Hanley was put in charge of rallying public concern and making arrangements for cars to convey large numbers of visitors over the rough thirty-kilometre road to Balfour on the following Sunday. In anticipation of a future career direction, Hanley was a speaker at the Nelson GWVA October meeting on the subject of "Insurance for Women."

Before long, Hanley appeared to have recovered from the travails of war and slowly established himself in the Trail business community. His injured left knee was a frequent source of pain and complaint and kept him from participating in the community's popular rugged sports. Nonetheless, he showed a spectator's keen interest in the local sporting scene, was a member of the provincial Conservative party and the Loyal Order of Servicemen Lodge, and district manager and partner, along with James Peverley Schofield, in a Monarch Life Insurance outlet. Jimmy Schofield was the son of the Trail Conservative member of the provincial parliament, James Hargrave Schofield, real estate and insurance agent. Pat Hanley, now in his late thirties, had finally settled into a community and a career.

Since 1896, Trail has been a hard-working and hard wrought town. The smelter, which processed the rich ores from the nearby Rossland mines, shaped the town and its people. After the Great War, Consolidated Mining and Smelting Company of Canada's (Cominco) operations with modern processes for the production of lead, zinc, gold and silver prospered. But Trail offered little to attract or entertain those accustomed to the cultural amenities of the city or even other growing towns in the province. There were few single working and professional women and even fewer opportunities for gentlemen of Pat Hanley's age to engage in an appropriate social life.

Mildred Neilson, a twenty-five-year-old graduate of Vancouver General Hospital School of Nursing, had joined the staff of Trail General Hospital in mid-1924. Along with several others of her profession, she lived at the Aldridge Nurses Home across the street from the Trail General Hospital and had come to know Patrick Hanley. Hanley was quite taken with Mildred and the two were known to have spent time together. As time would tell, Mildred did not return Hanley's growing interest in her. Her would-be suitor became quite distressed at her signs of rejection. At 10:00 a.m. on February 6, 1925, Patrick Hanley met with Mildred in the pleasant sitting room of the Aldridge Nurses Home. Hanley pulled out a revolver. A shot rang out. Mildred Neilson died with a bullet wound through her heart. There was a second shot and forthwith Hanley presented himself at the hospital across the street with a non-fatal gunshot wound in his side.

THE TRIALS OF PATRICK HANLEY

*M*urder in broad daylight: the victim—a young, attractive woman and a gentle angel of mercy; the perpetrator—a respectable but rather ordinary man, familiar to the community. The good citizens of Trail, Nelson and rural areas about the Kootenay were paralyzed with shock and grief. Newspapers headlined the "Slain Nurse" story. A brief formal announcement of the tragedy was manoeuvred on to page nine of the *Trail News* the very day of the murder. Within hours, reporters in Vancouver and Trail interviewed Miss Neilson's parents, police and the medical personnel who had come to her assistance in the final fifteen minutes of her life. From doctors at the Aldridge Nurses Home, reporters quoted the young woman's final words: "Dr. Williams, he shot me!"[1] Hanley's office mate, Jimmy Schofield, gave his candid statement: "I attribute Pat Hanley's unaccountable fatal shooting of Miss Neilson and wounding of himself, to his nervous breakdown and his nervous breakdown in turn to his suffering with his legs, which have never been right since the war."[2]

Schofield's reference to Patrick's nervous breakdown opened the door for further questions into Hanley's character and mental state since the war. Information about Hanley's early years being scanty, there is or was no evidence that he was of unstable personality or nervous demeanour at the age of twenty-eight prior to his enlistment in the Canadian Expeditionary Force. Due to the sensitivity of feeling for the victim at the Trail General Hospital, Hanley, suffering from his self-inflicted wound and general anxiety, was removed to the Sisters of St. Joseph's Mater Misericordiae Hospital in Rossland, where he was placed under armed guard and unavailable for comment.

Trail Tadanac Hospital, where Neilson had nursed and to which Hanley admitted himself February 6, 1925. Photo courtesy of the Trail Historical Society #7151.

Dr. J.B. Thom, who, along with Dr. C.S. Williams, attended the dying young woman, was also Trail's coroner. Under Thom's direction, within eleven hours of the crime, a Coroner's Jury of six reputable men was sworn in. At 9:00 a.m. on February 7, the first witness was called before the jury. Two hours of questioning and twenty minutes of consideration was all that was required for the jury to post its results: "The jury find that the deceased was murdered on Friday February 6, 1925 at about 11 a.m. on the second floor of the Aldridge building Trail, BC, by a bullet fired through the heart by Pat Hanley."[3]

An emotional funeral service for the young woman was held at Trail's Knox Presbyterian Church. Prominent businessmen carried her flower-adorned casket through streets lined with mourners to the CPR station. Mildred's father had come to Trail to escort his only daughter's remains to Vancouver, where a second service was held. Vancouver General Hospital Nursing school classmates clad in neat service uniforms acted as pallbearers at Grandview Methodist Church. The Trail Workmen's Committee of smeltermen raised funds for the erection of a suitable monument for the "unfortunate girl" at her burial site in Ocean View Cemetery, Burnaby. To this day, Mildred Neilson's monument—a

Dr. John Bain Thom, who tended the mortally wounded young nurse. Photo courtesy of the Trail Historical Society, #6666.

Mater Misericordiae Hospital, Rossland, where Hanley was transferred following the fatality of February 6, 1925. Photo courtesy of the Diocese of Nelson.

beautiful floral hedge encircling a coral marble urn—stands out from other grave markers on the gentle southern slope of the old cemetery.

The Great War Veterans' Association of Trail met to discuss the murder charges facing one of their number, but decided to take no action in the matter (other than to send a wreath of flowers for the casket): "The consensus of opinion was that Canadian law and justice would see that Hanley received fair representation, without any action on part of the association."[4] Indeed, the investigative reporters had assembled enough facts, events and background data (and especially opinions) that little remained for the police and judicial authorities and counsel to uncover. All that was required to present the case against Hanley was the registration of documents, preparation of witnesses, exhibits and evidence and the selection of a jury. The Grand Jury would decide Hanley's fate.

The Supreme Court of British Columbia assembled at the commanding, granite structure that was Nelson's courthouse on Wednesday, May 13, 1925. Patrick Hanley stood charged with murder. He pleaded "Not Guilty." Jury selection had been difficult. Two women called for jury duty had been challenged and Hanley was eventually tried by twelve worthy male peers, residents of Nelson and Kaslo. Since the *Trail News* was a weekly newspaper, the citizens of the Kootenay relied on the *Nelson Daily News* for up-to-date coverage of the trial. *Nelson Daily News* reporter Herbert H. (Bert) Currie vividly set forth the scene in the second-floor courtroom. A stickler for accuracy and detail, he described the demeanour of the accused, the presiding judge, Mr. Justice Murphy, Crown counsels James O'Shea (KC) of Nelson and Archie M. Johnson (KC) of Vancouver, and defence lawyers Eric Dawson of Nelson and A.H.

MacNeill (KC) of Vancouver. Currie was more than an experienced and competent reporter. He had studied law at Acadia University in Nova Scotia before joining the *Nelson Daily News* in 1909, and had begun reporting under then-editor William Garland Foster. Currie also served with the 54th Battalion in France and was instrumental in the formation of the Nelson branch of the Great War Veterans' Association. There is little doubt that the news reporter was well known to both prisoner Hanley and former city councillor, GWVA president and now resident writer, Annie Garland Foster.

Nelson Daily News *image of twenty-five-year-old nurse and murder victim Mildred Neilson of Trail. Photo courtesy of the* Nelson Daily News, *February 11, 1925 p. 1.*

The large second-floor interior courtroom was overflowing. A broad central staircase, illuminated by an arched stained-glass window at the midway landing, and the main floor foyer were also packed with curious spectators. Although not represented on the jury, more than half of those present were women. The formidable figure of Annie Garland Foster was among those women. What circumstances could possibly keep her away? Her knowledge of the participants, the local backdrop and her sympathies for both the accused veteran and the nursing sister would be compelling. The Nelson directory noted Mrs. Garland Foster was a resident of Nelson in 1925, although her career and interests were in transition betwixt health advocacy and literary pursuits. Her home address was not always predictable. But Annie would not have missed witnessing the murder trial!

The first day of the trial featured eight exhibits (photographs of the murder site, the fatal bullet, a bloodstained set of corsets) and the testimony of six Crown witnesses. Dr. Thom identified the photographs, told what he knew of Hanley's life in Trail and recalled the tragic futile moments when he attempted to save the young nurse's life. Cross-examination revealed that the accused was a patient of Dr. Thom and in the month preceding the shooting, Hanley was quite agitated and spoke of suicidal tendencies. Hanley was also concerned about his relationship with Miss Neilson. Thom offered reassurances and prescribed a "nerve sedative." Later, on the same night of Hanley's consultation with Thom, Schofield contacted the doctor on Hanley's behalf. In Hanley's room, located behind the Schofield insurance office, Hanley had become physically and emotionally distraught and was behaving quite irrationally. Dr. Thom suggested Hanley be taken to the Rossland Hospital. An interview with Thom the next day in Hanley's hospital room revealed that Hanley was still distraught.

In response to questioning by defence counsel, Thom offered the opinion that Hanley's mention of suicide did not necessarily indicate evidence of insanity. Next on the stand, Dr. C.S. Williams reiterated his efforts along with those of Dr. Thom to save Miss Neilson's life. Williams testified that he saw Hanley "fumbling with a revolver in his hand" and later, as they attended to the dying woman, he heard a second gunshot.

The sequence of events was picked up by a third witness, a friend and fellow nurse, Florence Eyton, who had spoken briefly to Hanley and Neilson in the lobby of the Aldridge Nurses Home, mere minutes prior to the murder. Florence saw Hanley soon after, when the self-wounded assailant ran across the street to the hospital where Eyton was now on duty. Another friend and nurse on duty at the time, Dorothy Ramson testified that she had known that Pat and Mildred were on friendly terms.

"James P. Schofield of Trail, Hanley's business partner, gave the sensational evidence of the day in regard to Hanley's weak physical and mental condition three weeks before the shooting occurred in Trail."[5] Ever since his return from the war, Schofield felt Hanley had exhibited increasing peculiarities. He recollected a disturbing series of encounters and conversations with the accused over the past several months involving an unusual insurance scheme, a tendency to lose his temper, agitation over social events and general nervous

Mildred Neilson's memorial at the Burnaby cemetery is tended and maintained to this day. Photo courtesy of Maurice Guibord, Vancouver, 2006.

distress that resulted in the visit to Hanley's room as explained by Dr. Thom. Hanley had then spent several days in a barely conscious state in the Rossland Hospital. When Jimmy Schofield brought Mildred Neilson to visit Hanley at the hospital, this seemed to settle him. Several days after release from hospital, Hanley took the train to Vancouver for some rest and a change of scene.

Throughout this intense first day of the trial, the prisoner showed little emotion (remaining "unperturbed," according to the *Trail News*). At the various adjournments, Hanley limped noticeably, leaning on the attendant constable.

Justice Murphy had "... constantly cautioned counsel, witnesses and even jurors so that no possible ground for a retrial should be found in the conduct of the case."[6] Nonetheless, when the court convened Thursday morning, owing to the omission of reading arraignment charges to the jury on the opening day, it ordered all questions put to witnesses examined on the previous day be read over to each witness by the court stenographer and confirmed by counsel and the witnesses before further evidence could be given. Without such consent to re-reading of the first day's proceedings, a new jury could be requested. Hanley and all counsel agreed to the re-reading of proceedings. Hence, the court and the members of the packed gallery did not hear new evidence until after 2:00 p.m.

Further exhibits were then revealed: revolver, shells, clothing, and an unopened, un-mailed letter from Hanley to Mildred. Trail's Chief of Police Benjamin Downes, the last witness for the Crown, gave his account of the events of February 6 and 8. On February 8, Downes charged Hanley with mur-der as he lay in a bed in the Rossland Hospital. Hanley's response to the charge was that he "... had not intended killing her, but had only wished to frighten her."[7] The police chief felt at that time that Hanley wanted to die and that he also might not survive the ordeal. Downes also read Exhibit #10 aloud to the court. This was Hanley's un-mailed letter to Mildred. The letter spoke of Hanley having paid a visit to Mildred's parents in Vancouver and his expected return to Vancouver. The Crown's case was thus concluded. Although it was now 4:30 p.m., the defence was called upon to address the jury. Mr. MacNeill announced (as was widely anticipated) that the line of defence would be that the accused was insane at the time of the shooting. With due respect, defence counsel offered the opinion that "a jury was a peculiarly poor tribunal for arriv-ing at a decision as to a man's sanity or insanity."[8] The defence would call upon two or three gentlemen who were competent in this regard to offer service to the jury.

The first witness for the defence was Dr. Monro, physician and surgeon, and Vancouver consultant to the Soldier's Civil Reestablishment Board to whom Hanley had been referred. On February 3, 1925, prior to the crime, Monro found no evidence of disability in Hanley's knee or leg. However, the doctor noted the patient suffered from "disability neurosis" or mental distress from fear of a permanent disability, a complaint not uncommon among returned soldiers. The court next heard from Frederick Castle of Vancouver, executive agent for Hanley's employer, Monarch Life Insurance Company. Castle, an elderly and experienced member of the firm, testified that he had recently worked for one month at the Trail office and found Hanley to be rather difficult to work with, "egotistic" and generally unpredictable and indifferent. Conversely, "Hanley

Nelson's Rattenbury-designed courthouse, where Patrick Hanley stood trial for murder 1925–1926. Photo courtesy of Touchstones Nelson: Museum of Art and History, #83.151.1.

might have been a crank, but was not so all the time."[9] A third witness and long-standing acquaintance of the accused, Mrs. Leila Christie had encountered Hanley on the recent train journey to Vancouver and found his behaviour on this occasion "nervous." Witness Fred Hosking met Hanley February 5 on his return trip to Trail and verified peculiar, erratic behavior.

May 15: the third day of the trial. Six full-length columns in the *Nelson Daily News* once more heralded the Hanley murder trial. The courtroom was more crowded than on previous days and again women and girls were the principal attendees. "Alienists" (an obsolete term for psychiatrists or psychologists) Dr. Donald W. McKay of Nelson and Dr. James G. MacKay of New Westminster took the stand as expert witnesses for the defence. McKay of Nelson concluded Hanley did not know what he was doing at the moment of Miss Neilson's murder. MacKay of New Westminster, who had examined Hanley on March 4, "... had reached the conclusion that the prisoner had a psychopathic personality... and belonged to the subdivision of the confusional type of mania-depressive."[10] When court resumed at 10:00 a.m. on Saturday, May 16, the defence concluded its argument. The press aptly summarized defence counsel MacNeill's address to the jury: "That Hanley was insane at the time of shooting Miss Neilson and therefore not guilty of murder, and that, because of the danger to society, he should be confined in some safe place, was the substance of the address."[11] It was

Nelson Gaol, adjacent to the courthouse, where Hanley awaited trial. Shown in 1954. Photo courtesy of British Columbia Archives collections, I 27275 cat. #07617.

the burden of the defence to prove insanity and through medical and corroborative testimony, the defence had done so. The Crown had offered no rebuttal to the medical evidence. Crown counsel Johnson then addressed the jury. Crown's role was not to secure a guilty verdict that the defence in essence had admitted, but to present all the facts and evidence before the jury. Johnson maintained that Hanley was sane at the time of the murder. The last word went to Justice Murphy. His charge to the jury was one of the longest on record in Nelson and the *Nelson Daily News* recorded every word and nuance. Murphy instructed the jury on the law regarding murder, the difference between culpable and non-culpable homicide, the reviewing of evidence and the rights of the accused. Guilty, not guilty, guilty of manslaughter or, in this case, not guilty because of insanity were the options before the jury. At 1:36 p.m., the jury retired to consider its verdict. Twice the jury returned to the courtroom to hear clarification of legal points. At 8:20 Saturday night, a hush hung over the largely male crowd in the Supreme Court. Jury foreman Sam Hunter announced that the jury was unable to agree upon a verdict. As Monday's paper exclaimed, "Prisoner Falls in Faint When Hears Result," and "Murder Jury Disagrees: Hanley Case Goes Over to the Fall Assizes." And there the matter rested until October 20, 1925, when the Supreme Court and the case of *R. vs Hanley* was *once again* called. Hanley spent the tedious interim five months at Oakalla Prison in Burnaby.

Justice J.A. [or W.A.] Macdonald (spelling and initials vary) of Vancouver presided at the Fall Assizes for 1925 in the Nelson Court House. Mr. J.W. deB. Farris joined O'Shea for the prosecution. Dawson and MacNeill returned to defend their client for a second time. Another all-male jury was under the watchful eye of a gallery of again predominantly women spectators. The prisoner appeared to be strong and in fair health. Three new witnesses added their testimony to the evidence repeated by the six recalled from Hanley's first trial. Nurse Neilson's father, George, told the Court that Hanley had told him that Mildred would never return to Vancouver. Hanley then qualified his remark that she might never again live in the city. A shopkeeper from Bellingham, Washington, identified the gun he had sold to Patrick Hanley, and Dr. Palmer, Rossland Hospital resident physician, stated "... that he would not say that Hanley was normal during his times in the Rossland Hospital [following the murder]."[12] On the second day of the trial, the two alienists—the two Dr. McKays (spelling varies)—were cross-examined at length and agreed "... they believed Hanley was suffering from manic-depressive insanity of the confusional or mixed type."[13] MacNeill again built his defence on the degree of insanity and declared a man of this condition should not go to the gallows, but should be confined in a "proper place." Four Hanley friends were then sworn in. In January, the friends had witnessed Hanley's fits and irrational behaviour in the room behind Schofield's office. All were unsettled by Hanley's strange "attacks."

Two more alienists then took the stand. For the prosecution, Dr. A.T. Mathers of Winnipeg declared Hanley was not insane or manic-depressive but rather suffered from hysteria. Mather's diagnosis was countered by that of a new defence expert, Dr. H.C. Steeves, who believed that the accused was not capable of distinguishing right from wrong. In summation, prosecutor Farris declared the facts pointed to a guilty verdict, while MacNeill based his case on the evidence of three alienists, a surgeon and two general practitioners. Hanley's defence counsel declared he was mentally unsound and not guilty on that basis. Justice Macdonald's charge to the jury leaned heavily on a discussion of legal insanity and presumption of innocence. The jury retired at 5:15 p.m., was polled again at 9:00 p.m. and rendered their failure to reach agreement to the court at 11:30 p.m. Following an all-night composing session at the *Nelson Daily News*, the public learned the next day the "Jury Disagrees in Pat Hanley Trial: Dismissed After 6 Hours Deliberation" and "Insanity Defence is Battleground."

For Hanley, it was back to confinement at Oakalla prison to await a third trial at the Spring Assizes. On May 4, 1926, Patrick Hanley found himself in the same Nelson setting with the same cast of characters—defence and prosecution counsels, exhibits, sheriffs and witnesses. Only Mr. Justice D.A. McDonald (no relation to Mr. Justice Macdonald of the October 1925 trial) and once again an all-male jury were new to their tasks. Procedures moved along quickly, with the Crown finishing its now-familiar case on the first day. Much of the detail of previous trials was omitted. The only sensation occurred when McDonald determined that Chief of Police Downes had not cautioned Hanley, in light of his disturbed state, sufficiently as to the implications of the murder charge. Witness Schofield updated the court on Hanley's personal financial state in February of the previous year. The fact was, Hanley was in debt and this could be a factor in his worrisome state. On day two of the trial, the defence heard more friendly witnesses and strong representation from alienists J.G. MacKay and H.C. Steeves. Although Hanley was in a better mental state than at the former trial, he was suffering from manic-depressive insanity of the confused type and was mentally irresponsible at the time of the slaying. Crown alienist Mather reiterated his judgment that Hanley was sane on February 6, 1925.

May 6, 1926, was the date Patrick Hanley would learn his fate. Defender MacNeill and Prosecutor Farris each addressed the jury and a silent, packed gallery for a little over an hour. His Lordship charged the jury and at 2:39 p.m. its members retired to consider. At 4:24 p.m., as the prisoner rose and the crowd fell silent, the jury foreman, Nelson grocer William Campion, responded to the Registrar's query:

"Gentlemen of the Jury, have you reached a verdict?"

"We have." stated Campion.

"Guilty."

With barely a moment's pause, Justice McDonald proceeded as required.

"Patrick Hanley, have you anything to say why the sentence of this court should not be passed upon you?"

"No, my Lord."

"The sentence of the court is that you be taken to the prison from which you came and there, on the second day of August next, be hanged by the neck until you are dead. And may the Lord have mercy on your soul!"[14]

Newspapers in Trail, Vancouver and Ottawa picked up the Hanley story, but it was quickly dropped from other British Columbia and local papers.

Mr. and Mrs. Neilson of Vancouver, Mildred's parents, view their daughter's memorial and gravesite at Ocean View Cemetery in Burnaby. Photo courtesy of Maurice Guibord and the City of Vancouver Archives. Photo by Stuart Thomson, VA 99-3049.

This concludes (in part) the "Tale of the Missing Pages"—the sequence of events that parallelled the years of the life of Annie Garland Foster that she intentionally cut from her memoir.

When composing "Passing Through," Annie must have relived the three Hanley trials and the tension and emotion surrounding those days. Six excised typed pages would have contained details and impressions far removed from those available through court records and newspaper reports. It is a shame she elected to obliterate her comments from her personal record.

Akin to her earlier secrecy about names of people and places, this excision of critical life events and observations mystifies the researcher, the reader and the anxious, sympathetic biographer.

JUSTICE DEFERRED

*I*n 1926, Palmer Rutledge was a twenty-three-year-old outgoing chap who engaged in all the extreme sports of the day. Palmer was brought up in Nelson and Trail and at the age of ninety-seven he still vividly recalled the events and murder trial of his mate, Pat Hanley. According to Palmer, Pat was an okay fellow but affected by the war. He just couldn't stand being rejected by the nurse. Joe Irving was fourteen when Pat Hanley visited his older sister Violet at the Irving family home in Trail. Violet knew the young murder victim. It was not unusual to own a revolver or for a vet "to go off his rocker. It happened a lot." Both elderly men were uncertain as to Hanley's ultimate fate. Time just moved on.

But in May 1926 there was no time to ponder or forget. Eighty-seven days and Pat Hanley would hang. On the day following Hanley's sentencing, Judge McDonald sent his record of the proceedings to the Secretary of State in Ottawa. For Annie Garland Foster, the case was not closed. Justice had not been served to either victim or perpetrator. She grieved for the young nurse whose life had been so violently and irrationally cut short. And yet her years of experience in studying and nursing the men affected by the horrors of war had given her a unique understanding of their separate miseries.

At her new apartment on Bute Street in Vancouver's West End, Annie's typewriter was put into action. On May 9, Annie H. Foster (the signature she used on that occasion) composed a lengthy letter to her Conservative Member of Parliament, H.H. Stevens. Mrs. Foster had earlier approached him on the matter of condemning "unfortunate," insane men, so Stevens was alerted to the concerns of one of his more vocal constituents. The Hanley case was another instance of injustice to prisoners and in this regard the correspondent was not entirely alone. Although the John Howard Society would not set up its office in Vancouver until 1931, Agnes MacPhail, Canada's first woman Member of Parliament, had since 1922 pursued the unsuitable topics of prison reform and parole offices. Since Annie had witnessed the first of the condemned man's three trials, she was in a strong position to comment. To Stevens she confessed, "I must say if ever a jury was befuddled about the legal interpretation of insanity, that one was...."[1] The Crown and defence alienists appeared to be in agreement that the prisoner was insane. The jury should then have found the man not guilty due to insanity and there would have been no further pain or trials. Annie went on to comment knowledgeably about manic depression without revealing her professional training on the subject. Nor did she refer to her personal acquaintance with the accused, but she critically observed "... that the local prejudice was so blasting that it was a crime to try the case in the Kootenay at all."[2] Surprisingly, she did not suggest a course of action Mr. Stevens should take but merely concluded, "I think something should be done for him at once."[3] She hinted that she might be in Ottawa before long and would be glad to see him there.

Upon receipt of her missive, Stevens, to his credit, immediately passed it along to the Honourable Ernest Lapointe, Canada's Minister of Justice. Stevens averred Mrs. Foster was "... a very responsible woman... who has been engaged in sociological work for many years" and urged the Minister to deal with her concerns "... according to the dictates of the law of humanity."[4] Lapointe promised "exhaustive investigation" and dispatched Dr. Harvey Clare of the Homewood Sanitarium in Guelph, Ontario, to Nelson. Dr. Clare was charged to give an opinion on Hanley's present "mentality" and judge whether the prisoner detained in Nelson's gaol was insane at the time of the crime for which he had been sentenced. Meanwhile, the deputy minister of justice requested a summary of the final judgment as well as some personal observations from trial judge McDonald. These were forthcoming, along with copies of other reports and correspondence. They were received by the Remission Branch of the Justice Department on June 7 and in no time landed on the desk of Michael F. Gallagher, chief of the Remission Branch. Gallagher, who would now deal with the Hanley file, had a reputation as a hard-line administrator of a very restrictive parole system. He felt indulgence of convicts would undermine the authority of the courts.

As the calendar turned over to June, the Hanley case took off in a curious and dangerous direction. An Ottawa solicitor heard of the Hanley case. This solicitor conferred with Gallagher regarding his own friend, who also suffered bouts of insanity resulting from World War I experiences. The solicitor's veteran

The British Columbia Penitentiary, New Westminster, constructed in 1878 and photographed in 1938, was home to many BC residents until 1980. Photo courtesy of New Westminster Public Library Historical Photographs, #1609.

friend was a married man with a child. His name was G.V. Hanley, and he was a member of British Columbia's Princess Patricia Light Infantry. Files were drawn from the Department of National Defence and the British Columbia Provincial Police. Urgent correspondence from the Deputy Minister of Justice to the Department of National Defence cited "Patrick Hanley—also referred to as Sergeant G.V. Hanley P.P.C.L.I." Confusion now set in! This was an extremely serious, incriminating case of mistaken identity.

Although a discrepancy in the first names was indeed noted, a veteran who knew G.V. Hanley well identified him, using as evidence the single photo of Patrick Hanley on file in the Department of Justice, as one and the same person as Patrick Hanley.

As late as July 12, word came to Hanley's defence counsel, A. MacNeill, that the Justice Department was seriously considering Hanley's case, but great importance was placed on the matter of Hanley's alleged marriage. Had Hanley been free to court Miss Neilson? There was no evidence proving that Patrick Hanley was *not* married, and clemency was less likely to apply to a man who was untrue to his wife and family. Proof of Hanley's bachelorhood must be obtained immediately and at all costs.

The materials under review in June by the Justice Department included a plea from Hanley, through his West Kootenay Member of Parliament, W.K. Esling, requesting that he be shot rather than hanged. This petition was denied as the law prescribed hanging. Of primary significance was Dr. Clare's report commissioned early on by Justice Minister Lapointe. Clare interviewed Hanley in Nelson and at the Oakalla Prison Farm near New Westminster June 1–3. On June 12, Clare succinctly reported: "I now believe that he [Hanley] was suffering from insanity when he committed the act, and that he has not completely recovered at the present time. My opinion is that his mental trouble will not completely recover at any time. I do not believe he was responsible for the act he committed; and I expect that he will be a mental case for the rest of his life."[5] Annie Garland Foster, having visited the inmate at Oakalla added with some reservation that Hanley had had an attack of his "malady," but doubted authorities at the institute had paid any attention.

In Ottawa, Remission Chief Gallagher (with the identity crisis not yet resolved) got the shock of his strident career on July 15 when he was alerted to a night telegram sent to recently appointed Minister of Justice E.L. Patenaude. It was signed by Mrs. W. Garland Foster, and said: "Will arrive Tues. re Hanley case Please Hold Open."[6] Gallagher's hastily telegraphed reply stated: "Trip to Ottawa not necessary but your representation should immediately be mailed."[7] Annie must have chuckled at the sense of urgency her telegram had evoked. In fact, Annie was on her way to visit her Foster in-laws and family in Ottawa, her sister and family in Maine and to attend a University of New Brunswick alumni gathering in Fredericton. The perceived assault on the Ministry of Justice would be no inconvenience.

On July 20, Annie paid her visit to the Langevin Building on Parliament Hill and deposited with the minister's private secretary copies of two most interesting documents. Both were hand-printed letters dated July 13, 1926, addressed to Mrs. W.G. Foster and signed by Pat Hanley. One letter challenged the so-called marriage issue by listing in great detail his whereabouts and the people, officers and staff with whom he was acquainted from the time of his enlistment until his discharge. All could vouch for his unmarried status. The letter ended with the obvious conclusion that time would be required to contact all these parties and records. If the case hinged on this point, a postponement would be necessary. The second letter was a directive to Annie on how to dispose of his body should the execution take place. He wished to be buried at Ocean View Cemetery in Burnaby (as was Mildred Neilson). Diagrams depicted the grave marker and inscription he desired.

With the clock ticking ever faster, the British Columbia executive council of the Canadian Legion wrote a formal letter to the Governor General in Council advocating that executive clemency be exercised towards Patrick Hanley. This letter was not received until July 21. Legion members had been forthcoming with the opinion that Hanley had at times appeared violently insane. The letter also cleared up the identity matter of the two soldiers named Hanley and expressed the hope that the error would not confuse the situation!

Meanwhile, creation of the following sequence of documents was under way. Gallagher, on behalf of the Deputy Minister of Justice, wrote rather cautiously

Lord Byng of Vimy, Governor General of Canada 1921–1926, signed P.C. Order-in-Council 1167 on July 22, 1926, commuting Hanley's sentence. Photo courtesy of Canada Patent and Copyright Office/Library and Archives Canada/C-033239.

to the Minister of Justice. "After a careful analysis of all the evidence adduced at the last trial, considering all relevant material now on record, and having special regard to the expert alienist's report [Dr. Clare]... the undersigned [Gallagher] is inclined to the view that the death sentence may well be commuted to a term of life imprisonment."[8] On July 21, Minister of Justice Patenaude, recommended to Governor General Byng that the death penalty be commuted to life imprisonment. The next day Byng set before the Privy Council of Canada all documents relating to the Hanley trial and petitions. In consequence, Lord Byng signed P.C. Order-in-Council 1167 which stated "… that the sentence of death so passed upon the prisoner be commuted to a term of life imprisonment in the British Columbia Penitentiary."[9]

The unbearable frustration and drama of Hanley's imminent execution was over. All participants and actors in the drama were notified by telegram. The warden of Oakalla informed Hanley and he was removed to the British Columbia Penitentiary. Hanley's reaction went unrecorded. The Department of Justice tersely notified Annie at her sister's home in Franklin, Maine: "Matter no longer Urgent." Upon her return to Vancouver, Annie wrote to Gallagher on August 13 expressing gratitude for the information. But he also drew fire from Annie as she requested an explanation for a comment in the *Ottawa Citizen* and the *Vancouver Province* noting that she had been in Ottawa for several days and had made personal intercessions on Hanley's behalf. Annie had indeed delivered documents to the Justice Department and had paid a personal visit to her deceased husband's friend, the recently elected Prime Minister Honourable Arthur Meighen, but her visit was not about the Hanley case. Gallagher responded with a blunt denial of having communicated names of applicants in clemency cases to the press.

Young Palmer Rutledge, still a resident of Trail in 1926, was of the opinion that Hanley had influential friends who had gotten him off the noose. In 2001, the name of Mrs. Garland Foster rang a bell in this regard.

A WRITER'S WORK

Annie Garland Foster's move to Vancouver in 1924–25 was deliberate and calculated. Before leaving her career in the health and welfare fields, she posed for a sentimental professional photograph in which she wore her traditional white nurse's uniform, her greying hair very visible beneath a starched shoulder-length veil. Then off came the veil! Notebooks, scrapbooks and foolscap were piled beside the typewriter, initially in her Nelson, then her Vancouver apartments.

Nelson and her careers in civic affairs, teaching and even health care were now in the past. Annie's instinct had always been to observe, report and comment openly on a wide variety of topics. Now she would transform her avocation into a career as a writer resident in the city, with the cultural resources, libraries, and archives that were essential to her new life. As a politician, advocate for veterans and health care for women and children and widow of a journalist of considerable reputation, Annie had acquired a roster of influential political and cultural acquaintances upon whom she could call for advice and assistance. As witnessed by her campaign to save Hanley from the gallows, she was not averse to "networking."

The Hanley trials, her emotional and strategic involvement in the commutation of his sentence, as well as her family visits to the east, had taken a great deal of Annie's time and thought. Her journalistic and research endeavours—that were critical to her financial state—had been put aside for several months. Prior to April 1926, Mrs. W. Garland Foster (or variations on that name) had nearly fifty articles and stories to her credit. Nineteen of these had appeared in the *Vancouver Province,* but from April to October 1926 there were no articles with her byline. She was obviously in a transition mode. Her time and energies were directed towards saving a man's life and arranging travels to eastern Canada.

Her life story in "Passing Through" (following the six-page gap) was blithely resumed as if nothing untoward had taken place in those shadowy months and years: "Meanwhile I had moved to Vancouver, where I had some encouragement to go on with my writing."[1]

Annie wrote from life experience, study and strong personal convictions. Her oldest existing manuscript, "Nelson Then and Now," written in 1921, was a short enthusiastic summary of that young city's history. Ironically, the Nelson story was first published in the *Vancouver Province* in May 1925, just as readers were suddenly focussing on the trial of the deranged murderer, Patrick Hanley, which was taking place in the landmark courthouse of that charming frontier city.

Without a doubt, Annie gained the most satisfaction seeing her name in print in the *Canadian Bookman*. Although distinctly Canadian, the journal, which commenced publication in 1919, had a narrow literary focus and a certain associated prestige. In March 1921, an assembly of Canadian authors (Annie was not among them) held a national conference at McGill University in Montreal, calling together nearly a hundred and fifty authors. An impressive executive committee and council were elected. Attendees included political activist and novelist Nellie McClung, Isabel Eccleston Mackay, Robert Service, Bliss Carman, Charles G.D. Roberts, Duncan Campbell Scott and Florence Randall Livesay—all soon to be, if not already, Canadian literary icons. Thus the Canadian Authors Association (CAA), which briefly adopted the *Canadian Bookman* as its official organ, was created.

The authors' association and the

Vancouver's classic Georgia Hotel, which Annie Foster used as a temporary home and address during the 1920s and 1930s. Photo courtesy of the City of Vancouver Archives, #Hot N36, location: 183-D-2.

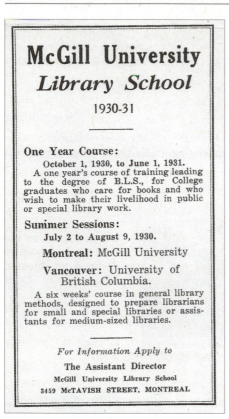

McGill University
Library School
1930-31

———

One Year Course:
October 1, 1930, to June 1, 1931.
A one year's course of training leading to the degree of B.L.S., for College graduates who care for books and who wish to make their livelihood in public or special library work.

Summer Sessions:
July 2 to August 9, 1930.

Montreal: McGill University

Vancouver: University of British Columbia.
A six weeks' course in general library methods, designed to prepare librarians for small and special libraries or assistants for medium-sized libraries.

———

For Information Apply to
The Assistant Director
McGill University Library School
3459 McTAVISH STREET, MONTREAL

McGill University in Montreal advertises its new Library School in Canadian Bookman, *a literary journal, in 1930. Image courtesy of* Canadian Bookman *v.12 #4, p. 43, 1930.*

journal soon, however, went their separate ways. The journal broadened its scope to include the creative arts and theatre and adopted a decidedly Canadian nationalistic direction, which was entirely compatible with Annie's leanings. The CAA organization "… persisted with the administrative notion that those who ardently desired to write are as important in their own way as those who write."[2] This too reflected Annie's sentiments and was most encouraging. Both CAA and *Canadian Bookman* were destined for greatness in their own respective ways, while the more political and critical *Canadian Forum* duelled with both the CAA and the *Bookman* for political credibility and objectivity.

The CAA quickly established branches across the country and Annie became an eager charter member of the Vancouver group. In August 1926, the Vancouver and Mainland Branch hosted the national convention. The group became known for its general good humour and good-time gatherings. In Vancouver, members preferred hiking and boating trips over the option of listening to a lecture by austere prairie novelist, Frederick Phillip Grove. Annie was preoccupied with the Hanley affair at the time and it is unlikely she attended the convention. However, the energy of the convention would have been a good tonic and the literary companionship definitely afforded good company. Delegates would have recognized Mrs. W. Garland Foster as the contributor of passionate articles in the *Canadian Bookman* on the quality of Canadian magazines, book and play reviews and a particularly delightful July 1923 front-page article on the poetry of her old Fredericton and Nelson acquaintance, Jane [Nain] Elizabeth Roberts MacDonald.

The literary career of Mrs. Garland Foster progressed in measured annual stages. In 1924, she composed lengthy, rather didactic articles on weaving as a home industry (for which she had acquired a fascination while in Britain) and food values for the highly respectable family magazine, *National Life*. She wrote: "The trouble with us is that we no longer know the source of our food or the way it is prepared… we buy package food."[3] How prophetic!

From August 1925 and through the following decade, Annie's bread and butter was the popular Magazine section of the *Vancouver Province*. Readership of the weekend edition of the newspaper far outstripped any other literary or national special-interest journal and remuneration was somewhat reliable. More than once, Annie gave credit in her articles to Lukin Johnston, creator and editor of the Magazine section, for her success as a journalist and short story writer. Johnston built up a roster of remarkable, talented young writers who were regularly featured in the magazine. Several became national figures — Bruce Hutchison (historian, journalist), F.H. Soward (diplomat and academic), Don Munday (mountaineer-adventurer), Dorothy Livesay (poet), Dorothy Bell (newspaper publisher) and the very capable H.H. Currie (a reporter from the *Nelson Daily News,* who wrote tales with a Kootenay or Interior British Columbia theme). These young writers rubbed bylines with the more experienced Richard Gosnell (British Columbia's first Provincial Librarian and Archivist) and Major J.S. Matthews (founder of the City of Vancouver City Archives).

Lukin Johnston, editor of the Magazine section, became a legend in life and in death. He left his birthplace in Surrey, England, in 1906 at the age of eighteen and wandered about the Kootenay Lake district. Later he joined the *Vancouver Province,* then the *Victoria Colonist,* followed by service overseas in World War I with the Canadian Expeditionary Forces. In view of the time Johnston spent in the Kootenay, his newspaper vocation and Annie's later reference to him, it is very likely that the Garland Fosters were early acquaintances of Lukin Johnston.

Initially, Mrs. W. Garland Foster was encouraged (or assigned) to write moralistic little animal tales for children's enjoyment. Unfortunately, "Woolly Bear Caterpillar" and "The Sad Case of Willie Mouse" were not Annie's forte. Within months, Johnston recognized that her talent

Lukin Johnston, magazine editor for the Province *(shown here in his 1929 book* Beyond the Rockies), *encouraged Annie Foster to pursue a career in writing and journalism. Photo courtesy of Hilary Johnston.*

lay elsewhere and allowed her to select topics that reflected her experiences and passionate beliefs: English cathedrals, historical biography and, more often, local and Native history and ethnography. But Johnston's integrity, reputation and effectiveness led to his promotion in 1928 as chief Southam News correspondent in London, where he was extremely successful and respected.

In November 1933, Europe was being introduced to a new political force in Germany, Chancellor Adolf Hitler. On November 16, 1933, Lukin Johnston interviewed Herr Hitler in Berlin at considerable length. Johnston wired his report to Southam News: "… Hitler unequivocally declared that Germany is ready to consider any invitation to recommence negotiations for disarmament or the limitation of armaments so long as she was invited on terms of absolute equality."[4] It was a headline-grabbing interview! Following the Hitler interview, Johnston boarded a steamer for Norwich, England… and was never seen again. He inexplicably disappeared some time after 2:30 a.m. on November 18, and was last seen sleeping in a chair on deck. Had he suffered a heart attack, wandered to the rail and slipped overboard? Or was there a darker explanation of this tragedy? Diplomatic and press circles were shocked. Tributes poured in to the Southam News agency and the Vancouver newspapers. Annie Foster was one of many who owed Johnston a deep measure of gratitude. He had been a fine mentor and had opened many doors for her.

Although the newspaper stories paid the bills, Annie needed time to pursue her own interests. A fifteen-minute streetcar ride took her to the Carnegie Library and the city's museum at Main and Hastings Streets. There she met librarians, collectors and archivists who shared her interests and her desire to uncover Vancouver's incongruously recent past. She became a member of the Vancouver Art, Historical and Scientific Association (VAHSA) and between October 1926 and June 1929 had six articles published in the association's *Museum Notes*. The June 1929 article explained how the VAHSA acquired works for its art gallery and recounted the personal and artistic background of Vancouver painter, Mary Riter Hamilton. Mrs. Hamilton was an unauthorized "War Artist" who painted evocative scenes of French and Flemish battlefields, just after the guns were silenced. Two hundred and twenty-seven Hamilton paintings were shown at the Public Archives of Canada in Ottawa in 1927 (and many are still in the nation's inventory). Annie would have seen these images during one of her visits there. The two women, having much in common, became friends.

It was also at the Carnegie Library that Annie had an encounter that would govern a good portion of her life for the next five years. She attended an evening lecture on the poetry and life of Mohawk-Canadian poet, Pauline Johnson. Pauline Johnson, a sentimental national figure, had passed away in near-penury in Vancouver in 1913. Her story had not been told, yet many inquiries were made about her. A biography was needed. Was Mrs. Garland Foster interested? She was: "At that moment the idea… which had been in my mind for some time got considerably speeded up."[5] It would be a risk. Many of her current interests and responsibilities would have to be put aside. Where would the money come from? And how did one undertake such a formidable task with no guarantee of acceptance by a Canadian publisher?

Nonetheless, in 1926 Annie accepted the challenge to write the first biography of Pauline Johnson. No articles by Mrs. W. Garland Foster appeared in the *Vancouver Province,* or in any other journal for that matter, in 1927. Annie had acquired a fascination for West Coast Native culture and

Portrait of Pauline Johnson from The Mohawk Princess. *Annie Foster was Johnson's first biographer. Photo courtesy of the Nelson Public Library.*

artifacts—although a true connection to the Native people eluded her—and it was not difficult to apply this interest to Pauline Johnson, one of Canada's first Native cultural figures. She established correspondence with the helpful folk at the Legislative Library in Victoria who had to date supported her coastal Native research and would now help in relation to Johnson's *Legends of Vancouver.* By March, Annie was off to Toronto, Brantford (Johnson's home), and quite likely Montreal, where she buried herself in press clippings, interviews, reviews and study of Pauline's own compositions. There was also her own family in Maine, New Brunswick and Ottawa to visit.

Nearly a year had passed since Hanley had been spared the gallows, yet Annie maintained her watch and continued to assemble material relevant to his case. Never one to miss any opportunity to further her cause, while still in Maine, Annie wrote to her old correspondent, Mr. Gallagher of the Remission Branch in Ottawa, reminding him of their communications regarding Patrick Hanley. She requested an appointment for October 1927, begging him to note she was employing no influential nabob or intermediary in making this request.

Since August of the previous year, Annie had, on occasion, taken the interurban tram to New Westminster to visit Patrick Hanley in confinement at the British Columbia Federal Penitentiary. She had become very concerned about the inflammatory and painful condition of the war wound in Hanley's thigh. It was steadily worsening and the authorities in charge seemed to pay little attention. Gallagher, as before, rebuffed her suggestion for an appointment. Hence, he was soon in receipt of a lengthy letter (postmarked Maine) outlining Hanley's medical condition. The letter also mentioned the matter of the injustice of the trials and sentencing. In November, Hanley's condition required emergency surgery, and Annie's diagnosis and concern were vindicated. In her acknowledgement to Gallagher she replied, "Surely, surely, if the facts are presented to [the Minister of Justice] he will be able to devise some way of permitting this man to vindicate his honour while at the same time destroying the prenicious [sic] precedent which has been established by this case."[6] Mr. Gallagher, the Hanley case was not closed.

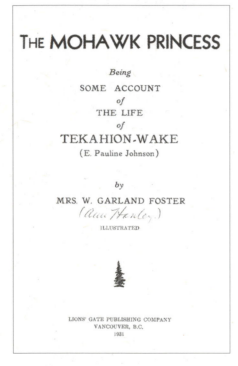

THE MOHAWK PRINCESS

Being

SOME ACCOUNT
of
THE LIFE
of
TEKAHION-WAKE
(E. Pauline Johnson)

by

MRS. W. GARLAND FOSTER
(Ann Hanley)

ILLUSTRATED

LIONS' GATE PUBLISHING COMPANY
VANCOUVER, B.C.
1931

The Nelson Public Library's copy of The Mohawk Princess, 1931, biography of Canadian poet E. Pauline Johnson, by Annie H. Foster. This copy was signed by the author and donated to Notre Dame University of Nelson. Image courtesy of the Nelson Public Library.

Having assumed a full-time career as a biographer and writer, Annie felt she needed an office, a den, a retreat, indeed, a "Studio" where she could spread her books and papers and concentrate on her work. She found the ideal summer cottage on the disorganized cliff road above the ocean at White Rock, British Columbia. There was a garden, solitude, frequently sunshine, and it was accessible by train or a less than two-hour bus ride from Vancouver. The village was home to eight hundred permanent residents and the wide bay area was known as Semiahmoo—an attractive connection to the local Coast Salish culture and subject matter for several articles. A small apartment on Nelson Steet in Vancouver's West End, or occasionally, a suite at the Georgia Hotel downtown, would be her winter and permanent address. From her retreat at the "Studio," Annie administered and balanced the several portfolios she had taken on. When penitentiary authorities withdrew her visitation and correspondence privileges with Hanley in March 1928, she appealed this decision (without success) to Gallagher. He was probably not amused by her remark that she was considering writing a novel based on the circumstances of the Hanley case.

Writing, in whatever form, was now paramount. An author's reliance on the assistance of others to provide the documents and references essential to research led Annie to enroll in Canada's first graduate course in library science. In October 1930, Mrs. W. Garland Foster was a rather mature fifty-five-year-old student at McGill University Library School in Montreal. Library school was at times tedious and some of her fellow students were intolerable, misplaced academics, but the studies served their purpose in helping her organize materials for publication, write book reviews and research references. While a student in Montreal she managed to contribute rather lightweight articles for the *Vancouver Province* and maintain contacts in Vancouver; but following right along from her McGill graduation in May 1931, Annie proceeded to her alma

mater in Fredericton, for a master's degree in English and West Coast studies. Her Pauline Johnson biography, *Mohawk Princess,* published in 1931 by Lion's Gate Publishing of Vancouver, served in lieu of a master's thesis. This degree was complemented with courses in short story writing taken at the University of Washington in Seattle.

In the 1930s, amidst the lectures and assignments, Annie had numerous major research projects under way. There were updates to Pauline Johnson, but Prime Minister (and William Garland's friend) Arthur Meighen, the Russian Doukhobors of western Canada, CPR pathfinder Walter Moberly and the Haida of the Pacific coast occupied a good deal of her time and resources as well. She was preparing a lifetime writing agenda.

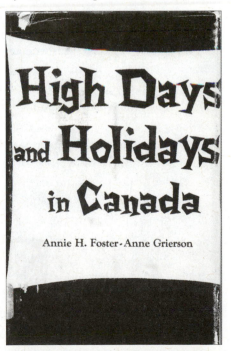

Cover of Annie's second volume, High Days and Holidays, *a standard for Canadian school and reference libraries. Image courtesy of the author.*

Patrick Hanley, from his cell at "the Pen" in New Westminster was also engaged in writing. In November 1930, prisoner #3129 composed a neatly organized and logically drawn, four-page petition addressed to the Minister of Justice applying for a "reduction of sentence or parole." The reasoned grounds for the request were enumerated as follows:

1. Doubt as to legal culpability
2. Denial of justice on the part of the Crown
3. Error on the part of the trial court
4. Economical and sociological reasons
5. Compassionate grounds[7]

Each point was supported by a convincing statement and argument. It is difficult to imagine that the petition was entirely of Hanley's composition. (But Mrs. Garland Foster was in Montreal at the time and Hanley had few other visitors.) Via the warden, Gallagher informed the prisoner: "In response the prisoner may be told that his case has been considered but that it is not deemed one in which his release, under license, can be recommended. You may also inform this inmate that for some years past it has not been the practice to grant, in any case, a reduction of sentence."[8] Gallagher was certainly correct in his statement about reductions in the number of paroles granted. Between 1932 and 1938 the number of regulations governing all manner of prison controls increased nearly tenfold. As a general rule the public was indifferent to prison reform or lack of it. There were fewer men on the street looking for jobs and fewer handouts if such men were detained in prison. Refusal of Hanley's 1930 petition resulted in a letter from Annie to Minister of Justice Hugh Guthrie and a reply that her plea was "quite out of the question."

Another year, another petition, another rejection courtesy of Mr. Gallagher—1932, 1934, 1937, 1938. Each year, Annie directed more military data, logic and pleas to the appropriate Solicitors General and Ministers of Justice. On December 2, 1937, she re-opened a cheeky correspondence with Gallagher: "You must have missed my letters through the years, but as there is nothing to add to my previous statements in the case of Patrick Hanley, there seemed nothing else to do, but to deprive you of my correspondence! However, recently, there has been something else."[9] The "something else" was a warning that others, for example, a former penitentiary chaplain, were taking an interest in Hanley's prolonged confinement. Gallagher hoped to put a stop to further annoying correspondence by informing the "Dear Madam" in December 1938 that the papers in the Hanley matter would not come under review until July 1941.

By 1939, Annie Garland Foster had come to the present and the final chapter of her "Passing Through" memoir. She was in a very reflective mood: "Twenty years after the war and the things that followed it have become a bad dream from which I long ago recovered."[10] The guns of war were again looming. She spoke of the "end of life," of having taken life too seriously, of making adjustments to old habits. Yet, she recognized that her dominant preoccupation was that of welfare worker—social activist, in twentieth-century parlance. In wanting to do and to help, she had not always been successful for herself or for those she tried to help: "Later, applying judgment to past experience, I decided that I was getting nowhere, so decided to concentrate on one individual, help him solve his problems and give him the best build up possible in order to let him find himself, if he can."[11] That one individual was, of course, Patrick Hanley. And although she had decided to conclude her memoir in 1939, Patrick Hanley's story had not yet come to a conclusion. Was she afraid the story might not have a satisfactory conclusion? Had she run out of ways and means to continue the struggle on his behalf? She had signed off on her memoir. "Passing Through" was concluded and would provide no more answers.

HANLEY WALKS

There were times when Annie longed for the quiet and simplicity of her "Studio" retreat, but she also took her own advice against isolating herself just to concentrate on writing. While living in Vancouver, she kept up her professional and social commitments. She became a director (1928–1929) and long-time member of the Vancouver Art, Historical and Scientific Association—the group that had nudged her into the local history arena. As president of the Vancouver and Mainland Branch of the Canadian Authors Association (1937–1938), she was also a member of the national council of the Canadian Authors Association and rubbed shoulders with some rather erudite literary company.

It was gratifying for Annie to be recognized in the association's journal as the author of *Mohawk Princess* and one of five of Vancouver's most successful authors for 1931. *Mohawk Princess* was a serious-minded, seriously researched biography, not a book to be lightly considered or chatted about by the average reader. It remained, until 1965, the standard biography (and a favourite of school and public libraries) of Pauline Johnson. In a minor "Pauline renaissance," starting in 1981, four more biographies were published, culminating in Charlotte Gray's *Flint and Feather: The Life and Times of E. Pauline Johnson*, published in 2002. Pauline and Annie have stood the test of time and continue to be popular with the discriminating collector of early Canadian literature.

Although the Depression brought reduced sales of books, magazines and newspapers and it was often assumed authors would write for no remuneration, Annie continued working with the CAA and drama and radio groups. The CAA activities complemented Annie's overtly patriotic involvement with the

Women's Branch of the Canadian Club. Formed in 1906 for the purpose of "promoting passion for Canada," the Canadian Club was designed for those of Mrs. Garland Foster's nationalistic fervour. When Lady Tweedsmuir, wife of the Governor General, visited Vancouver in 1936, Annie was honoured to present her with a copy of her Pauline Johnson biography. In 1938, Annie travelled to the interior of the province on a lecture tour. She spoke to women's Canadian Clubs in Rossland, Trail, Vernon and her former city of Nelson. Naturally her topics were Pauline Johnson and various anecdotes and curious facts from British Columbia history.

With the advent of the 1940s, Mrs. W. Garland Foster contributed fewer and fewer articles to the *Vancouver Province*. As a writer she had already completed several significant publications and had on her desk drafts of several works-in-progress. All represented considerable primary research. From all this research and poring-over of catalogues, she had encountered hundreds of references to works by British Columbian authors. She knew that this information, which she had recorded on 3 x 5-inch cards would be of interest to others. Annie therefore sought out additional references and compiled what she felt was the most useful piece of work in her entire personal bibliography.

It was not definitive, visually attractive or a bestseller, but "The British Columbia Authors' Index," compiled by Mrs. W. Garland Foster, MA and BLS, was a trailblazer in a bibliographic sense. In 1941, mimeographed copies of the eighty-four-page index (which excluded school textbooks or government publications) were sent to all public and educational libraries in the province. For the rest of her life, Annie endeavoured to keep this listing somewhat up to date, if only for her own use.

About this time, possibly as a diversion from the weightier concerns at the penitentiary and in the academic publishing industry, Annie took a renewed interest in her teaching profession. She produced a "health book for Canadian schools," which never saw publication, but a collaborative work with her friend Anne Grierson, *High Days and Holidays in Canada: A Collection of Holidays Facts for Canadian Schools,* published by Ryerson in 1938, has been a standard reference work for teachers and librarians until very recently. It was last reprinted in 1967.

Annie was always attracted to the heroes of discovery, adventure and rectitude, and as a child she absorbed such tales. For enjoyment and satisfaction, she created *The Makers of History* and Ryerson published the volume in 1946 as part of its *Gallery of Heroes* series for children. Leif Ericsson to Thomas Edison to Sir Wilfred Grenfell to Giuseppe Garibaldi and a dozen others were lionized as the makers of world history. Surprisingly, no Canadians qualified as makers of history. The book was reprinted in 1972 in an American Biography Index Reprint Series.

There may have been very good reasons why several of Annie's lengthy, most serious and thoughtful manuscripts remain unread and unpublished in the archives of the University of New Brunswick and the City of Nelson, British Columbia. There is now no likelihood that these books or critical essays will ever be published. Three of those manuscripts in the UNB collection, however, have attracted the attention of two graduate students at her alma mater, the University of New Brunswick. These students were amazed to realize that examples of Mrs. Garland Foster's research and composition had not been read by more than a handful of literary critics, colleagues or casual researchers.

Her manuscripts were not truly significant for their intellectual content, but rather for the forceful point of view she frequently adopted and the mindset of a very Canadian woman of her era. The depth of Annie's research was considerable (for the decade in which she was writing) and there are few Canadian female writers of non-fiction with whom to draw comparisons. In her MA thesis, Shannon Armstrong sets Annie's unpublished memoir "Passing Through," so heavily relied upon here, alongside her biography of Pauline Johnson. The similarities of the two characters are few—gender, country of birth, literary and poetic ambition. Mrs. Garland Foster, the biographer, in spite of her sensitivity and diligent research, could not accurately represent Johnson's cultural heritage. And her overt Canadian nationalism was quite distinct from the nationalism of the Mohawk Princess herself. Armstrong describes Garland Foster's efforts to depict an ethnicity not her own as an example of "cultural appropriation."

Until 1981, with the publication of Betty Keller's biography, Annie's was the only known biography of Pauline Johnson. As Johnson's popularity fluctuated, it seemed there was less and less interest in her style of poesy and her traditional Native stories. During the years the *Mohawk Princess* was a successful publication, Annie had also sold five brief articles that dealt with Johnson's life and works. She did, however, eventually appear to recognize the passing appeal of the biography. She noted to her friend Flora Burns in 1959, "of course were I writing it now, I should probably develop it quite differently."[1] Madeline Bassnett, a UNB archives student, was also quite taken with "Passing Through" and edited the work to twenty-nine pages. Bassnett also analyzed and drew insight into members of the Ross family from the dozen or so photographs in the collection. Annie had a way of fascinating and affecting lives!

"Indian Trails in Maple Land: Myths of Haida Land," a ninety-page collection of thirty-one Haida oral tales, also rests unread in the Annie Harvie Garland

Foster fonds at UNB. The title is a misnomer. The "maple" is not indigenous to the Haida homeland, Haida Gwaii (formerly known as the Queen Charlotte Islands). Annie Garland Foster gives no indication that she had ever visited the islands or, indeed, ever met a member of the Haida Nation. Annie was simply drawn to the richness and inherent value of the traditional Haida stories; she saw an opening in Canadian literature for a compilation of wonderful tales and was probably unaware of the conventions that governed the retelling of stories from an oral tradition. Annie wrote under the assumption that the Haida, along with other Native peoples, shared a Canadian identity with most other Euro-Canadians. Shannon Armstrong regrets that the writer "… valued her Western readership's understanding more than the voices of the Haida people."[2] Armstrong's thesis examines these and many more facets (mostly critically) of this collection of Haida stories. It appears that Annie was in need of a friendly but critical editor. Her style and grammar were also sometimes rudimentary.

A third unpublished typescript at UNB also describes a sector of the Canadian population that did not fit the 1930 Euro-Canadian colonial image. Shannon Armstrong identified the Doukhobors as another marginalized "subaltern group" that came under Annie Garland Foster's scrutiny. "The Canadian Doukhobors: A Study in Communism" was a 174-page manuscript that the author had genuinely hoped to see in print. The story of the Russian Doukhobors' journey to Canada in 1899 and their efforts to retain their cultural identity was very little known (and greatly misunderstood) in the mid-1930s. A much younger Annie Ross, however, had had first-hand knowledge of this "peculiar" people. She had first encountered the pacifist, agricultural community while teaching in Saskatchewan in 1907, then again in the Kootenay country of British Columbia around Cascade, Grand Forks and Nelson. Annie had first written about this unusual people[3] for *Saturday Night* in 1924. There she revealed the internal tensions within the community, describing leader Peter Verigin as "… a poseur of the most pronounced type…."[4] As a chronological history, "The Canadian Doukhobors" covered the material satisfactorily, but Armstrong again objects to Annie creating a history for a people who are not her own and whom she did not understand. Annie's terminology in describing various Doukhobor groups as "fanatics," "restless," "bizarre" and the community as "the problem," rather than a people, would be unacceptable in the twenty-first century. In 1936, when the story of the Doukhobors in Canada was far from over and the "peculiarities" arising from their beliefs far from resolved, Annie left her readers with hope "… that the Doukhobours will endeavour to adapt themselves to the citizenship of the country in which they reside."[5]

In her readings, writing and research, Mrs. W. Garland Foster came across as a great Canadian patriot. The theme of justice was also never far from her thoughts. And yet in her experiences with the individual she had resolved to champion, Patrick Hanley, Canadian justice was certainly not seen to be done. Remission Branch Director Gallagher never went long without receiving an initiative on behalf of Hanley. In February 1940, the Reverend Howard

The Reverend J. Dinnage Hobden of the John Howard Society of Vancouver was instrumental in obtaining Patrick Hanley's release from prison in 1945. Photo courtesy of the Rotarian, *v.92 #6 1958 p. 32–33.*

Ireland, retired penitentiary chaplain, respectfully advised Gallagher that claims of justice and well-being would best be served if Hanley was released. Hanley himself rewrote and resubmitted his previous petitions—twice in 1940. The review hinted at for 1941 did not produce a change of opinion and a history of the case prepared in 1942 appeared only briefly to tip the scale in Hanley's favour.

Nonetheless Hanley's list of supporters was growing. The very respected and compassionate executive secretary of the John Howard Society of British Columbia, Reverend J. Dinnage Hobden, wrote to Gallagher in October 1941 with interesting and relevant information: "There is at his [Hanley's] disposal a fully furnished cottage at White Rock, a rural settlement 30 miles from Vancouver, which has a property of 60 x 120 feet and has good garden facilities. It is expected that this would be transferred to him outright, so that it could be used as an asset in exchange for other property at any time."[6] There would be no doubt in Gallagher's mind from whence the offer for property in White Rock came!

W.B. Drader, a veteran and former comrade-in-arms of Pat Hanley, also came forward with a proposal. He needed help farming 160 acres near Lytton, British Columbia. Hanley could be of assistance there. Drader supplied references for his own character, but his offer was dismissed and an explanation regarding the rejection was deemed "contrary to our practice" by the authoritative Mr. Gallagher.

When the good Reverend Hobden of the John Howard Society was advised there would be no clemency, he pressed the case and requested psychiatric opinion be obtained from the staff at Vancouver General Hospital. This may (or may not) have led to Hanley being subjected to interviews with two more medical men. Dr. Manchester, an elderly gentleman with out-of-date methodology, found a "paranoidal type of mentality," while Dr. Davidson, a man of more modern techniques, found Hanley co-operative and concluded in his report of

March 1, 1943, that "there is no evidence of a psychosis at the present time....
There was nothing brought out in the history that would suggest that he is
dangerous or that there would be any risk in giving him his freedom."[7]

In January 1943, D. Wilson from the Remission Branch in Ottawa had con-
ducted some on-site investigation. He interviewed the prisoner and Reverend
Hobden, as well as a Mrs. Garland Foster: "Mrs. Foster recited at length the
efforts she had made from time to time to obtain Hanley's release.... She also
stated that if it would induce a favourable decision she would not only give
Hanley a home but would also marry him."[8] This was a gesture the Department
of Justice was not accustomed to acknowledging!

An *internal* communiqué of May 22, 1943, to the Minister of Justice, the
Honourable Louis St. Laurent, considered the recent Drader, Hobden and
Davidson correspondence: "In the circumstances, the undersigned has the honour to advise that PATRICK HANLEY be released, under the restraint of the Ticket of Leave, upon the additional condition that he immediately report to the Rev. J. Dinnage Hobden of the John Howard Society, Vancouver, B.C., and place himself under his directions; all arrangements to be made to the satisfaction of the Warden."[9] The undersigned was none other than M.F. Gallagher.

Louis St. Laurent, future Prime Minister of Canada. As Minister of Justice and Attorney General (1941–46), he played a key role in reviewing Hanley's petitions for release. Photo courtesy of Library and Archives Canada/C010461'.

If this document had been made public in any way, there would have been considerable cause for celebration. Gallagher's more liberal tone was seconded by Warden Meighen's annual reviews of 1943 and dragging on into 1944. However, the conflict-
ing opinions of the doctors, Davidson and Manchester, caused the Minister of
Justice to equivocate and call for further psychiatric assessment. Meanwhile,
Annie had introduced herself by way of correspondence to Mr. St. Laurent and
informed him that Mr. Hanley would soon be in receipt of a life insurance
policy amounting to $2,000. (No doubt she was responsible for the annual
premiums while Hanley was incarcerated.)

Dr. J.P.S. Cathcart, Chief Neuropsychiatrist for the Department of Pensions and National Health was provided with a selection of background reports. He immediately set off for New Westminster where he spent June 24, 1944, entirely in the company of prisoner #3129. Cathcart's report of July 11 was five typewritten single-spaced foolscap pages. So thorough was the report that it could stand alone as an analytical biography of Patrick Hanley. A very brief, casual preliminary report dated July 3, 1944, and addressed to Gallagher at the Remission Branch summarized Cathcart's findings: "The gist of these notes and the impressions, is that this convict is not insane, nor is he presenting any mental symptoms whatever, further I have my doubts whether he was ever insane in the usual meaning of that term."[10] Cathcart would discuss his findings soon with Dr. Davidson and Dr. Mathers (of the 1925–6 trials) and the warden. The doctors ultimately concurred with Cathcart's conclusion that there was no evidence of psychosis and likely never was.

In December 1944, Annie, unaware of these momentous discussions within the Department of Justice regarding Hanley's mental state, reminded the Honourable Minister of Justice of her nearly twenty-year involvement in efforts to obtain Hanley's parole. Her plea to be allowed more frequent visits, should it not be the intention of the Ministry to ever release him, was somewhat pathetic and heart-wrenching. This appeal elicited the customary note from Gallagher informing her that the matter had been referred to the Acting Superintendent of Penitentiaries.

On March 9, 1945, in an internal memorandum from a Mr. Warnock to his superior in the Remission Branch, Mr. Gallagher summarized the numerous documents created by alienists, psychiatrists, jury and judge that had considered Hanley's sanity over the past twenty years. If he was sane, when was he sane? Warnock concluded the case was worthy of clemency. Five days later, Gallagher typed a memo to the Minister of Justice using exactly the same wording of recommendation that he had in May of 1943 (see endnote 9)! The Minister then pencilled a notation to the effect that refusal of clemency would not be "within clemency practice."

As the final parole documents were being prepared, the insightful Mr. Warnock of the Remission Branch did rather unhelpfully point out that if Hanley was not insane at the time of the murder, then there was no reason to commute the death sentence. Might not war injuries and their consequences have been the basis for early clemency and commutation? However, once the order was given, red tape appeared to dissolve. A Ticket of Leave Licence document was issued to Patrick Hanley on May 27, 1945, with copies distributed throughout the bureaucracy. To the standard conditions of release, the following was added:

"That he immediately report to Reverend J. Dinnage Hobden of Vancouver and place himself under his supervision; all the arrangements to be made to the satisfaction of the Warden."[11] In the continued correspondence exchanged on behalf of Mr. Hanley, the Under-Secretary of State, Ph. Thibault, informed Mrs. W. Garland Foster of Hanley's liberation. Hanley would be required to present himself once a month indefinitely to the chief of police in Vancouver.

On April 5, 1945, Patrick Hanley "walked." He was escorted from the British Columbia Penitentiary by the Reverend Hobden.

WHITE ROCK AT HOME

*A*nnie Ross Foster was seventy years old when she wed Patrick Hanley. She had been a widow for nearly twenty-seven years. Her groom was a fifty-seven-year-old bachelor. Although Annie had told Mr. Wilson of the Remission Branch in January 1943 that she would marry Hanley if that would "induce a favourable decision," it was by no means a condition of Hanley's Ticket of Leave that he should accept or offer a proposal of marriage to Mrs. Garland Foster. Inducement or not, Annie and Pat (as he would henceforth be called) exchanged vows on April 21, 1945—sixteen days following his release. Pat joined his wife at her residence, "The Studio," in White Rock. Respectability had been achieved.

Gallagher and the Minister of Justice would no longer receive correspondence from Mrs. W. Garland Foster or Annie Foster. Instead, they would receive petitions to discontinue the requirement of Hanley's monthly reports by mail to the Vancouver City Police. Correspondence was now signed simply "Ann Hanley."

Her chief antagonist, Michael F. Gallagher, finally, after having served the Ministry of Justice with extreme (undue) bureaucratic diligence for twenty-eight years, retired in 1952. However, in February 1948, he expedited Mrs. Hanley's appeal to relieve her husband of the onus of reporting monthly to the Vancouver police. On the basis of a police report that "... he had conducted himself very favourably to date, ... and was in the employ of a real estate firm..."[1], Gallagher recommended that Hanley's Ticket of Licence be varied to require him to report monthly by mail to the Commissioner of the Royal Canadian Mounted Police in Ottawa. The variance was signed by the Governor

Simply Ann Hanley, retired writer and community worker, at her home in White Rock, BC, 1964. Ninety years of age, the writer poses for the camera, content in the company of her papers, her memories and her typewriter. Photo courtesy of the White Rock Museum and Archives.

General, Alexander of Tunis, on February 7, 1948. How the change in destination of reporting was perceived as a concession is rather peculiar!

Possibly Gallagher was mellowing or finally becoming attuned to changing attitudes towards parole and rehabilitation of prisoners. In 1949, he offered the kindly and capable Reverend Hobden of the British Columbia John Howard Society a position as the western representative of the Remission Branch. Before long, Hobden took the opportunity to raise the matter of the Hanley case. On April 8, 1949, he wrote to his superior regarding Hanley, noting the high esteem that the gentleman now enjoyed in White Rock: "There is no question but what his wife's influence has been an important factor in the acceptance of Hanley by the community."[2] Within the week, the Governor General signed another remission request and Hanley was relieved of making any report, monthly or otherwise, on his Ticket of Leave, so long as he was of good deportment. Patrick Hanley was truly a free man. A conclusive RCMP report written in January 1955 confirmed his various business activities over the previous ten years and his general standing in the community. Throughout the course of the previous decade, Annie and Pat (and no doubt, their closest friends) tried to ensure that almost no one became aware of Pat's serious criminal record.

Nonetheless, there was an underground current of speculation about the man from Annie's past who had suddenly become her husband. Neither Pat nor Annie denied or corrected the local perception that Pat had been a wartime friend of her first husband, William Garland Foster. This seemed a very plausible explanation for their long-standing, if remote, friendship. Under any circumstances or conditions, the woman had taken a serious risk in linking her life with a man she hardly knew outside of a prison setting. Nearly twenty years had passed since they both resided and worked in the Nelson–Trail area.

This was not a marriage based on love or affection, nor was it entirely a marriage of "convenience." Hanley needed a benefactor/benefactress. He emerged into a world much different than the one from which he was removed in 1926. In 1945, a new generation of young men was returning from yet another devastating war and was experiencing the same traumas that had so affected his life. Business practices and social situations had changed immensely during his years of confinement. Annie, although thoroughly accustomed to managing her own affairs, needed assistance in her beloved garden and possibly a companion. The marriage was largely a measure of Annie's lifelong tenacity to a cause and a case.

By all unofficial accounts, Pat Hanley of the 1940s, 1950s and 1960s was a somewhat brusque and unpleasant fellow. He was still quick to take umbrage and had difficulty settling into a career. Initially he purchased a dry-cleaning and tailoring business in White Rock, but within a year gave this up for a position with a real estate firm. In 1950, he established Moss and Hanley Ltd., a realty and life insurance outfit. Hanley's office quarters migrated several times up and down the Johnston Street and 152nd Street business section of White Rock. He experienced a rift with the Fraser Valley Real Estate Board in 1960 but continued in business until 1969, when he finally retired at the age of eighty-one.

One old friend of Annie's observed, many years after her death, that Pat "did not make her happy." This statuesque, matronly woman was a presence in the White Rock community. Mrs. Foster/Hanley's literary and organizational abilities and intelligence were held in awe by those she encountered. It did not appear that Patrick Hanley was capable of appreciating a very great kindness that had been given to him, nor the woman ultimately responsible for saving his life.

Marriage, such as it was, did not seriously interfere with Annie's literary career. She had several major research projects in progress and she had a backlog of topics to investigate. In 1946, Annie was also in a mood to take inventory of her life, her achievements and her unfulfilled literary dreams. She busied herself with her papers, index cards, typewriter and the correspondence that already occupied several cabinets and files in her "Studio" home. Some sort of order, with an eye to the preservation of her published and unpublished words and works, should be established.

In 1945, Dr. Alfred Goldsworthy Bailey, head of the History Department at the University of New Brunswick, had written to Annie. Bailey inquired about her well-being as an early graduate of the university and about her literary career. He asked her if she would care to write a brief account of the intellectual influences she experienced as an undergraduate. Annie responded with a brief reflection on the intellectually stimulating times of fifty years ago. Her rather dreamy article was published in a November 1946 edition of the student newspaper, *The Brunswickan*. Annie noted that one of the paramount forces in her academic experience, and a man for whom she had a great affection, was Dr. Loring W. Bailey, professor of sciences and mathematics. Coincidentally, Loring Bailey was the grandfather of Dr. Alfred Bailey.

Annie had attended University of New Brunswick reunions and functions whenever she visited Fredericton or her family in Maine. Her commitment to her alma mater was sincere and based as well on her deep heritage in the province of New Brunswick. In 1946, Annie commenced depositing her papers and manuscripts with the University Library. She had every confidence in Dr. Bailey, who was also chief executive officer for the library (1946–1960). Hence, the archival fonds of Annie Harvie (Ross) Foster Hanley was created at the University of New Brunswick Archives. Into the fonds, Annie committed her unpublished manuscripts, including her cherished "Passing Through" memoir, a selection of family photographs, newspaper and biographical clippings, copies of articles she had published and the occasional bit of correspondence. The fonds also contains three major works that Annie had great hopes would be published. Her biography of Conservative Prime Minister Arthur Meighen, on which she had laboured since 1940, underwent its final revision in 1960, and not long afterwards was quietly laid to rest in the file box at the archives. She presumed her subject, despite the clever title, "The Inscrutable Canadian," was

PAGE 8 First Section - The Woodstock Bugle, Wednesday, July 17, 1974

Obituaries

ANNIE HARVIE (ROSS) HANLEY

The funeral of Annie Harvie (Ross) Hanley a one-time Woodstock resident, was held on Friday, June 21, 1974 from Chapel Hill Funeral Home, White Rock, B.C. She had been in ill health the past three years.

Mrs. Hanley is survived by her husband, Pat Hanley of White Rock, B.C., two nieces, Mrs. Robert Blaisdell, Franklin, Maine, Mrs. Marshall Crandall, Hallowell, Maine, and two nephews, J.R. Ross, Caledonia, N.S., and Dr. C.G. Ross, Woodstock.

Annie Harvie (Ross) Hanley was born Feb. 15, 1875, in Fredericton, one of three children of Robert Fulton Ross and Christine (Doak) Ross. J. Loggie Ross and Mrs. Margaret Homer died before her.

Mrs. Hanley attended grade school in Woodstock, receiving a county scholarship to the University of New Brunswick in 1892. She graduated in 1896 with a Bachelor of Arts degree, majoring in English and a grammar school teaching license.

She trained as a nurse next in Philadelphia Polyclinic under one of the world renounced Florence Nightingale's graduates. She was employed as matron of Woodstock's first hospital on Broadway Avenue in 1903 for one year and then returned to hospital and private nursing duties in Philadelphia. On a doctor's recommendation she then went west where she taught school in Regina and Saskatoon, and later in 1909 after moving to Nelson, B.C., she taught and served as school principal.

In 1914 she married her first husband, Capt. W. Garland Foster, one time editor of Nelson Daily News. Later when her husband was posted overseas, she joined him in England where she worked as a nursing sister with the British Red Cross for nearly two years. After the death of her husband, less than two months before the Armistice in November 1918, she returned to British Columbia and Nelson where she was elected to the city council.

In the mid-twenties she began writing seriously with her overseas experiences providing the material. This included magazine articles for the Province and book length writings after moving to Vancouver in 1926. Her first book was "The Mohawk Princess" on the life of Pauline Johnson. She was a charter member of the Canadian Author's Association from 1920. Attended McGill University in 1932 where she took a library course. Later earned her master's degree in English at the University of New Brunswick and studied at the University of Washington. For several years prior to 1973 she was actively researching and writing a book on the life of the late Dr. W.D. Rankin, of Woodstock, which was never published.

In 1927 she took up summer residence in White Rock, and spent her winters in Vancouver where she pursued her writing career, resulting in several books and hundreds of published articles, some of which are in the Woodstock public library. In 1945 she married Patrick Hanley, and moved to White Rock for year-round residence.

Woodstock, New Brunswick, and the Woodstock Bugle of July 17, 1974, remember one of the city's more accomplished personalities, Annie Harvie (Ross) Hanley. The condensed obituary gives little recognition to her works as Mrs. Garland Foster. Image courtesy of Charles Gordon Ross.

by then out of fashion or her efforts unappreciated. Judgment has already been passed on Annie's "The Canadian Doukhobor" and "Indian Trails in Maple Land" manuscripts. The "Index of British Columbia Authors" and its supplements, although never published, was of great advantage to researchers and librarians who came across it in public and academic libraries. Until authorized and systematized bibliographies and *Books in Print* annuals appeared, Annie's 3 x 5 cards proved very useful. In correspondence with the University Archives, she bequeathed publication rights to her unpublished manuscripts to the University of New Brunswick. She would not give up hope that her works would one day be of interest to historians and researchers. Her fonds also contains a typewritten document, "Partial Check List Fugitive Articles Etc.," which is just as the title suggests—an incomplete list of the lesser or brief articles that saw print under Annie's byline between 1923 and 1945. The "Fugitive List" of approximately a hundred and forty entries shows the depth and variety of articles she wrote out of interest and of need, and leads to a closer understanding and appreciation of Annie Ross Foster Hanley and her works.

Not all of Annie's works are in the care of the archivists at the University of New Brunswick. British Columbia's Touchstones Nelson: Museum of Art and History owns two hefty manuscripts: "Plant Hunters and Plant Breeders" (329 pages) and "Heroes of Health: 31 heroes from Hippocrates to Otto Meyerhoff" (187 pages). Have these manuscripts ever been revealed to the light beyond the Archives Room at Touchstones Nelson? Possibly only the Nelson archivist and this biographer are aware of the existence of these typescripts. What a shame. Each manuscript represents an immense amount of concentration and composition, and information that remains valid after sixty years.

Special Collections at the University of British Columbia Library holds a sixteen-page biographical manuscript of Rocky Mountain surveyor, Walter Moberly. The City of Trail and the Provincial Archives of British Columbia have original typescripts of Annie's 1938 article on the construction of the Dewdney Trail, the first government-sponsored wagon route west–east across southern British Columbia. This article was unfortunately usurped by the publication of two similar articles by reputable provincial historians in British Columbia historical journals about the same time. Provincial Librarian Dr. W. Kaye Lamb also detected a couple of errors in Annie's research and could not, therefore, recommend her Dewdney Trail study for publication.

When Annie ceased trying to keep her "Index of British Columbia Authors" up to date, she undertook what at first appeared to be a more reasonable bibliographic challenge. She would assemble an "Index of British Columbia Newspapers" in the form of a list of newspapers past and present. She accomplished this feat without the aid of previous catalogues or databases by ferreting out names of newspapers from directories and histories but primarily through letters and more letters of inquiry to major libraries and archives. Mrs. Hanley's polite, but lengthy, queries to Provincial Librarian and Archivist Willard Ireland during the early 1960s finally elicited a response: "I am afraid … we cannot cope with your enquiry."[3]

Some of Annie's newspaper file cards remain, unedited and unpublished, in safekeeping in the Touchstones Nelson archives. In the late 1960s, Annie entrusted her "Index of British Columbia Newspapers" file to the librarian of Notre Dame University of Nelson. When that institution closed, the local Kootenay collection of documents and photographs was transferred to the city's Museum and Archives (now Touchstones Nelson).

It is quite probable that some of Annie Foster Hanley's essays and research have simply gone missing and others may not have been written. There is no trace of a "Fathers of Confederation" text supposedly written in 1962, a health book for children, a draft work on Dr. W.D. Rankin of Woodstock, New Brunswick, a radio drama called "His Last Duchess" or several children's tales.

There was always something or someone next on her agenda. Annie longed to write a biography of Sir George Eulas Foster (1847–1931), the New Brunswick and Canadian diplomat for whom she had undertaken a study on the English toy industry in 1916. Sir George's political career was lengthy and frequently controversial. He was often satirized in the press and on one occasion held up as a "pecksnif"—one addicted to fatuous and hypocritical talk of benevolence. Annie felt he was a fascinating figure to present in print and had bid for the opportunity to contribute to a biography. However, Sir George's widow, Lady Foster, wanted strict editorial control of the text and William S. Wallace was chosen to write the Foster memoir, which was published in 1933. Wallace, Chief Librarian at the University of Toronto and editor of the *Canadian Historical Review*, was pretty stiff competition for an author with only one biography to her credit. Ultimately, as Annie confessed to Dr. Bailey in 1947, "in the end I was glad [that I did not get the contract], as I am afraid I might have been more difficult than Wallace was about cutting. It was just too bad that the love affair was passed over, as it showed Sir George in a quite different attitude than he seemed in later years."[4]

Regardless of a continuing economic need to write and pursue a career in writing Annie (and later Pat) were in the forefront of civic events and issues in White Rock. They always took time to respond to needs and causes to be addressed in the growing community. Pat was still very much a newcomer (and a curiosity) in White Rock, but in 1945, Annie became chairman of the newly formed Women's Civic League. The league's initial purpose was to protest against a 40 per cent increase in tax rates but it moved on to urge progress on sewage system installation as well.

In 1947, a movement to raise funds and build a hospital in the adjacent growing neighbourhood of Surrey was underway. Pat and his friend Bob Grierson initiated a similar project aimed at acquiring a hospital for White Rock. The gentlemen opened an account, deposited fifty dollars each, rallied the local business community, called a public meeting and thus created the White Rock Hospital Society. It was not until November 1952 that sod was turned for the construction of a forty-five-bed White Rock Hospital, but Pat and Ann Hanley are remembered as ardent, early supporters of the community health facility. As White Rock loyalists, and like many business people in the White Rock

The City of Nelson, BC, remembers Annie Garland Foster, teacher, politician, veterans' and public health advocate, journalist. In 2006, a recently developed street near Miss Ross's Hume School was named Foster Place. Back row: author Frances Welwood, Agnes Gibson Baker (see photo p. 160), Michelle Mungall (City Councillor). Front row: Foster Place residents Kyle and Ashley Hall, children of Nelson Daily News *editor Bob Hall. Photo by Ron Welwood.*

community, Pat and Annie also supported the secession of White Rock from the Municipality of Surrey, favouring instead the incorporation of the Municipality of White Rock, which came about in 1957.

Like many seniors, especially those with a passion for history, Annie became engrossed in her own family story. She had outlined her Scottish-Canadian heritage quite capably in a very human way in her "Passing Through" memoir and in a twelve-page document entitled "Some Account of the Families of James Ross, Donald McDonald, Joseph Story, James Doak and Their Descendants," specially compiled for the University of New Brunswick Archives. However, she recognized that within her mother's family, the Doaks of the Doaktown, New Brunswick, settlement, there were more stories to tell. Unlike most family history followers, the medical and genetic aspects of marriage and intermarriages within families also motivated Annie. Although she was not qualified to make more than casual observations in this regard, she felt such information would be useful to future generations. Annie collaborated with a Fredericton relative, Mrs. Louise Bamford, on the Doak history. In 1968, when she was ninety-three, Annie wrote to her friend Gretchen Gibson in Nelson describing her collaboration. Louise would do the genealogical research, while Annie provided anecdotal materials—with special interest in the family feuds. Annie completed her share of the project in July 1969. However, "The Doaks of Doaktown" was never completed. The authors disagreed on what material to include and gracefully parted company on the project. Annie could not continue alone and it was 1989 before Louise published *The Bamford Saga.* This volume was a genealogical

216 PASSING THROUGH MISSING PAGES

compilation of some Doak family lineages. There were no stories, scandals or adventures such as Annie envisaged.

⟶

Letters—Annie had written and received thousands of them over the years! Regrettably, very little correspondence of a personal nature has survived. There are a few personal exchanges with her long-time Nelson friend, Gretchen Phair Gibson, and the friendly archival banter with Dr. Alfred Bailey of the University of New Brunswick. As a researcher, Annie would have appreciated the insights revealed in personal correspondence, yet she made no effort to include her letters among her papers.

Charlotte Gray, a noted Canadian biographer, feels that sometimes letters are more revealing than even journals or diaries. Letters are more calculated and organized and the writer aims to convey a definite impression and tone. Like journals and diaries, memoirs are a one-way conversation, anticipating no conversation or response. Annie's "Passing Through" is an example of that one-way conversation.

In the years following the completion of "Passing Through," Annie was extremely selective in the materials and written information she willed to future generations. There may be the occasional reference to Pat in the few personal letters, but there are certainly no references to the Hanley criminal case. Most copies of Annie's letters on deposit in archives and government files are formal communications and deal with matters of fact, requests and forceful opinions. Particularly in the Hanley case, the letters are the material of judicial and government files only.

The lengthy correspondence between Remission Branch Chairman Gallagher and Mrs. Garland Foster was formal but took on the manner of a personal exchange. Undoubtedly both correspondents formed definite opinions as to how the other spoke, dressed and comported himself/herself. A fictionalized face-to-face encounter would have been a memorable moment. Gallagher would have addressed Mrs. Foster as "My good woman"; Annie would have replied in stern but charming tones, "Sir, I beg you to consider…."

Although Annie did not share her correspondence regarding the Hanley case, we must remember that there are in existence many memoranda, reports, judgments, analyses, internal correspondence and documents comprising the Hanley file that passed across Ministry of Justice and other government desks between 1926 and 1955. The names Annie Foster and Ann Hanley are on a good number of these documents. I daresay Annie would be rather piqued to realize that in the twenty-first century it is now possible to learn the details of what was for her a very lengthy and very private crusade.

One of Annie Foster Hanley's most loyal and trusted friends was Margaret Lang Hastings of White Rock. Margaret was a newspaperwoman with the *White Rock Sun,* a local historian and a great admirer of the spirit and dedication of her literary mentor. On a personal level, Margaret was very protective of Annie's private life. Mrs. Hanley was charming, intelligent and encouraging. The reporter never forgot Annie's birthday. On or near Annie's 89th, 93rd, 94th and 95th birthdays, the *White Rock Sun* featured an article and photograph of the community's literary wonder. The biographical data was always the same. Annie had three careers (teacher, nurse and writer), two husbands, a great-great-grandfather who lived to be 104, hundreds of published articles, and had just completed a manuscript and was in the throes of researching another. Mrs. Hanley could be counted on to supply a positive get-up-and-go quotation. On her ninety-fourth birthday, she explained: "Once committed to writing you just cannot give it up!"[5]

"It has been a long life...."[6] mused Annie on the final page of her memoir in 1939—when she was sixty-three. At age ninety-nine, Annie Harvie Ross Garland Foster Hanley passed away on June 18, 1974, at the Florence Nightingale Private Hospital in Whalley, British Columbia, not far from her home and studio at White Rock. One and a half years later, Pat Hanley died, on December 16, 1975.

L'ENVOI

Reflecting on Annie's long and productive life one finds elements of sadness, humour, intelligence and determination, but few expressions of joy or happiness. Her Ross and Doak family history and upbringing were not unusual; Annie was neither challenged nor privileged in ways uncommon to her contemporaries. What made Annie Ross Foster Hanley the woman she became was her ability and her willingness to make a difficult decision when it was required of her and to carry through with grit and conviction until the goal was accomplished or it was time to change direction. These attributes were exemplified by her thirty-year marathon in championing the legal, medical and what would later be called "the human rights" case of Patrick Hanley.

The schoolgirl and schoolteacher Annie or Nan Ross; the nurse, officer's wife, politician and writer Annie Garland Foster; and Ann Hanley, the senior activist and journalist—all made independent, career and personal choices considerably more significant than those asked of most women during her time. Choices of a different nature were made when, in 1939, she examined her life and selected for her memoir anecdotes she deemed to be of interest and value to "future psychologists." Choices were many, but regrets were few. If only she hadn't taken it all quite so seriously and shown a little levity along the way!

Annie was extremely serious about her academic and nurses' training. It was a great privilege for a young woman at that time to receive such educational opportunities. She would never cease learning. Her aptitude and near-obsession with various manifestations of mental illness permitted her an elemental insight into the phenomenon of post-traumatic stress disorder.

The women's movement proved a conundrum in her early years. It was unattractive to be a suffragette in the early twentieth century, but the reality and the desperate effects of the Great War on women and children led Annie to realize that there was no other choice. Respect for women and the dignity of the person overrode her reluctance to brazenly speak out. Within months of her widowhood, she became (although in denial of the title!) the epitome of the suffragette. In taking on candidacy for public office, she urged women to join her in exercising their new franchise and responsibility.

Annie Garland Foster Hanley was not a particularly charismatic figure, although she was respected, capable and frequently intimidating. She was much more than the sum of her writings. In fact, Annie is an example of a person with unexceptional (even modest) literary abilities, but with a decidedly forceful point of view, who made a living and through her varied professions, made a difference.

Her life is worth recording. With no immediate family to preserve her memory and her accomplishments, Annie made another "choice" in 1990—this time, posthumously. The Nelson Museum was then creating an exhibition in honour of the women of early Nelson. Quite unexpectedly, Annie rose from her seat at the 1920 Nelson City Council table and invited this author to tell her story. Only the briefest outline of Annie and William Garland Foster's Nelson days along with some crumbling newspaper clippings and a series of cross-references were available in the archives file folder marked "Annie Garland Foster." Had Annie anticipated the much later observation of a thoughtful writer and editor? Did she realize that the biographer does not find the subject; rather, the subject finds the biographer?

AFTERWORD

*N*inety-nine years and nearly as many accomplishments. Thirty-seven years since her death and Annie Harvie Ross Garland Foster Hanley remains an enigmatic but also magnetic figure. My investigation into her life has been as thorough as reasonably possible and yet I cannot be confident that I have neatly explained or justified my friend Annie's actions, her dreams, her loves or even her ambitions.

One hopes that at the end of her long life, Annie was content with her victories, big and small. She was obviously encouraged sufficiently by her accomplishments to continue her efforts for social and personal justice until the very last years of her life. Annie must have realized that she did make a difference.

She had saved a man from the gallows. She had nursed the wounded of World War I and obtained a measure of assistance for the widows and children of the fallen. Like many others, she brought education, national pride and health protection to the children of remote rural communities. At a time when women were barely credited with the right and ability to vote in public elections, Mrs. Garland Foster dared to put herself forward to challenge the voters and the male opponents for civic election in a tight-knit, but very young and inexperienced city.

Annie Ross was a product of her times, her country and her upbringing. Her life was governed by a sense of propriety, patriotism, conduct and responsibility. Education expanded her horizons but also challenged the rules and manners inculcated in her upbringing. Following her mid-life experiences during World War I, Annie found herself conflicted or confused by injustices and suffering resulting from rigid adherence to pre-war rules of governing and behaviour. In many incidences she came into opposition with the old ways and the old way of thinking… and yet, she clung to the security of accepted rules of personal behaviour and gentility. The world had changed irrevocably. She must change with it and foster the positive aspects generated by the cataclysmic times. Balance must be sought also in her personal life. She must make a living. Teaching, nursing, writing would serve this purpose as well as engage her passions and talents. Annie Harvie Ross Garland Foster Hanley is not a figure of national significance or notoriety. Nonetheless, as a personality she is unique, intriguing and now her story has been told.

It has been a fascinating and sometimes frustrating experience to walk, read and talk with Annie as she searched for a pathway "passing through" traditional conduct and twentieth-century notions of justice and social responsibility.

Not until deep into my fascination and research with Annie did I realize that I was encountering elements of my own upbringing in Vancouver of the 1940s and 1950s. I was also recalling the conflicts and questioning inherent in the lives of "my two Marys," to whom this book is dedicated. My mother, Mary Devereux Clay (1908–1997), was a self-educated, caring woman who spoke and wrote her mind on political and religious issues with authority and respect. My sister, Mary Catherine Clay Paterson (1940–1987), was in the forefront of the establishment of women's centres and transition homes in North Vancouver. She too was a caring mother who spoke her mind on matters of concern to the women's movement of the 1980s. I am proud to have shared in the lives of all three women.

August 2011

ACKNOWLEDGEMENTS

INDIVIDUALS

Special thanks to Ron Welwood and Verna Relkoff.

Ted Affleck	Shannon Armstrong	Agnes Gibson Baker
Louise Bamford	Madeline Bassnett	Patricia Belier
Isabell Brinley	Ian Currie	Anne Edwards
Alistair Fraser	Ralph Friesen	Margaret Lang Hastings
Joe Irving	Ted Jones	Percy Livingstone
Floyd Low	Shirley Miller	Greg Nesteroff
Tim Pearkes	Alan Ramsden	Patricia Rogers
Andrew Ross	Dr. Gordon Ross	Palmer Rutledge
Michael Savill	Greg Scott	Ken Welwood

INSTITUTIONS

Especially University of New Brunswick Archives and Special Collections for permission to quote extensively from manuscripts in the Annie Harvie (Ross) Foster Hanley fonds MG L7.

Nelson, British Columbia and Area
City of Nelson
City of Trail Archives: Sarah Benson
Golden and District Museum: Colleen Palumbo

Touchstones Nelson: Museum of Art and History, Shawn Lamb Archives:
    Shawn Lamb, Laura Fortier
Nelson Municipal Library: Helen Blum and Anne DeGrace
Selkirk College Library: Judy Deon

Vancouver, British Columbia and Area
British Columbia Courthouse Library Society
Davis and Company, Vancouver
Fraser Valley Real Estate Board
Jewish Historical Society of British Columbia: Diane Rogers, Cyril Leonoff
Simon Fraser University Library
University of British Columbia Library, Special Collections
Vancouver Art Gallery Library
Vancouver City Archives
Vancouver City Museum
Vancouver Public Library, Northwest Collection
White Rock Museum and Archives: Hugh Ellenwood

Victoria, British Columbia
British Columbia Archives
Legislative Library of British Columbia
McPherson Library, University of Victoria
Victoria Public Library

Saskatchewan and Manitoba
Manitoba Legislative Library
Mortlach Historical Society: Marilyn Forbes
Rosthern Community Library
Saskatoon City Archives
Saskatoon Public Library, Local History Department
University of Saskatchewan Library, Special Collections: Linda Fritz

New Brunswick
Atlantic Salmon Museum, Doaktown
Carleton County Archives, Woodstock
Harriet Irving Library, Archives and Special Collections, University of
    New Brunswick
L.P. Fisher Public Library, Woodstock: Greg Campbell

Museum Services, Heritage Branch, Wellness, Culture and Sport,
    New Brunswick
Provincial Archives of New Brunswick
School Days Museum, Fredericton
University of New Brunswick Alumni Association

Canada
Dalhousie University Archives, Halifax, Nova Scotia
Library and Archives Canada
Mills Memorial Library, McMaster University, Hamilton, Ontario
University of Toronto Library

United States and Britain
British Library, Rare Books Division
McLean Hospital, Belmont, Massachusetts
Providence Rhode Island Public Library
Shaw-Savill Lines, Great Britain: Mike Foreman
Thomas Jefferson University Archives and Special Collections, Philadelphia,
    Pennsylvania
University of Pennsylvania Public Service Archives and Records Centre,
    Philadelphia, Pennsylvania

APPENDIX

WORKS BY ANNIE GARLAND FOSTER

The author has attempted to locate or identify the written works of Annie Harvie Ross (Garland) Foster Hanley. Other than her "Partial Checklist of Fugitive Articles" and a helpful list of what she felt were her significant writings compiled for her newspaper friends, Annie did not attempt to ensure there existed one complete list of her published, unpublished or in-progress works. Many items from her "Fugitive" list could not be verified, yet they have been noted in this bibliography.

BOOKS

Foster, Annie H. and Anne Grierson. *High Days and Holidays in Canada*. Toronto: Ryerson, 1938.

Foster, Annie H. *Makers of History*. Toronto: Ryerson, 1946.

———. *Mohawk Princess: being some account of the life of Tekahion-Wake E. Pauline Johnson*. Vancouver, BC: Lion's Gate Publishing, 1931.

VERIFIED NEWSPAPER ARTICLES (LISTED IN CHRONOLOGICAL ORDER)

"Landmarks of Nelson: Queen City of the Kootenays." *Vancouver Province*, 10 May 1925: 3.

"Remarkable Discovery of Work of Famous U.S. Artist." *Vancouver Province* Magazine, 22 May 1925: 3.

"The Dr. Briggs Collection." *Vancouver Province*, 30 August 1925.

"Rover Drinks from the Fountain." *Vancouver Province* Magazine, 6 September 1925: 8.

"How the Woolly Bear Spent His Months in the Winter." *Vancouver Province* Magazine, 4 October 1925: 8.

"Little Willie Mouse Learned a Sad Lesson." *Vancouver Province* Magazine, 18 October 1925: 8.

"Mistletoe Tradition." *Vancouver Province* Magazine, 20 December 1925: 3.

"Famous Coast Indian Stone." *Vancouver Province*, 15 March 1926: 3.

"How Canada's Parliament Moved to Ottawa." *Vancouver Province* Magazine, 4 April 1926: 83.

"The University of New Brunswick—Alma Mater." *Vancouver Province*, 18 April 1926.

"Ely Cathedral." *Vancouver Province* Magazine, 3 October 1926: 9.

"The Vancouver Water Clock." *Vancouver Province* Magazine, 28 November 1926: 3.

"Bones for Fido." *Vancouver Province*, 4 February 1928: 6.

"Canterbury Cathedral." *Vancouver Province* Magazine, 19 February 1928.

"Memory of Indian Poetess Links East and West." *Vancouver Province* Magazine, 4 March 1928: 4.

"Romance of the Mohawk Brooches." *Vancouver Province* Magazine, 6 May 1928: 5.

"Romance of the Mohawk Brooches Part II." *Vancouver Province* Magazine, 27 May 1928: 3.

"Church Has Seen Eleven Centuries." *Vancouver Province* Magazine, 10 June 1928: 5.

"City's Art Gallery in 1887." *Vancouver Province* Magazine, 15 July 1928: 4.

"Beauties of Skidegate." *Vancouver Province* Magazine, 30 September 1928: 9.

"First Mayor of Vancouver Drew No Salary." *Vancouver Province*, 28 October 1928: 9.

"Growing Old Gracefully." *Vancouver Province* Magazine, 13 January 1929.

"First Gold Rush in BC." *Vancouver Province* Magazine, 17 February 1929.

"Chasing Literature." *Vancouver Province*, 20 February 1929.

"Distinguished Canadian Artist." *Vancouver Province* Magazine, 3 March 1929.

"The Dream Girl of the Pacific." *Vancouver Province* Magazine, 10 March 1929.

"A Word-picture of Lisbeth." *Vancouver Province*, 21 April 1929: 5.

"From Hand to Mouth." *Vancouver Province*, 6 May 1929.

"Old Contemptibles." *Vancouver Province* Magazine, 19 May 1929.

"A True Bear Story." *Vancouver Province*, 6 July 1929: 6.

"Another Bear Story." *Vancouver Province*, 2 August 1929: 6.

"Buttered Toast." *Vancouver Province*, 1 September 1929: 6.

"Pomegranate." *Vancouver Province*, 24 November 1929: 6.

"Constancy." *Vancouver Province*, 20 February 1930: 6.

"In Semiahmoo Bay." *Vancouver Province* Magazine, 23 February 1930: 8.

"The Snowdrop." *Vancouver Province*, 12 March 1930: 6.

"Christmas Customs." *Vancouver Province* Magazine, 21 December 1930.

"Leaving Cats." *Vancouver Province*, 3 July 1931: 6.

"Chee Chee Protests Mr. Robin." *Vancouver Province*, 18 July 1931: 11.

"Adolescent Child Requires Patience and Understanding." *Vancouver Province*, 18 August 1931.

"Wanted—a Wife Unemployed." [byline Timothy O'Farrell] *Vancouver Province*, 17 October 1931.

"Youth and Optimism." *Vancouver Province*, 9 January 1932: 9.

"Maxstoke Castle." *Vancouver Province* Magazine, 29 November 1935: 9.

"Discovering Mount Baker." *Vancouver Province*, 4 July 1936: 6.

"Helen Randal—Popular Registrar of Nurses." *Vancouver Province*, 19 June 1937: 4.

"Hallowe'en." *Vancouver Province*, 30 October 1937: 6.

"Santa's Reindeer." *Vancouver Province*, 24 December 1937: 3.

"West Coast Totem Poles." *Vancouver Province*, 15 August 1942.

VERIFIED JOURNAL OR MAGAZINE ARTICLES (LISTED IN CHRONOLOGICAL ORDER)

"Magazines and Canadian Idealism." *Canadian Bookman* (May 1923): 131.

"Honey Sources of Kootenay." *Gleanings in Bee Culture*, Vol. 51 (November 1923): 735.

"Canadian Magazines." *Canadian Bookman* (December 1923): 341.

"Weaving—A Home Industry." *National Life* (April 1924): 20–1.

"Food Values." *National Life* (May 1924): 11, 19, 24.

"A Doomed Utopia." Saturday Night (14 June 1924): 3, 5. Reprinted on website "Explosion on the Kettle Valley Line: the death of Peter Verigin," http://www.canadianmysteries.ca/sites/verigin/archives/newspaperormagazinearticle/1656en.html.

"Lord Dunsany's Plays." *Canadian Bookman* (October 1924): 211.

"On Reflecting Canadian Life." *Canadian Bookman* (December 1924): 249.

"Drift Inn." *Western Home Monthly* (January 1925).

"Famous Old Mines of the Kootenay." *Mining Truth,* Vol. 11 (16 July 1925): 5–6.

"The Reward of Persistence." *Canadian Bookman,* Vol. 7, No. 11 (November 1925): 187.

"Stone Images and Implements, and Some Petroglyphs." *Museum Notes* (Art, Historical and Scientific Association of Vancouver), Vol. 1, No. 3 (October 1926): 14–6.

"The Case for Canadian Magazines." *Canadian Bookman,* Vol. 8, No. 11 (November 1926): 338–9.

"Graphic Arts of the Haidas." *Museum Notes* (Art, Historical and Scientific Association of Vancouver), Vol. 3, No. 1 (March 1928): 5–8.

"The First Art Association in Vancouver." *Museum Notes* (Art, Historical and Scientific Association of Vancouver), Vol. 3, No. 1 (September 1928): 3–4.

"The First Mayor of Vancouver." *Museum Notes* (Art, Historical and Scientific Association of Vancouver), Vol. 3, No. 3 (September 1928): 11–13.

"S.L. Howe, First Reeve of Point Grey." *Museum Notes* (Art, Historical and Scientific Association of Vancouver), Vol. 3, No. 3 (September 1928): 18–19.

"A Diana of the Mountains." *Western Home Monthly* (September 1929): 82, 85, 87.

"Les Pauvres and Its Artist." *Museum Notes* (Art, Historical and Scientific Association of Vancouver), Vol. 4, No. 2 (June 1929): 65–68.

"An Interesting Little Theatre Movement." *Western Home Monthly* (October 1929): 34, 84.

"Coals to Newcastle." *Western Home Monthly* (May 1930): 33, 49.

"The Difference." *Canadian Bookman,* Vol. 12, No. 4 (April 1930): 84.

"Drab Lives." *Canadian Bookman,* Vol. 13, No. 6 (1931): 124–5.

"The Lyric Beauty of Pauline Johnson's Poetry." *Canadian Bookman,* Vol. 16 (1934): 37, 43.

"Canadian Communists: The Doukhobor Experiment." *American Journal of Sociology,* 41 (1935): 327–40.

"Pauline Johnson's Gift to Vancouver." *Canadian Bookman,* Vol. 18, No. 6 (June 1936): 7–8.

"British Columbia Indian Lands." *Pacific Northwest Quarterly,* Vol. 28 (1937): 151–162.

"False Gods." *Dalhousie Review,* Vol. 18 (October 1938): 337–42.

"The Sonnet in Canadian Literature." *The British Annual of Literature,* Vol. 1 (1938).

"White Poppies." [sonnet] *The British Annual of Literature,* Vol. 2 (1939): 90.

"Flowers the Queen Saw." *Good Gardening* (September 1939).

"Vegetarians by Contract." *Dalhousie Review,* Vol. 20 (April 1940): 71–3.

"The Kitsilano Masks." *Canadian Geographical Journal,* Vol. 28, No. 2 (February 1944): 84–7.

"The Cup That Cheers." *The Garden Beautiful,* Vol. 9 (May 1946): 17–18.

"Bee Flowers." *The Garden Beautiful,* Vol. 9 (July 1946): 29–30.

"Intellectual Influences at UNB in the Nineties." *The Brunswickan* (29 November 1946): 7–9.

"Global State of Mind." *Saturday Night,* Vol. 64 (23 October 1948): 35.

"Andrew Onderdonk, Master Builder." *Pacific Northwest Quarterly,* Vol. 49, No. 4 (October 1958): 146–9.

"Pauline." *Canadian Author and Bookman,* Vol. 43 (Spring 1968): 18.

UNPUBLISHED MANUSCRIPTS/SOME UNVERIFIED (LOCATION SUPPLIED IF KNOWN)

Foster, Annie H. "Health Book for Canadian Schools." Submitted to Ginn and Co., Toronto, no date.

Foster, (Mrs.) W. Garland, comp. "British Columbia Authors' Index." Mimeographed, 115 pp. [Copies available at UBC Special Collections, Vancouver Public Library, UNB Archives].

Foster, (Mrs.) W. Garland. "The Canadian Doukhobors: A Study in Communism." Typewritten manuscript, 1935–1936. 175 pp. [UNB Archives & Special Collections. Annie Harvie (Ross) Foster Hanley fonds MG L7 Series 2, Box 2, File 5].

———. "The Dewdney Trail." Typewritten manuscript, 1938, 4 pp. [City of Trail BC Archives].

———. "His Last Duchess." Radio Drama, c. 1934 [no location].

———. "Intellectual Influences at UNB in the Nineties." Typewritten manuscript (photocopy), c. 1945 [University of New Brunswick Archives, MG L7, Series 2, Box 2, File 11].

———. "Indian Trails in Maple Land: Myths of Haida Land." (retold) Typewritten manuscript, c. 1946, 90 pp. [UNB Archives & Special Collections. Annie Harvie (Ross) Foster Hanley fonds, MG L7, Series 2, Box 2, File 10].

———. "The Inscrutable Canadian: A Life of the Right Honourable Arthur Meighen, K.C." Typescript, 1932–1935, 490 pp. and revised manuscript, 1960, 433 pp. [UNB Archives & Special Collections. Annie Harvie (Ross) Foster Hanley fonds, MG L7, Series 2, Box 1, Sub-series 2, File 2–3].

———. "A Little Garden by the Sea." n.d. [no location].

———. "Nelson Then and Now." Typescript, 1921–1923, 13 pp. [UBC Library. Special Collections].

———. "Partial Checklist of Fugitive Articles Etc. 1923–1945." Typescript, 1945, 5 pp. [UNB Archives & Special Collections. Annie Harvie (Ross) Foster Hanley fonds, MG L7, Series 2, Box 1, Sub-series 2, File 1].

———. "Passing Through: Pictures From the Life of Mrs. W. Garland Foster, née Annie H. Ross." Typescript, 1939, 248 pp. (missing pp. 227–232) [UNB Archives & Special Collections. Annie Harvie (Ross) Foster Hanley fonds, MG L7, Series 2, Box 2, File 6].

———. "Peter, a Spaniel—His Book." n.d. [no location].

———. re: Red Cross Anthology of Poetry. c. 1944 [no location].

———. "Walter Moberly, Pathfinder of the West." Typescript, c. 1940s, 16 pp. [UBC Library. Special Collections].

Hanley, Ann. re: Dr. W.G. Rankin of Woodstock, New Brunswick. c. 1960s [no location].

———. "Fathers of Confederation." n.d. [no location].

———. "Heroes of Health: 31 heroes from Hippocrates to Otto Meyerhoff." Typescript, 1945+, 187 pp. [Touchstones Nelson: Museum of Art & History. Archives. Annie Garland Foster fonds].

———. "Plant Hunters and Plant Breeders." Typescript, 1945+, 329 pp. [Touchstones Nelson: Museum of Art & History. Archives. Annie Garland Foster fonds].

———. "Prosody." n.d. [no location].

———. "Rocket, a Fox Terrier." n.d. [no location].

———. "Some Account of the Families of James Ross, Donald McDonald, Joseph Story, James Doak and Their Descendants." Typescript, 1959, 12 pp. [UNB Archives & Special Collections. Annie Harvie (Ross) Foster Hanley fonds, MG L7, Series 2, Sub-Series 2, Box 2, File 7].

UNVERIFIED NEWSPAPER, JOURNAL OR MAGAZINE ARTICLES (LISTED IN CHRONOLOGICAL ORDER)

"While East Is Bound in Snow." *Vancouver Province*, 21 April 1923.

"Nutrition and Food." *Canadian Home Journal* (May 1923).

"Has Canada an Emigration Problem." *Winnipeg Free Press*, 8 September 1923.

"Wild Salads." *Western Home Monthly* (October 1923).

"Happy Home Bees." *Gleanings* (November 1923).

"The Voice of the Prophets." *National Life* (December 1923).

"My Favorite Book." *National Life* (February 1924).

"Arbutus." *National Life* (February 1924).

"Twinflower." *National Life* (March 1924).

"Basis of Citizenship." *National Life* (July 1924).

"A New Idea in W.I." *Canadian Home Journal* (August 1924).

"Helping Nature." *Canadian Horticulture and Home Magazine* (October 1924).

"Nelson Mountaineering." *Canadian Pacific Rail...* [sic] (November 1924).

"Burial of Czar of Russia in Canada." *Saturday Night* (24 November 1924).

"Memories—A Lullaby." *Canadian Bookman* (December 1924).

"Snake and Mouse." *Vancouver Province*, 4 October 1925.

"First Clergyman...Vancouver." *Vancouver Province*, 24 October 1925.

"Toys." *Vancouver Province*, 27 December 1925.

"Pauline and McBride." *Vancouver Province*, 3 January 1926.

"Crystal Gardens." *Canadian Pacific Rail...* [sic] (January 1926).

"Trailers of Death." *Vancouver Province*, 6 March 1926.

"The Philosophy of Used Cars." *Vancouver Province*, 22 March 1926.

"A Link with the Past (Sechelt Image)." *Catholic Bulletin* (26 March 1926).

"O'Hagan Letter." *Vancouver Province*, October 1926.

"Pioneer of Three Provinces." *Saturday Night* (27 November 1926).

"Golden of the Selkirks." *Vancouver Province*, 28 December 1926.

"The Chinook Jargon." *Vancouver Province*, January 1928.

"Spring Comes to Stanley Park." *Western Tribune*, May 1928.

"Two Reviews of Pirandello Plays." *Vancouver Province*, 30 September 1928.

"Totem Poles." *Edmonton Journal*, 12 January 1929.

"Northern Winter Port." *Vancouver Province*, 3 February 1929.

"West Coast Handicraft." *Edmonton Journal*, 4 May 1929.

"B.C. Whaling Station." *Western Home Monthly* (September 1929).

"Caduceus." *Vancouver Province*, January 1930.

"Crocus." *Vancouver Province*, March 1930.

"Sunsets at Semiahmoo." *Vancouver Province*, 8 December 1931.

"Wells of the Cariboo." *Canadian Magazine*, Vol. 81 (June 1934): 15–16.

"Gardenia." *Vancouver Province*, February 1936.

"E. Pauline Johnson." *Vancouver Province*, March 1936.

"Easter Lilies." *Vancouver Province*, April 1936.

"Pauline Johnson's Vancouver Legends." *Vancouver Province*, 4 November 1936.

"Founders of Old Fort Langley." *Vancouver Province*, 23 January 1937.

"R.P. Stevens." *Vancouver Province*, 26 January 1937.

"Abbott House." *Outlook* (January 1938).
"Abbott House." *Vancouver Province*, 19 January 1938.
"White Rock." *Vancouver Province*, n.d., 1938.
"Garden Path." *Garden Beautiful* (May 1939).
"Dressing the Soldier." *Vancouver Sun*, September 1939.
"Miramichi Buttons." *Vancouver Province*, 25 September 1941.
"Murray Tweeds." *Montreal Star*, 24 December 1942.
"Masks." *New World*, July 1942.
"Cauliflowers—Sowing Seeds for Victory." *Montreal Star*, 22 August 1942.
"More About Cauliflowers." *Montreal Star*, 1943.
"The Herb Garden." *Montreal Star*, April 1945.
"More Wild Vegetables." *Montreal Star*, 1945.

LETTERS TO THE EDITOR, VANCOUVER PROVINCE (LISTED IN CHRONOLOGICAL ORDER)

Red Cross Nurse is Bitterly Opposed to Liquor, 14 November 1926: 14.
In favour of three-coloured traffic light at Granville and Hastings, 15 July 1928: 10.
Employment of Oriental-trained nurses in Canadian hospitals, 6 March 1932: 2.
University, 21 August 1932: 14.
The weight of learning, 22 July 1933: 10.
First Vancouver novels, 15 May 1942: 4.

BOOK REVIEWS / SOME UNVERIFIED

"The Song of Seasons." *Canadian Bookman* (July 1923): 175–6.
"Wild Geese." *Vancouver Province*, 17 January 1926.
"The Living Forest." *Canadian Bookman* (February 1926).
"Chris in Canada." *Canadian Bookman* (February 1926).
"Along the Ottawa." *Canadian Bookman* (5 February 1926): 4.
"Woodrow Wilson, Life and Letters." *Vancouver Province* Magazine, 29 April 1928: 4.
"Persephone." *Vancouver Province*, 3 April 1928.
"Gorman's Hawthorne." *Vancouver Province*, 10 June 1928.
"Intimacies in Canadian Life and Letters." *Vancouver Province* Magazine, 24 June 1928: 4.
"The Development of English Biography." *Vancouver Province*, 14 April 1929: no page.
"Each in His Own Way." *Vancouver Province* Magazine, 23 June 1929: 4.
"The European Starling on His Westward Way." *Vancouver Province* Magazine, 21 July 1929: no page.
"Grandeur and Misery of Victory." *Canadian Bookman,* Vol. 12, No. 5 (May 1930): 108.
"Phillipa." *Canadian Bookman,* Vol. 12, No. 11 (November 1930): 236.
"Life of Adams." *Vancouver Province*, 12 January 1931.
"Sir Charles G.D. Roberts: a biography." *Vancouver Province*, 10 July 1943: no page.

ENDNOTES

THE STUDIO

 1. Annie Harvie (Ross) Foster, "Passing Through: Pictures from the life of Mrs. W. Garland Foster, née Annie H. Ross," (Annie Harvie [Ross] Foster Hanley Fonds, MG L7, University of New Brunswick Archives & Special Collections, typed manuscript, 1939), 1.
 2. Ibid., 1.

"SCOTSMEN ALL"

 1. Mrs. Patrick Hanley, *Some Account of the Families of James Ross, Donald McDonald, Joseph Story, James Doak and Their Descendants* (Annie Harvie [Ross] Foster Hanley Fonds, MG L7, University of New Brunswick Archives & Special Collections, Sept. 1, 1959), 1.
 2. "Passing Through," 74.
 3. Ibid., 65.
 4. *Some Account of the Families*, 6.

HOMESTEAD AT MANNERS SUTTON

 1. "Passing Through," 7.

MILL TOWN

 1. "Passing Through," 28.
 2. Ibid., 29.
 3. Ibid., 32.
 4. Ibid., 36.
 5. Ibid., 41.

FREDERICTON SCHOOL AND FAMILY

 1. "Passing Through," 42.

THE DOAKS OF DOAKTOWN

 1. "Passing Through," 47.
 2. Ibid., 57.
 3. Ibid., 48.
 4. Ibid., 61a.
 5. Ibid.

WOODSTOCK HOME

1. W.O. Raymond, "The Founding of Woodstock," © R. Wallace Hale, http://www.rootsweb.com/~nbcarlet/historyarticles/foundingofwoodstock.htm.
2. "Passing Through," 86.
3. Ibid., 87.
4. Ibid., 100.
5. Bob Sander-Cederlof, "E.P. Roe," http://bobsc5.home.comcast.net/books/eproe.html.
6. "Passing Through," 96.
7. Ibid., 98.

THE UNIVERSITY OF NEW BRUNSWICK

1. "Passing Through," 103–104.
2. Ibid., 103.
3. Scott Wade and Hugh Lloyd, *Beyond the Hill* (Fredericton: Students' Representative Council: Associated Alumni and Senate, UNB, 1967), 177.
4. "Account of Entry to U.N.B.—Mary K. Tibbits," (Hathaway VF No. 983). http://www.lib.unb.ca/archives/mtibbits.html.
5. Wade, 128.
6. "Passing Through," 109.

FACULTY AND FRIENDS

1. "Passing Through," 111.
2. Ibid., 117.
3. Ibid., 118.
4. Mrs. W. Garland Foster, "The University of New Brunswick—Alma Mater of Many Famous Canadians," *Vancouver Sunday Province*, April 18, 1926.
5. "Passing Through," 117.
6. Mrs. W. Garland Foster, "Intellectual Influences at UNB in the Nineties" (Annie Harvie (Ross) Foster Hanley Fonds, MG L7 Box 2, UNB Archives & Special Collections, c. 1945), 1.
7. Ibid., 2.
8. "Passing Through," 113.
9. Ibid., 118–118a.

AN AMERICAN NURSE

1. "Passing Through," 120.
2. Butler Hospital for the Insane, Providence, R.I., Reports of the Trustees and Superintendent (January 27, 1897), 35.
3. "Passing Through," 126.
4. Ibid., 127.
5. Ibid., 128.
6. Ibid., 131.

7. Ibid., 126.

8. Ibid., 135.

MATRON OF WOODSTOCK'S HOSPITAL

1. "Passing Through," 140.

2. Ibid., 145.

"WESTWARD HO!"

1. "Passing Through," 148.

2. Ibid., 149.

3. Ibid.

4. Ibid., 154.

5. Ibid., 156.

6. Ibid., 157.

7. Ibid., 162.

8. Ibid., 159.

9. Ibid., 160.

"INLAND PARADISE"

1. "Passing Through," 163.

2. Ibid., 165.

3. *Nelson High School 1901–1956*. (Souvenir Edition, March 10, 1956), no page.

4. "Passing Through," 164.

5. British Columbia. Sessional Papers. *Dept. of Public Schools Report, 1908.*

6. *Nelson Daily News*, March 31, 1910, 5.

7. "Passing Through," 167.

MRS. GARLAND FOSTER

1. "Passing Through," 168.

2. Ibid., 170.

3. Ibid.

4. Ibid., 171.

5. Lloyd Roberts, *The Book of Roberts* (Toronto: Ryerson Press, 1923), 108.

6. "Passing Through," 172.

7. Ibid., 173.

8. *Nelson Daily News*, January 18, 1915, 7.

9. "Passing Through," 177.

10. Ibid., 178.

WAR ALARUMS

1. Susan Mann, ed., *The War Diary of Clare Gass, 1915–1918* (Montreal: McGill-Queen's University Press, 2000), xlii.

2. Annie Garland Foster, Wartime Diary (White Rock Museum & Archives, 1995–17 File 1 Diary), 2.

3. Ibid., 3.

4. "Passing Through," 180.

5. Wartime Diary, 6–7.

6. Ibid.

7. Ibid., 8.

8. Susan Mann, *Margaret Macdonald: Imperial Daughter* (Montreal: McGill-Queen's University Press, 2005), 31.

9. "Passing Through," 184a.

10. Wartime Diary, 15.

SISTER IN SERVICE

1. Mann, *Margaret Macdonald*, 68.

2. Ibid., 89.

3. "Passing Through," 187.

4. Ibid., 195.

5. *Nelson Daily News*, August 25, 1916, 8.

6. Ibid.

7. John Beswick Bailey, *Cinquante-quatre: Being a Short History of the 54th Canadian Infantry Battalion* (Belgium[?], 1919), 11–12.

8. "Passing Through," 189.

9. Ibid., 192.

10. Wartime Diary, 36.

11. "Passing Through," 194.

12. Bailey, 13.

13. "Passing Through," 197.

14. "Brunner Mond Explosion 1917," http://eastlondonhistory.com/silvertown-explosion-1917/.

15. "Passing Through," 202.

16. Ibid., 200–201.

17. Ibid., 203.

HOMECOMING

1. "Passing Through," 204.

2. Ibid., 205.

3. Isabel McKay Brinley to F. Welwood, correspondence, February 7, 1991.

4. "Passing Through," 212.

5. Ibid., 210–211.

6. Ibid., 211.

7. Ibid., 212–213.

8. "William Garland Foster," London Gazette (Issues No. 31480, No. 31183, 1919), http://www.gazettes-online.co.uk/archive.

9. *Kootenay Outlet Reflections: A History of Procter, Sunshine Bay, Harrop, Longbeach, Balfour, Queen's Bay* (Procter-Harrop Historical Book Committee, 1988), 96.

10. "Passing Through," 219.

11. *Nelson Daily News*, August 14, 1919.

12. Ibid., September 3, 1919.

13. "Passing Through," 220.

14. Ibid.

CIVILIAN LIFE

1. "Passing Through," 222.

2. *Nelson Daily News*, January 12, 1920.

3. Ibid., January 16, 1920, 4.

4. Alexander D. McRae to Mrs. Annie Garland Foster (Correspondence, White Rock Museum & Archives, 1955–17 file 4).

5. *Nelson Daily News*, February 3, 1920, 2.

NELSON CIVIC AFFAIRS

1. Annie Garland Foster, Notebook, back cover (White Rock Museum & Archives, 1995–17, File 2).

2. Cyril E. Leonoff, "Silver King Mike of the West Kootenay, British Columbia, 1849–1922," *Western States Jewish History* (Vol. XXXVII, No. 3 & 4, Spring/Summer 2005): 246.

3. *Saturday Night* (April 1920), no page.

4. *Nelson Daily News*, April 1, 1920, 6.

5. Ibid.

6. Ibid., September 14, 1920, 5.

7. Ibid., September 16, 1920, 2.

8. Ibid., June 9, 1920, 6.

9. Prior to 1949, cases from a provincial appellate court could bypass the Supreme Court of Canada and appeal directly to the Judicial Committee of the Privy Council in London. *Bishop of Vancouver Island v. City of Victoria* became an important Canadian decision and has been followed in principle and considered in over seventy-five subsequent cases.

10. *Nelson Daily News*, September 14, 1920, 5.

11. Ibid., November 9, 1920, 6.

12. Ibid., November 23, 1920, 3.

13. Ibid., December 8, 1920, 8.

14. Ibid., December 15, 1920, 3.

15. Ibid., January 8, 1921.

16. "Passing Through," 223–224.

CHAMPION OF VETERANS

1. *Nelson Daily News*, January 6, 1921, 3.

2. Ibid., August 20, 1920, 5.

3. Ibid., September 9, 1920, 3.

4. Women's Institute, Nelson, Minute Book, January 1921 (Touchstones Nelson: Museum of Art and History).

5. Ibid., February [18th] 1921.

6. Nelson's first Mayor, John Houston, dubbed Nelson "Queen City of the Kootenays" on August 1, 1899 when the first spike for the electric street railway system was driven.

7. Gretchen Gibson, "A Few West Kootenay Authors," *Cominco Magazine* (Vol. 4, No. 6, June 1943): 5.

8. "Passing Through," 224.

9. British Columbia. Sessional Papers, 1925. *Report of the Provincial Board of Health* by H.E. Young, MD, Provincial Health Officer, N5.

10. *Nelson Daily News*, September 2, 1921, 3.

11. Ibid.

12. Ibid.

13. Ibid., September 5, 1921, 2.

14. *Calgary Herald*, September 9, 1921, 1 (White Rock Museum & Archives, 1995–17 File 2).

15. Ibid.

16. *Nelson Daily News*, January 9, 1922, 3.

17. Women's Institute, Nelson, Minute Book, February 1922 (Touchstones Nelson: Museum of Art and History).

18. "Passing Through," 224–5.

19. *Skowhegan Reporter*, December 7, 1922.

20. *Nelson Daily News*, June 9, 1924, 5.

21. Ibid., June 20, 1924, 9.

22. "Book Review Contest," *Canadian Bookman* (Vol. 5, No. 6, June 1923): 158.

MISSING PAGES

1. *Nelson Daily News*, August 25, 1916, 8.

2. Veteran Affairs Canada, "Canadians on the Somme," http://wwii.ca/content-63/world-war-i/canadians-on-the-somme/.

3. Ibid.

4. Attestation Papers. Lt. Patrick Hanley. Library and Archives Canada. Ministry of the Overseas Military Forces of Canada Fonds. Accession 1992-93/166/Box 4014-50 (Army Form B 103).

5. Ibid. (Army Form I 1237, Medical Case Sheet).

THE TRIALS OF PATRICK HANLEY

1. *Nelson Daily News*, February 7, 1925, 1.

2. Ibid.

3. *Nelson Daily News*, February 9, 1925, 1.

4. Ibid., February 10, 1925, 1.

5. Ibid., May 14, 1925, 1.

6. Ibid.

7. Ibid., May 15, 1925, 9.

8. Ibid., 2.

9. Ibid., 9.

10. Ibid., May 16, 1925, 2.

11. Ibid., May 18, 1925, 1–2.

12. Ibid., October 21, 1925, 7.

13. Ibid., October 22, 1925, 1.

14. Ibid., May 7, 1926, 1.

JUSTICE DEFERRED

1. A.G. Foster to H.H. Stevens, Correspondence, May 9, 1926, Library and Archives Canada. Department of Justice fonds, Vol. 1540, File No. cc250, part 1, Patrick Hanley documents, 1925–1955.

2. Ibid.

3. Ibid.

4. Ibid., H.H. Stevens to Lapointe, Correspondence, May 14, 1926.

5. Ibid., Dr. H.Clare, Memorandum to Minister of Justice, June 12, 1926.

6. Ibid., telegram, July 15, 1926.

7. Ibid., telegram, July 16, 1926.

8. Ibid., M. Gallagher Report to Minister of Justice, July 15, 1926.

9. P.C. Order-in-Council 1167, July 22, 1926, Library and Archives Canada. Privy Council Office fonds. Vol. 1392, PC 1167. Patrick Hanley documents, July 22, 1926.

A WRITER'S WORK

1. "Passing Through," 233.

2. Lynn Harrington, *Syllables of Recorded Time: The Story of the CAA, 1921–1981* (Toronto: Simon and Pierre, [Dundurn Press] 1981), 8.

3. Mrs. W. Garland Foster, "Food Values," *National Life* (May 1924): 11, 19, 24.

4. *Vancouver Province*, November 18, 1933.

5. "Passing Through," 233.

6. Foster to Gallagher, Correspondence, November 28, 1927, Library and Archives Canada. Department of Justice Fonds. Vol. 1540, File No. cc250, part 1. Patrick Hanley documents, 1925–1955.

7. Ibid., Hanley to Minister of Justice, Petition, November 30, 1930.

8. Ibid., Gallagher to the Warden, BC Penitentiary, Correspondence, December 12, 1930.

9. Ibid., Foster to Gallagher, Correspondence, December 2, 1937.

10. "Passing Through," 239.

11. Ibid., 240.

HANLEY WALKS

1. Ann Hanley to Flora Burns, Correspondence (University of Victoria Special Collections, Burns Family Fonds 1885–1964, SC 019).

2. Shannon K.L. Armstrong, "Exploring the Unseemed Texts of the Archive: Canadian Identity and Cultural Appropriation in the Unpublished Works of Ann Hanley (Mrs. W. Garland Foster)." (M.A. thesis, Department of English, University of New Brunswick, 2003), 27.

3. Maude Alymer, *A Peculiar People: the Doukhobors* (New York: Funk and Wagnall, 1904).

4. Mrs. W. Garland Foster, "A Doomed Utopia: the Doukhobors and Their Troubles— How Peter Verigin Plays Upon the Ignorance of His Followers," *Saturday Night* (Vol. 39, No. 30, June 14, 1924): 5.

5. Mrs. W. Garland Foster, "The Canadian Doukhobors: a Study in Communism" (University of New Brunswick Archives & Special Collections, MG L7 Box 2, File 5, typed manuscript, c. 1936), 174.

6. Dinnage Hobden to Gallagher, Correspondence, October 10, 1941, Library and Archives Canada. Department of Justice fonds. Vol. 1540, File No. cc250, part 1. Patrick Hanley documents, 1925–1955.

7. Ibid., Dr. Geo. A. Davidson to Warden, BC Penitentiary, Correspondence, March 1, 1943.

8. Ibid., D. Wilson to Warnock, Correspondence, Remission Branch, January 6, 1943.

9. Ibid, M.F. Gallagher to Minister of Justice, Correspondence, May 22, 1943.

10. Ibid., J.P.S. Cathcart to M.F. Gallagher, Correspondence, July 3, 1944.

11. Ibid., *License under the Ticket of Leave Act,* Patrick Hanley, March 27, 1945.

WHITE ROCK AT HOME

1. M. Gallagher and Alexander of Tunis, *Remission Register,* February 7, 1948, Library and Archives Canada. Department of Justice fonds. Vol. 1540, File No. cc250, part 1. Patrick Hanley documents, 1925–1955.

2. Ibid., Hobden to Gallagher, Correspondence, April 8, 1949.

3. Willard Ireland to Ann Hanley, Correspondence, May 19, 1961 (Provincial Archives of British Columbia, Provincial Archives Correspondence, GR 1738, Box 68, File No. 3).

4. Annie H. Foster to Alfred G. Bailey, Correspondence, February 27, 1947 (Alfred G. Bailey fonds, UARG 80, Series 8, Case 34, File 17, University of New Brunswick Archives & Special Collections).

5. Margaret Lang, "Woman of Many Careers…," *White Rock Sun,* February 8, 1968, 14.

6. "Passing Through," 248.

BIBLIOGRAPHY

PUBLISHED WORKS

Books

Adams, John Coldwell. *Sir Charles God Damn Roberts*. Toronto: University of Toronto Press, 1986.

Affleck, Edward L. *Kootenay Lake Chronicles*. Vancouver: Alexander Nicolls Press, 1978.

_____. *Sternwheelers, Sandbars and Switchbacks*. Vancouver: Alexander Nicolls Press, 1973.

Art Gallery of Greater Victoria. *Mary Riter Hamilton 1873–1954*. Victoria: Art Gallery of Greater Victoria, 1978.

Bailey, John Beswick. *Cinquant-Quatre: being a short history of the 54th Canadian Infantry Battalion*. (Belgium? 1919). Touchstones Nelson: Museum of Art and History.

Bamford, Louise M. *The Bamford Saga, 1764–1989*. Fredericton: I.M. Bamford, 1989.

Barrett, Art and Laine Dahlen. *A Humorous Look at Nelson's History*. Rev. by Bob Murray et al., Nelson, BC: Kootenay School of Art, [1971].

Beam, Alex. *Gracefully Insane: The Rise and Fall of America's Premier Mental Hospital*. Cambridge, MA: Public Affairs, 2000.

Beaver Valley and Pend d'Oreille Historical Society. *Beaver Valley and Pend d'Oreille: Oral Histories from Early Settlers of Fruitvale, Beaver Falls, Columbia Garden, Montrose, Park Siding and the Pend d'Oreille River Valley, 1892–1945*. [Trail, BC]: Hall Printing, 1997.

Bossence, Gail. *A Time to Remember: A History of Mortlach and District*. Mortlach, SK: Mortlach History Book Committee, 1983.

Bruce, Henry. *Down Home: Notes of a Maritimes son*. Toronto: Key Porter Books, 1988.

Bull, Natalie. *Woodstock Walkabout*. Woodstock, NB: Carleton County Historical Society, c. 2000.

Butler Hospital for the Insane, Providence RI. Reports of the Trustees and Superintendent, January 27, 1897.

Cairns, Alex and A.H. Yetman. *The History of the Veterans Movement 1916–1925 and the Canadian Legion 1926–1935*. Special edition of the *Manitoba Veteran*, v. 1, 1961.

Cleverdon, Catherine. *The Woman Suffrage Movement in Canada*. 2nd ed. Toronto: University of Toronto Press, 1974.

Connell, Allison. *A View of Woodstock: Historic Homes of the 19th Century*. Fredericton NB: New Ireland Press, 1988.

Dunleavy, Janet E. and Gareth W. Dunleavy. *Douglas Hyde: A Maker of Modern Ireland*. Los Angeles: University of California Press, 1991.

Foster, Annie H. and Anne Grierson. *High Days and Holidays in Canada: A Collection of Holidays Facts for Canadian Schools*. rev. ed. Toronto: Ryerson, 1956.

Foster, Annie H. *Makers of History*. Series: Gallery of Heroes. Toronto: Ryerson, 1946.

_____. *Mohawk Princess: Being Some Account of the Life of Tekahion-Wake E. Pauline Johnson*. Vancouver: Lion's Gate Publishing, 1931.

Francis, Daniel. *L.D. Taylor: Mayor and the Rise of Vancouver*. Vancouver: Arsenal Pulp Press, 2004.

Giles, L.C. and Bramshott and Liphook Preservation Society. *Liphook and Bramshsott and the Canadians*. Bramshott and Liphook Preservation Society, 1986.

Glanville, Alice. *Schools of the Boundary 1891–1901*. Merritt, BC: Sonotek, 1991.

Golden and District Historical Society. *Golden Memories*. 1982.

Graham, Clara. *This Was the Kootenay*. Vancouver: Evergreen Press, 1963.

Gray, Charlotte. *Canada: a Portrait in Letters 1800–2000*. [Toronto]: Doubleday Canada, 2003.

____. *Flint and Feather: The Life and Times of E. Pauline Johnson—Tekahionwake*. Toronto: HarperFlamingo Canada, 2002.

Hanic, Edna and David Scott. *Nelson: Queen City of the Kootenays*. Vancouver: Mitchell Press, 1972.

Hansen, Linda Squires. *Those Certain Women: A History of the Associated Alumnae, UNB*. Associated Alumnae of the University of New Brunswick, 1982.

Harrington, Lynn. *Syllables of Recorded Time: The Story of the Canadian Authors Association, 1921–1981*. Toronto: Simon and Pierre [Dundurn Press], 1981.

Hogg, Peter W. *Constitutional Law of Canada*. 4th ed. Toronto: Carswell, 1997.

Howay, F.W. and E.O.S. Scholefield. *British Columbia from the Earliest Times to the Present*. vol. IV. Vancouver: S.J. Clarke Publishing Company, 1914.

Jessen, Michael. *City of Nelson Diamond Jubilee 1897–1972*. Commemorative Souvenir edition. [Nelson, BC: Nelson Daily News, 1972.]

Joyce, Art. *Hanging Fire and Heavy Horses: A History of Public Transit in Nelson*. Nelson, BC: City of Nelson, 2000.

Kootenay Outlet Reflections: A History of Procter, Sunshine Bay, Harrop, Longbeach, Balfour, Queen's Bay. Procter-Harrop Historical Book Committee, c. 1988.

Lamb, Shawn. *100 days, 100 years: A Collection of Nelson's Top News Stories*. Nelson, BC: Nelson Daily News, 1997.

Lang, Joan. *Lost Orchards: Vanishing Fruit Farms of the West Kootenay*. Nelson, BC: J. Lang, 2003.

Lang, Margaret. *Along the Way*. White Rock, BC: M. Lang, 1967.

Little, Nina Fletcher. *Early Years of the McLean Hospital*. Boston, MA: Francis A. Countway Library of Medicine, 1972.

Mann, Susan, ed. *The War Diary of Clare Gass, 1915–1918*. Montreal and Kingston: McGill-Queen's University Press, 2000.

____. *Margaret Macdonald: Imperial Daughter*. Montreal and Kingston: McGill-Queen's University Press, 2005.

Maude, Alymer. *A Peculiar People: The Doukhobors*. New York: Funk and Wagnall, 1904.

McMullen, Lorraine ed. *Re(Dis)covering Our Foremothers: 19th Century Canadian Women Writers*. Series: Reappraisals Canadian Writers. Ottawa: University of Ottawa Press, 1990.

Meighen, Right Honourable Arthur. *Overseas Addresses June–July 1921*. Toronto: Musson, 1921.

Miller, Muriel. *Bliss Carman: Quest and Revolt*. St. John's, NF: Jesperson Press, 1981.

Mills, Ed. *Canadian Inventory of Historic Buildings*. Canada National Historic Sites, 1977.

Morton, Desmond. *Fight or Pay: Soldiers' Families in the Great War*. Vancouver: University of British Columbia Press, 2004.

Ramsay, Bruce. *Ghost Towns of British Columbia*. Vancouver: Mitchell Press, 1963.

Roberts, Lloyd. *The Book of Roberts.* Toronto: Ryerson, 1923.

Roland, Charles G., ed. *Health, Disease and Medicine: Essays in Canadian History.* Toronto: Hannah Institute for History of Medicine, 1984.

Ross, Malcolm. *Our Sense of Identity: A Book of Canadian Essays.* Canadian Literature Series. Toronto: Ryerson, 1954.

Sealey, Douglas. "Douglas Hyde in New Brunswick 1890–1." In *The Untold Story: The Irish in Canada,* vol. 2, edited by Robert O'Driscoll and Lorna Reynolds, 237–247. Toronto: Celtic Arts of Canada, 1988.

Strong-Boag, Veronica and Carole Gerson. *Paddling Her Own Canoe: The Times and Texts of E. Pauline Johnson (Tekahionwake).* Toronto: University of Toronto Press, 2000.

Tarasoff, Koozma. *Spirit Wrestlers: Doukhobor Pioneers' Strategies for Living.* Ottawa: Spirit Wrestlers Publishing, 2002.

Thirkell, Fred and Bob Scullion. *Frank Gowen's Vancouver 1914–1931.* Surrey, BC: Heritage House, 2001.

Wade, Scott and Hugh Lloyd. *Behind the Hill.* [Fredericton]: Students' Representative Council, Associated Alumni and Senate U.N.B., 1967.

Woodcock, George. *British Columbia: A History of the Province.* Vancouver: Douglas & McIntyre, 1990.

Woodcock, George and Ivan Avakumovic. *The Doukhobors.* Toronto: Oxford University Press, 1968.

Journal articles

"Annie Garland Foster." *Saturday Night* (April 1920): no page.

Belier, Patricia. "Passing Through: Pictures from the Life of Mrs. W. Garland Foster (née Annie H. Ross)." *The Officers' Quarterly* 12.1 (Spring 1996): 7–9.

"Bishop of Vancouver Island v. City of Victoria." Supreme Court of British Columbia. *Western Weekly Reports* 1 (1920): 120–8.

"Bishop of Vancouver Island v. City of Victoria." *Court of Appeal Reports* 3 (1920): 493–509.

"Book Review Contest." *Canadian Bookman* 5.6 (June 1923): 158.

Canadian Bookman, 1923–1926.

Canadian Author and Bookman, 1931–1943.

Collings, Judge Philip. "My Bones Turned to Water: Memoirs of a Brief Association with the Late D.N. Hossie, Q.C." *Advocate* 51 (1993): 247–249.

Coyne, Vince. "A Medical Miracle: Our Hospital Owes its Life to Volunteers." *Sounder* (September 1989): 4–8.

Duff, A. Wilmer. "Douglas Hyde in Canada." *Toronto Saturday Night* 8 (October 1938).

Foster, Mrs. W. Garland. "A Doomed Utopia: The Doukhobors and Their Troubles—How Peter Verigin Plays upon the Ignorance of his Followers." Saturday Night 30 (June 14, 1924): 3, 5. (reprinted at http://www.canadianmysteries.ca/sites/verigin/archives/newspaper ormagazinearticle/1656en.html).

Foster, Mrs. W.G. "'Les Pauvres' and its Artist." *Museum Notes, Art, Historical and Scientific Association of Vancouver,* Vol. 4, No. 2 (June 1929): 65–8.

Gibson, Gretchen. "A Few West Kootenay Authors." *Cominco Magazine,* Vol. 4, No. 6 (June 1943): 2–5.

Leonoff, Cyril E. "'Silver King Mike' of the West Kootenay, British Columbia, 1849–1922." *Western States Jewish History* XXXVII: 3 & 4 (Spring/Summer 2005): 239–254.

Mulvihill, James. "The 'Canadian Bookman' and Literary Nationalism." *Canadian Literature,* Vol. 107 (Winter 1985): 48–59.

Welwood, Frances. "Lukin Johnston and *The Province.*" *British Columbia History,* Vol. 43, No. 2 (Summer 2010): 10–18.

Welwood, Ron. "The University Club of Nelson and the Provincial University Question, 1903–1910." *British Columbia Historical News,* Vol. 22, No. 2 (Spring 1989): 10–14.

Newspapers

The Bugle. Woodstock, NB, January 25, 1984.

Foster, Mrs. W. Garland. "Landmarks of Nelson." *Vancouver Province* Magazine, May 10, 1925: 3.

Foster, Mrs. W. Garland. "The University of New Brunswick—Alma Mater of Many Famous Canadians." *Vancouver Sunday Province,* April 18, 1926.

Golden Star. Golden, BC, Sept. 3, 1910; July 1, 1911.

Joyce, Art. "Portraits of Women I: Annie Foster." *Nelson Daily News,* August 27, 1999: 9.

Joyce, Art. "William Garland Foster: Editor & Manager 1908–1914." *Nelson Daily News,* April 22, 1999.

Lang, Margaret. "Woman of Many Careers…" *White Rock Sun,* February 8, 1968: 14.

Nelson Daily News. June 12, 1915; January 12, 1920–January 15, 1921; February 7, 1920; June 2–25, 1924; February 7–12, 1925; May 14–18, 1925; October 20–23, 1925; May 4–7, 1926; May 1, 1928; November 18–December 2, 1933; April 27, 1952.

Skowhegan Reporter. December 7, 1922.

Trail Daily Bulletin. May 5–7, 1926.

Trail News. February 6, 13, 20, 27, 1925; May 15, 22, 1925; October 22, 29, 1925.

Vancouver Daily Province.

Vancouver Sun, March 7, 1926; November 1933.

Reference and government documents

British Columbia. *Gazette,* Pt. 1.

British Columbia. Sessional Papers, 1908–1916. *Department of Public Schools Annual Report.*

British Columbia. Sessional Papers, 1925. *Report of the Provincial Board of Health by H.E. Young, MD Provincial Health Officer.*

British Columbia. Sessional Papers. 1939. *Annual Provincial Board of Health Report.*

Canada. *Census of Canada,* 1906—Assiniboia.

Canada. *Statutes of Canada* 1920, C 54: "Returned Soldiers' Insurance Act."

Canadian Annual Review.

Canadian Men and Women of the Times, 1898.

Canadian Parliamentary Guide.

Canadian Yearbook.

London Gazette. Issue No. 31480, July 17, 1919, and No. 31183, February 14, 1919, http://www.gazettes-online.co.uk/archive (accessed 20 March and 16 May 2006).

"Roberta Catherine MacAdams Price…First Women in Provincial and Territorial Legislature."

Library and Archives Canada, www.collectionscanada.ca/women/002026-269-e.htm (accessed 27 March 2006).

"Schofield, J.H." *Who's Who in British Columbia,* 1934. Victoria: S.M. Carter.

Statistics Canada. *Canada Census,* 1881.

Websites

Baird, William T. "70 Years of New Brunswick Life Autobiographical Sketches." Saint John, NB: Press of E. Day, 1890. Our Roots. http://www.ourroots.ca/f/toc.aspx?id=3064 (accessed 11 March 2007).

Bitner, Ruth and Leslee Newman. "Saskatchewan History Centennial Timeline, 1905–2005." Saskatchewan Western Development Museum. http://olc.spsd.sk.ca/DE/Saskatchewan100/1905.html (accessed 16 March 2006).

"A Brief History, Kettle Valley Steam Railway." http://kettlevalleyrail.org/history.htm (accessed 7 June 2006).

Brissenden, Constance. "History of Metropolitan Vancouver Hall of Fame." www.Vancouverhistory.ca/whoswho_Y.htm (accessed 6 June 2006).

"Brunner Mond Explosion 1917." http://eastlondonhistory.com/silvertown-explosion-1917/ (accessed 9 June 2006).

Canada. National Parole Board. "History Parole in Canada." http://www.npb-cnic.gc.ca/about/part2_e.htm (accessed 20 February 2007).

Copley, Hilda to Mrs. Foster, Correspondence, Canadian Casualty Station, Oct. 15, 1918. http://www.54thbattalioncef.ca/images/NCopley.jpg From The Collection of © http://members.shaw.ca/cef54/. Retrieved from http://www.54thbattalioncef.ca. Floyd Low and Patricia A. Rogers © Keepers of the Flame 1997–2010 on 11 May 2010.

Cranbrook Archives, Museum and Landmark Foundation. "The Crowsnest Pass Railway Route." http://www.crowsnest.bc.ca/ (accessed 2007).

"Doaktown Historic Site." http://www.gnb.ca/0007/heritage/doak.asp (accessed 12 March 2007).

Edwards, Gail. "The History of the Book in BCL a state of the art review." www.hbic.library.utoronto.ca/fconfbc_en.htm (accessed 13 May 2006).

"Electoral History of BC 1871–1986." www.elections.bc.ca/elections/electoral_history/ (accessed 6 June 2006).

"The Federated Women's Institutes." http://www.fwic.ca/fact.htm#history (accessed 11 May 2010).

Fisher, Robert. "John and Mary Fisher." 2004. www.familyheritage.ca/otherfishers.pdf (accessed 15 March 2006).

General Federation of Women's Club. "Notable Club Women." http://www.gfwcct.org/notableclubwomen.htm (accessed 21 March 2006).

Government of Saskatchewan. "Saskatchewan Community Profile—Mortlach." http://www.saskbiz.ca/communityprofiles/CommunityProfile.Asp?CommunityID=626 (accessed 16 March 2006).

Great Canadian Rivers. Miramichi. www.greatcanadianrivers.com/rivers/miramichi/history-home.html (accessed 15 March 2006).

Haslemere Educational Museum. "Hutcheson Museum." http://www.haslemeremuseum.co.uk./about.html (accessed 9 June 2006).

"Here Is to your Health…" Philadelphia Department of Public Health.
http://www.phila.gov/health/history/parts/part_3.htm (accessed 16 March 2006).

Higginbottom, Peter. "Percy House Hospital." http://www.workhouses.org.uk/ (accessed 12 March 2007).

"History McLean Hospital: Brief History from Charlestown to Belmont." McLean Hospital, Belmont, MA. www.mclean.harvard.edu/about/history (accessed 9 June 2006).

"Hospitals in the UK—Great War Forum." http://19141918.invisionzone.com/forums/index.php?showtopic=187&st=40 (accessed 1 February 2007).

Howe, Jonas. "King's New Brunswick Regiment." http://personal.nbnet.nb.ca/halew/KNBRegt.html (accessed 15 March 2006).

"Inauguration of the Buildings of UBC at Point Grey Congregation for the Conferring of Honourary Degrees October 16, 1925": 5.
http://www.library.ubc.ca/archives/pdfs/misc/Document_4.pdf (accessed 6 June 2006).

Lambert, R.S. "Miramichi Fire of 1825" from "Redcoat Sailor."
http://www3.bc.sympatico.ca/charlotte_taylor/Folder1/Miramichi_Fire_of_1825.htm (accessed 15 March 2006).

Low, Floyd and Patricia A. Rogers. "54th Battalion Canadian Infantry, 1915–1919."
http://members.tripod.com/apollon_2/ (accessed 15 March 2006).

"Loyal Edmonton Regiment." Loyal Edmonton Regiment Museum.
http://www.lermuseum.org/ler/mh/interwar/index.html (accessed 25 March 2006).

Margaret Chase Smith Library. "Margaret Chase Smith." http://www.mcslibrary.org/bio/biog.htm (accessed 10 June 2006).

Pankhurst, Emmeline. "My Own Story 1914." In "Internet Modern History Sourcebook," edited by Paul Halsall. http://www.fordham.edu/halsall/mod/1914Pankhurst.html (accessed 9 June 2006).

Pugh, Margaret. "The Black Watch" from "The 42nd Royal Highland Regiment, the Black Watch (Nashwaak)": 69–71.
http://www3.bc.sympatico.ca/charlotte_taylor/Folder1/Black_Watch.htm (accessed 15 March 2006).

"RAMC Hospitals in the Great War." http://www.1914-1918.net/hospitals.htm (accessed 1 February 2007).

Raymond, W.O. "The Founding of Woodstock." © R. Wallace Hale.
http://www.rootsweb.com/~nbcarlet/historyarticles/foundingofwoodstock.htm (accessed 15 March 2006).

"The Roll of Auxiliary Home Hospitals in the U.K. 1914–1919."
http://www.juroch.demon.co.uk/UKhospitals.htm#Middlesex (accessed 9 June 2006).

Sander-Cederlot, Bob "E.P. Roe": 6. http://bobsc5.home.comcast.net/books/eproe.html (accessed 13 March 2007).

"Seeing you." American Newsreel, Ann Arbor, Michigan, 1958. www.emd.ca/artist/seeingyou.html (accessed 25 March 2006).

Shaw Savill. "Megantic." http://www.shawsavillships.co.uk/megantic.htm (accessed 20 March 2006).

"Silas Weir Mitchell." http://www.whonamedit.com/doctor.cfm/959.htm (accessed 16 March 2006).

Smedman, Lisa. "Veterans had to fight for their rights." Vancouver Courier On-Line.

www.vancouver.com/issues05/062205/entertainment/062205en4.html (accessed 22 April 2006).

The Society for Psychical Research, Kensington, London. "The Society for Psychical Research." http://www.spr.ac.uk/index.php3 (accessed 18 March 2006).

Spartacus Educational. "Voluntary Aid Detachment." www.spartacus.schoolnet.co.uk/ FWWnurses.htm (accessed 9 June 2006).

Turner, Greta "Shottermill." http://www.johnowensmith.co.uk/books/s2h1873855400.htm (accessed 9 June 2006).

University of New Brunswick. "Historical Sketch of UNB." http://www.unb.ca/welcome/historical_sketch.html (accessed 11 May 2010).

University of New Brunswick. "UNB in Fredericton, 177th Encaenia." http://www.unb.ca/graduation/encaenia/177/origin/html (accessed 6 March 2006).

University of New Brunswick Archives & Special Collections. "Roberts Family Chronology." http://www.lib.unb.ca/archives/finding/roberts/chron.html (accessed 10 March 2007).

_____. "Account of entry to U.N.B.—Mary K. Tibbits." http://www.lib.unb.ca/archives/finding/alumnae/mtibbits.html (accessed 12 March 2007).

University of Pennsylvania, School of Nursing, Center for the Study of the History of Nursing. "Nursing in Historic Philadelphia: A Walk through Time." www.nursing.upenn.edu/history/PDF/walk.pdf (accessed 16 March 2006).

van der Meer, Jitse M., ed. "Facets of Faith and Science," vol. IV. http://www.redeemer.on.ca/pascal/book4.htm (accessed 16 March 2006).

Veterans Affairs Canada. "Canadians on the Somme." http://wwii.ca/content-63/world-war-i/canadians-on-the-somme/ (accessed 1 February 2007).

Village of Doaktown. "Doaktown Historic Site." http://www.doaktown.com/attract.html (accessed 15 March 2006).

Village of Doaktown. "Doak Historic Site/Squire Doak." http://www.doaktown.com/squire.html (accessed 15 March 2006).

Warner, Marina. "Heroes and Icons. The Time 100." http://www.time.com/time/time100/heroes/profile/pankhurst03.html (accessed 9 June 2006).

Young, D.M. "Campbell, Dugald" in Dictionary of Canadian Biography Online. www.biographi.ca/EN/ShowBioPrintable.asp?BioId=36428 (accessed 15 March 2006).

UNPUBLISHED

Correspondence

Ted Affleck to F. Welwood re A.G. Foster. August 11, 28, 2001.

Louise Bamford to F. Welwood re A.G. Foster. April 9, 1991.

Isabel McKay Brinley to F. Welwood re A.G. Foster. February 7, 1991.

Annie Hanley to Gretchen Gibson. April 8, 1968.

Percy Livingstone (former Surrey City Administrator) to F. Welwood. April 9, 1991.

Interviews

Ted Affleck, Vancouver, BC, 1991.

Agnes Gibson Baker, Nelson, BC, 1991.

Judge Leo Gansner, Nelson, BC, 1991.
Margaret Lang Hastings, White Rock, BC, 1991.
Jack Horswill, Nelson, BC, 1991.
Palmer Rutledge, Vancouver, BC, November 14, 2000.
Joe Irving, Crescent Valley, BC, February 25, 2005.

Manuscripts

Bassnett, Madeline. "Public Portraits, Private Selves: Great Events and the Every Day Life of Annie Harvie (Ross) Foster Hanley." Unpublished paper, 2003. University of New Brunswick.
———. "Passing Through: Pictures from the Life of Mrs. Garland Foster (née Annie H. Ross). By Annie Harvie (Ross) Foster." [edited version] Unpublished paper, 2003. University of New Brunswick.
Bolton, Freeda Hume. "Happiness is Remembering." Typewritten ms., 1983. Nelson Municipal Library. Nelson, BC.
Foster, Annie Garland. Wartime Diary. White Rock Museum & Archives, 1995–17 File 1, Diary.
Foster, Mrs. W. Garland. "The Canadian Doukhobors: A Study in Communism." Typewritten ms. [c. 1936]. University of New Brunswick Archives & Special Collections, MG L7, Series 2, Box 2, File 5.
———. "Indian Trails in Maple Land: Myths of Haida Land." Typewritten ms. [c. 1946]. University of New Brunswick Archives & Special Collections, MG L7, Series 2, Box 2, File 10.
———. "Intellectual Influences at UNB in the Nineties." Typewritten ms. (photocopy), c. 1945. University of New Brunswick Archives, MG L7, Series 2, Box 2, File 11.
———. "Nelson Now and Then." Typewritten ms. (photocopy), 1923. University of British Columbia Library, Special Collections.
Hanley, Annie Harvie (Ross) Foster. "The Doaks (in NB)." Typewritten, 3 pp. ms. (photocopy), 1972. Andrew Ross.
———. "Passing Through: Pictures from the Life of Mrs. W. Garland Foster née Annie H. Ross." Typewritten ms. (photocopy), 1939. University of New Brunswick Archives & Special Collections, MG L7, Series 2, Box 2, File 6.
———. "Some Account of the Families of James Ross, Donald McDonald, Joseph Story, James Doak and Their Descendants." Typewritten ms. (photocopy), 1959. University of New Brunswick Archives & Special Collections, MG L7, Series 2, Box 2, File 7.

Miscellany

"Alfred G. Bailey fonds." University of New Brunswick Archives & Special Collections. UARG 80, Series 8, Case 34 file.
"Annie Garland Foster." White Rock Museum & Archives, 1995–17 file 2.
"Attestation Papers." Lt. Patrick Hanley. Library and Archives of Canada. Ministry of the Overseas Military Forces of Canada fonds. Accession 1992–93 166 Box 4014–50.
"Burns Family fonds, 1885–1964." University of Victoria Special Collections, SC019.
"Canadian Authors Association." Vertical File. Vancouver Public Library.

City of Nelson, BC. Bylaws. 1920.

City of Nelson, BC. Minutes of City Council, Nelson BC, 1920.

City of Nelson, BC. Tax Assessment Rolls.

City of Trail, BC. Archives. 85–1 "Schofield, James H."

"Fisher Family (and Foundry)." Vertical File. Carleton County Archives, Woodstock, NB.

"The Fisher Memorial Hospital." Vertical File, n.d. Carleton County Historical Society.

King, Mrs. Nellie. "History of the Carleton Memorial Hospital." Vertical File, 1974. Carleton County Historical Society.

Library and Archives Canada. Department of Justice fonds. Vol. 1540 File no. cc250, parts 1–3. Patrick Hanley documents 1925–1955.

Library and Archives Canada. Privy Council Office fonds. Vol. 1392 PC 1167. Patrick Hanley documents, July 22, 1926.

"Nelson High School 1901–1956." Souvenir Edition. 10 March 1956, no page.

Provincial Archives of BC. Provincial Archives. Correspondence, GR 1738, Box 68, File no. 3.

"Trial Book." Nelson Supreme Court Assizes, 1920s.

University Club of Nelson. Minute Book. Touchstones Nelson: Museum of Art and History, Nelson, BC.

Women's Institute Nelson. Minute Book. Touchstones Nelson: Museum of Art and History, Nelson, BC.

Dissertation

Armstrong, Shannon. "Exploring the Unseemed Texts of the Archives: Canadian identity and Cultural Appropriation in the Unpublished Works of Ann Hanley (Mrs. W. Garland Foster)." MA thesis, Department of English, University of New Brunswick, 2003.

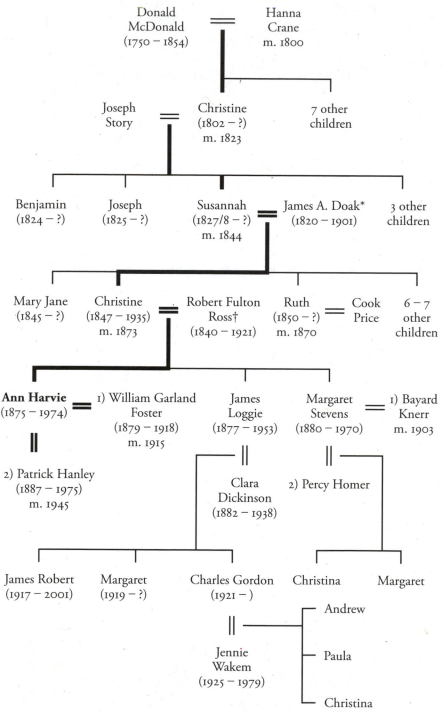

Donald McDonald (1750 – 1854) ══ Hanna Crane m. 1800

Joseph Story ══ Christine (1802 – ?) m. 1823 — 7 other children

Benjamin (1824 – ?) — Joseph (1825 – ?) — Susannah (1827/8 – ?) m. 1844 ══ James A. Doak* (1820 – 1901) — 3 other children

Mary Jane (1845 – ?) — Christine (1847 – 1935) m. 1873 ══ Robert Fulton Ross† (1840 – 1921) — Ruth (1850 – ?) m. 1870 ══ Cook Price — 6 – 7 other children

Ann Harvie (1875 – 1974) ══ 1) William Garland Foster (1879 – 1918) m. 1915

James Loggie (1877 – 1953)

Margaret Stevens (1880 – 1970) ══ 1) Bayard Knerr m. 1903

2) Patrick Hanley (1887 – 1975) m. 1945

Clara Dickinson (1882 – 1938)

2) Percy Homer

James Robert (1917 – 2001) — Margaret (1919 – ?) — Charles Gordon (1921 –) — Christina — Margaret

Jennie Wakem (1925 – 1979)

Andrew

Paula

Christina

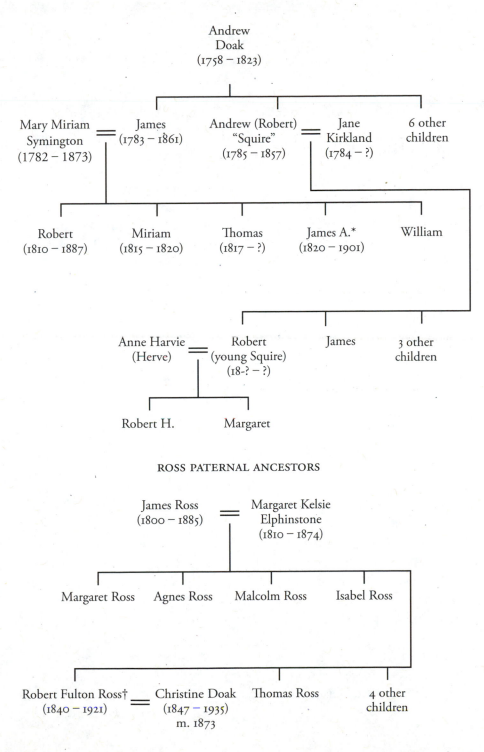

DOAK MATERNAL ANCESTORS

Andrew
Doak
(1758 – 1823)

Mary Miriam   James   Andrew (Robert)   Jane   6 other
Symington   (1783 – 1861) "Squire"   Kirkland   children
(1782 – 1873)   (1785 – 1857)   (1784 – ?)

Robert   Miriam   Thomas   James A.*   William
(1810 – 1887)   (1815 – 1820) (1817 – ?)   (1820 – 1901)

Anne Harvie   Robert   James   3 other
(Herve)   (young Squire)   children
                (18-? – ?)

Robert H.   Margaret

ROSS PATERNAL ANCESTORS

James Ross   Margaret Kelsie
(1800 – 1885)   Elphinstone
                (1810 – 1874)

Margaret Ross   Agnes Ross   Malcolm Ross   Isabel Ross

Robert Fulton Ross†   Christine Doak   Thomas Ross   4 other
(1840 – 1921)   (1847 – 1935)   children
                      m. 1873

INDEX

$\mathcal{S}$ ince the age of twelve, Frances Clay Welwood's ambition has been to write a book. In 1990, she encountered Annie Garland Foster and this dream slowly became a reality. They never met, as Foster passed away in 1974 at the age of ninety-nine, but Welwood spent nearly two decades painstakingly researching and gathering the details of this enigmatic woman's life and her important contribution to Canadian history. Welwood is an accomplished historian and has written articles for *BC History* (previously *BC Historical News*); *Manitoba History*; *Resolutions: Journal of the Maritime Museum of BC*; and local news media. She has recently been awarded the 2010 Yandle Prize for best article in *British Columbia History* for her story about Lukin Johnston. *Passing Through Missing Pages* is Welwood's first book. Frances lives in Nelson, BC.